# A HEAD START ON SCIENCE

## ENCOURAGING A SENSE OF WONDER

# A HEAD START ON SCIENCE

## ENCOURAGING A SENSE OF WONDER

WILLIAM C. RITZ, Editor

NATIONAL SCIENCE TEACHERS ASSOCIATION

Arlington, Virginia

NATIONAL SCIENCE TEACHERS ASSOCIATION

Claire Reinburg, Director
Judy Cusick, Senior Editor
Andrew Cocke, Associate Editor
Betty Smith, Associate Editor
Robin Allan, Book Acquisitions Coordinator

ART AND DESIGN
Will Thomas, Jr., Art Director
Joseph Butera, Graphic Designer—Cover and Inside Design
Kris Bohan, Illustrations

PRINTING AND PRODUCTION
Catherine Lorrain, Director
Nguyet Tran, Assistant Production Manager
Jack Parker, Electronic Prepress Technician

NATIONAL SCIENCE TEACHERS ASSOCIATION
Gerald F. Wheeler, Executive Director
David Beacom, Publisher

LIBRARY OF CONGRESS CATALOGING-IN-PUBLICATION DATA

A head start on science : encouraging a sense of wonder / edited by William C. Ritz.
    p. cm.
  Includes bibliographical references and index.
  ISBN 978-1-933531-02-1
  1.  Science--Study and teaching (Early childhood)--Activity programs.  I. Ritz, William C.
  LB1139.5.S35H4 2007
  372.3'5--dc22
                    2007006502

NSTA is committed to publishing material that promotes the best in inquiry-based science education. However, conditions of actual use may vary and the safety procedures and practices described in this book are intended to serve only as a guide. Additional precautionary measures may be required. NSTA and the author(s)s do not warrant or represent that the procedures and practices in this book meet any safety code or standard of federal, state, or local regulations. NSTA and the author(s) disclaim any liability for personal injury or damage to property arising out of or relating to the use of this book, including any of the recommendations, instructions, or materials contained therein.

Permission is granted in advance for photocopying brief excerpts for one-time use in a classroom or workshop. Permissions requests for coursepacks, textbooks, and other commercial uses should be directed to Copyright Clearance Center, 222 Rosewood Dr., Danvers, MA 01923; fax 978-646-8600; www.copyright.com.

# CONTENTS

## The Activities

# PREFACE

## Origin of This Activity Book

*A Head Start on Science: Encouraging a Sense of Wonder* is a book of 89 activities that have been used successfully by hundreds of teachers in Head Start programs across the country. For this book, they were modified to be used by an even greater variety of early childhood educators, including day care, preschool, and K–2 classroom teachers.

The book has its roots in a project that dates back to 1996. At that time, the Department of Science Education of California State University, Long Beach (CSULB), in cooperation with the Head Start Program of the Long Beach Unified School District, undertook a project called "A Head Start on Science." Support came from a grant from the Head Start Bureau of the U.S. Department of Health and Human Services.

The purpose of the project—which continues today—was to "demonstrate, evaluate, and replicate a summer institute prototype designed for Head Start teachers, teacher assistants, and home visitors." The goal has been to prepare institute participants to foster a lifelong interest in science among children in early childhood settings. For that to happen, Head Start educators themselves have to become more confident and enthusiastic about their own "sense of wonder" about the world.

During the first summer institute, participants were teachers and teacher aides from Head Start centers in Long Beach, California. An independent evaluator provided the project with data to refine the institute plans and materials for replication in Long Beach and elsewhere. Products to assist in sharing the prototype institute with others include a teacher's guide, a project website, a 12-minute descriptive video, and a "how to" manual for those planning to replicate the institutes.

More recently, a grant from the American Honda Foundation supported the establishment of a National Center for Science in Early Childhood at California State University, Long Beach. The center brought teams of educators from across the United States to participate in leadership training at CSULB during the summers of 2000 and 2001. As a result, there now exists a national network of over 20 "A Head Start on Science" dissemination and training centers.

From the beginning, overall guidance for the project was provided by a National Advisory Board made up of experts from Head Start, science education, and early childhood education programs. Day-to-day efforts of the project have been guided by persons with expertise in these same fields. Project staff are also actively involved in sharing what is being learned with Head Start, early childhood, and science education audiences across the country. We hope you will find, as earlier users did, that the activities will encourage a sense of wonder among our littlest scientists.

— William C. Ritz
Project Director
"A Head Start on Science"

# ABOUT THE EDITOR

William C. Ritz, professor emeritus of science education at California State University, Long Beach (CSULB), has been involved in science teaching and science teacher education all his professional life.

Bill's career began in the public schools of Western New York State, where he taught junior high science and biology for many years. During a four-year affiliation with the Eastern Regional Institute for Education (ERIE), his service as an elementary science consultant took him into classrooms throughout New York and Pennsylvania while he also completed doctoral studies in science education at SUNY at Buffalo. In 1970, Bill joined the science education faculty of Syracuse University, where he also directed the University's Environmental Studies Institute.

Since moving to California in 1977, he has taught both elementary and secondary science education courses at CSULB. Bill was elected to the Board of Directors of the National Science Teachers Association (NSTA) as its Teacher Education Director in 1983. He returned to the NSTA Board in 1988–1989 as president of the Association for the Education of Teachers in Science (AETS) and again in 1996–1998, as director for District XVI.

Author of more than 20 publications in science education, he has directed a number of funded projects at CSULB, including the Young Scholar's Ocean Science Institute, the Project to Improve Methods Courses in Elementary Science, Project MOST: Minority Opportunities in Science Teaching, and A Head Start on Science.*

---

\* A list of "A Head Start on Science" project staff and other collaborators is on p. 337.

# INTRODUCTION

## Our Theme

In 1956, Rachel Carson wrote a book about the time she spent along the Maine coastline with her nephew, Roger. From the time Roger was just a baby until he was more than four years old, he and Rachel shared adventures in the world of nature. She never set out to "teach" him anything, but rather to have fun and marvel at all the plants and animals, the sounds and smells encountered on walks through the woods and near the ocean. Roger, of course, learned a great deal as Rachel called his attention to various things and gave them names as well. He learned as the two of them made discoveries together.

In *The Sense of Wonder* she wrote, "If a child is to keep alive his inborn sense of wonder . . . he needs the companionship of at least one adult who can share it, rediscovering with him the joy, excitement and mystery of the world we live in" (Carson 1956)*. This curriculum, *A Head Start on Science*, was written to help adults facilitate young children's learning as they work as partners to explore their world. We hope your sense of wonder will be heightened as you observe children, as their curiosity leads them to answer their own questions about everything they see, hear, smell, and touch.

## Our Beliefs About Science Education and Young Children

- Early childhood teachers build on the "sense of wonder" present in all children.

- Young children learn about science through play.

- Doing science comes naturally for young children.

- The science processes that young children engage in are more important than learning science facts.

- Early childhood science teachers serve as "facilitators" of learning, as opposed to "instructors."

- As children engage in science experiences, adults observe children's actions and listen to their conversations so that they can follow children's leads.

---

* *The Sense of Wonder*. Copyright © 1956 by Rachel Carson. Copyright renewed 1984 by Roger Christie. Reprinted by permission of Frances Collin, Trustee.

- Science processes occur in all parts of the classroom and outdoors, not just at the science table.

- Children are intrinsically motivated when they have materials to enjoy, have some control over their learning, and enjoy success when involved in science processes.

- Children and adults should feel free to engage in science processes, understanding that exploration is more important than right or wrong answers.

- A primary role of the early childhood science teacher is to provide an appropriate learning environment and opportunities for children to explore, represent, and share their discoveries.

- Children learn best when they have their own science materials to explore.

- Trial and error, cause and effect are natural parts of the scientific learning experience.

- Science activities and materials need to be culturally relevant and part of a child's everyday world.

- Every child, regardless of gender and ability, needs to have equal access to science experiences.

- Young children with disabilities are best served in classrooms where they are involved in science processes along with typically developing peers.

- Adults need to model excitement and enthusiasm when involved in science processes and when planning and anticipating discoveries.

- Children who engage in active learning in early childhood programs are more likely to succeed in school and in life than children who attend more teacher-directed programs.

- Peer modeling, lively interaction, and conversation are essential parts of the early childhood science curriculum.

- When talking to children about science, it is important to honor their choice of words.

- In early childhood classrooms there should be a balance between child-initiated and teacher-initiated science activities.

- Effective early childhood teachers must be effective parent educators who involve families in their children's science activities.

# The Role of Questioning in Science

## Listen to Children

You will notice that we have included a caution in the "Getting Started" section of many of the activities in this curriculum: "Listen to what children say and observe what they do before asking questions."

## Follow Children's Leads

Another caution we have included is: "Follow children's leads when deciding which two or three questions to ask." If you observe children in their explorations and really listen to what they say, your questions and comments will follow their interests. If you see Jaime pick up a snail and study the bottom of the snail, your asking, "What do you see on the bottom of the snail?" or "What does the bottom feel like?" makes sense. Asking, "What do you think the snail eats?" (although a perfectly good question) does not make sense at this particular time. Instead it interrupts the child's concentration and pulls her attention away from something in which she is obviously interested.

## Don't Answer Too Quickly

Give children time to think and explore before asking questions. Children will often answer their own questions. Sometimes they are just thinking out loud. If Brian asks, "What do snails eat?" wait a bit then turn his question back to the group by asking, "How can we find out?" This keeps a group of children engaged as they begin to think about how to find out what snails eat. You may have planned to discuss the snail's hard shell today, but if the children are interested in finding out what snails eat, then follow their lead! Ask children what they think snails might like to eat, then spend the rest of the activity time putting out various foods to see which become "snail food."

## Ask Genuine Questions

The questions you ask should always be genuine. They should usually be questions to which you don't know the answer. If you ask a child, "How does that smell to you?" you really don't know the answer. On the other hand if you ask, "How many rocks are in front of you?" you know there are four and the child probably knows there are four. This type of question does nothing to further children's understanding. It can also interrupt the child's explorations and will often dampen a child's enthusiasm. Genuine questions lead to conversations, comfortable times when adults and children share thoughts and ideas, when both share control of the learning.

## What Kinds of Questions Are Best?

- Questions that follow children's interests or leads
- Questions to which you may not know the answer
- Questions that have many correct answers; each person has his or her own
- Questions that are genuine and lead to conversations

## Examples of the Best Questions

- "How would you describe it?"
- "What does it look/feel/smell/taste/sound like?"
- "How can we find out?"
- "Can you think of another way?"

# Encourage Children to Engage in Science Processes

Sometimes you will want to encourage children to engage in particular science processes. In that case your questions will be less open-ended but will still have many correct answers:

- "See if you can find other materials in the room that your magnets will attract?" (experimenting)
- "Are any of these rocks shinier than yours?" (observing, comparing)
- "What is the same about all these plants?" (observing, classifying)
- "What did you find out about what snails eat?" (communicating, classifying)

## Encourage Children to Use Science Tools

Sometimes you may want children to make regular use of the science tools:

- "What can you find out with the hand lens?"

- "Which one is the heaviest? Could you use the balance to find out?"

These questions encourage children to explore, to experiment, and to communicate their findings. They are not questions you use to quiz children to find out if they know the "correct" answer.

## Give Children Time to Answer

Once you ask a question, be sure to give children a chance to answer it! Science education innovator Mary Budd Rowe studied teachers' responses to children's questions. She advised waiting for at least three seconds after asking a question (longer for younger children). She called this "wait time." After the child answers a question, pause again for another three seconds. Often the child will add to his or her initial response or even change his or her answer.

## Comments and Questions That Facilitate Learning

Following is a list of comments and questions that will facilitate learning. Post them in your classroom where you can refer to them. Put some of your favorites on tag board and post them up high to remind you to use them when talking to children about science.

- "I'm not sure I understand what you mean. Try telling me again."

- "What makes you think so?"

- "Wow! Look at that!"

- "What would happen if ....?"

- "Tell me more ...."

- "Well, what do you think it is?"

- "I don't know. What could we do to find out?"

- "What do you think those (things) might be?"

- "I wonder what that (critter) might like to eat?"

- "Paul, you did a nice job of being gentle to that mealworm!"

- "Let's try that again!"
- "How does the top of that rock feel to you?"
- "How many pennies would it take to balance that rock?"
- "What could you do to make that marble roll farther?"
- "Please tell me what you did from beginning to end."
- "How could we find out which magnet is strongest?"
- "Does that (odor) (sound) (texture) remind you of anything else?"
- "How are the two objects alike? different?"
- "Which of the two blocks feels heavier?"
- "Which of these things belong together?"
- "Let's put all the things that go together into one group!"
- "What can we call that group?"
- "Does this remind you of something you've seen before?"
- "Can you think of a way to make your shadow longer?"
- "Try drawing a picture that shows me how the snail eats."

The final payoff in using these questions on a regular basis is that you will begin to hear the children ask them. When children can ask themselves questions that lead them to further explorations, then they are truly on their way to becoming scientists.

# The Importance of Science Processes

*A* *Head Start on Science* emphasizes encouraging a sense of wonder within young children through their use of the science processes. There are three ways of looking at the meaning of process. First, an emphasis on process usually implies a corresponding de-emphasis on science factual "content." But don't get the wrong impression! Science content is still there—children learn about their everyday world by examining and exploring such things as snails, plants, rocks, and shadows. But the emphasis is not on spoon-feeding them specific information about these objects and phenomena. Rather, they are encouraged to expand their perceptions of the world by learning how to observe such things as silkworms changing into moths, how to compare the smells of various foods, how to classify leaves collected on a walk, and how to communicate what they have learned.

A second meaning of process centers on the idea that how children learn science should resemble what scientists do. Scientists observe, classify, infer, carry out experiments, and communicate their findings. How have they become able to do these things? Presumably, they learned to do them, over a period of many years, by practicing them. We believe that just as the people of science have learned to gain information in these ways, the elementary forms of what they do can begin to be learned by very young children.

A third meaning of process introduces the idea of human intellectual development. From this point of view, processes are in a broad sense "ways of processing information." Such processing grows more complex as the individual develops from early childhood on. The intellectual skills that are developed allow a child to get much more information from a simple observation than they could have before these skills were developed. Therefore, a child observing a snail will see much more than just a slow-moving object in the grass. She or he will notice the sticky trail the snail leaves, will compare the snail to other slow-moving objects, will observe what the snail eats, and will begin to ask questions about and comment on the snail's environment and other things of interest.

There are four processes* that we feel are developmentally most appropriate for very young children:

1. Observing: seeing, hearing, feeling, tasting, and smelling

2. Communicating: oral, written, and pictorial

3. Comparing: sensory comparisons and linear, weight, capacity, and quantity comparisons

4. Organizing or Classifying: grouping, sequencing, and data gathering

---

*Adapted from American Association for the Advancement of Science (AAAS) Commission on Science Education. 1967. *Science—A process approach: Purposes, accomplishments, expectations.* Washington, DC: American Association for the Advancement of Science. Reprint, 1968.

# Using the Activities

The activities in *A Head Start on Science: Encouraging a Sense of Wonder* are developmentally appropriate for all children in early childhood education settings. Children as young as two years old will enjoy observing and exploring new and familiar materials. At the same time, primary-grade children will enjoy the challenges of experimenting and finding out more, while they organize their information and try out new ways to communicate the results. Every activity calls for active involvement of children and adults. Adults do not focus on teaching children science "facts," but rather encourage children to make discoveries on their own and to frame new questions.

Each activity includes the following components:

Investigation:        A simple description of the activity that includes the main point of the investigation.

Process Skills:        A list of the science-process skills children will use during investigation.

Materials:        A list of all materials needed to complete the investigation.

Procedure:        The procedure is divided into four sections:

*Getting started*:

Suggestions for beginning the investigation. Most include a caution for the adult to watch children and listen to what they say before asking questions.

*Questions and comments to guide children*:

Examples of questions and comments that will focus children's attention on the investigation. Listening to children is equally important to forming questions and making comments. As you listen and follow children's leads, decide which questions to ask, or which comments to make. Choose only a few; child talk should dominate as the investigation proceeds.

*What children and adults will do*:

A description of what children and adults will probably do as they engage in process skills. It is quite possible, however, that children's interests may move the activity in a different direction. Adults should take advantage of these "teachable moments" even if the activity does not go exactly as planned. For example, children may be fascinated by looking through a hand lens and may begin looking through a variety of transparent objects instead of just looking at their hands as the teacher had planned.

*Closure*:

A description of how the investigation might end. This includes various ways children might communicate their findings, including participating in discussion, drawing, or graphing. It sometimes involves including children in the clean-up process or in deciding where to store materials.

**Follow-up Activities:** Many of the investigations include suggestions for follow-up activities using the same or similar materials that will help children make additional discoveries. Of course children love repetition, so you may want to repeat a popular activity exactly the way it was originally presented before introducing variations.

**Center Connections:** Center connections remind you to keep the materials you have been using available to children so that they can continue to make discoveries on their own. Art connections suggest ways children can represent their work through painting, drawing, and making models.

# Introduction

Literature Connections:

Teachers can use the books in the "Literature Connections" lists in a variety of ways, including as read-alouds and for story dramatizations and expanding science content. When teachers use versions of the printed word—by recording children's observations and by displaying and reading related book—children increase their understanding of how printed language works. Thus it is important that written materials and books with science themes be an everyday part of the classroom environment.

The books listed in each activity include titles recommended by the Head Start on Science curriculum developers and by teachers who have used the activities in this book in their classrooms. A special effort was made to include books from the NSTA "Outstanding Science Trade Books for Students K–12" lists of the past decade.

Assessment Outcomes and Possible Indicators:

The "Head Start Child Outcomes Framework" (see Appendix A for the complete framework) is intended to guide early childhood education programs in their ongoing assessment of the progress and accomplishments of children and in their efforts to analyze and use data on child outcomes in program self-assessment and continuous improvement. The framework is composed of 8 general domains, 27 domain elements, and 100 examples of more specific indicators of children's skills, abilities, knowledge, and behaviors.

Science activities include many of the elements in all eight domains. (In fact you will find it almost impossible to find a developmentally appropriate science activity for young children that does not cross domains!) So, for example, any activity in which children are discussing what they are discovering will include indicators under the "Language Development" domain and the domain element "Speaking and Communicating." Possible indicators might be one of the following:

- Develops increased abilities to understand and use language to communicate information, experiences, ideas, feelings, opinions, needs, questions, and other varied purposes.

- Progresses in abilities to initiate and respond appropriately in conversation and discussions with peers and adults.

- Uses an increasingly complex and varied spoken vocabulary.

For each activity, we give the three to six most prominent domain indicators. As you conduct the activities with children, you will discover many other indicators that are not listed that you can measure for some of the children in your group. For example, you may notice a non-English-speaking child responding for the first time to directions given in English. Another child may spontaneously count to 10 while gathering rocks. Each of the eight child outcomes domain indicators has been identified for some of the activities, but only science indicators have been listed for all activities.

What to
Look For (Rubric):

Although you may use a rubric in your agency's assessment tool that uses different terms than ours, the rubric we provide—"What to Look For"—will easily convert into the measurements you are currently using. The following general rubric has been adapted for each activity.

| Not Yet | Lack of interest or curiosity about the subject |
|---|---|
| Emerging | Reluctant to participate in activities where the subject is examined; only looks; shows some curiosity about the subject |
| Almost Mastered | Willing to look, touch, listen, and discuss subject either in a group or independently; shows curiosity and may begin to ask questions |
| Fully Mastered | Independently notices; willing to explore; listens and describes and asks about the subject; shows a strong natural curiosity |

Family Science Connection (in English and Spanish): A Family Science Connection concludes almost every activity. These connections, which are intended to be photocopied and sent home with students, extend the learning that has taken place at school and involve the whole family in a pleasurable learning activity. The suggested materials can easily be found in the home or in the nearby outside environment. Directions are simple and open-ended, allowing family members to make choices depending on their particular interests and the availability of materials. Family members are also offered suggestions for comments or questions to use to stimulate children's curiosity.

# Teaching Respect for Living Things

Young children are often highly attracted to animals, insects, and many reptiles—especially those that can fit in the palms of their hands. These creatures bring squeals of joy and excitement from most children as their faces light up with wonder, watching the uniqueness of all tiny creatures. Bringing "critters" into your early childhood setting can be a marvelous decision. You simply need to plan for the proper care of them.

A sound first step is to select creatures such as insects (e.g., consider caterpillar-to-butterfly kits). Small reptiles and fish are also popular choices; however, reptiles and sometimes fish require a constant heat source, which calls for the use of electrical components in the classroom, which in turn can pose electrical dangers. It is also wise to steer clear of "hairy" critters that often have the dander that can cause allergic reactions or asthmatic flare-ups. Using the internet, your local pet store, or biological supply houses as resources, learn about the habitat and food needed for the critter of your choice. Encourage the children to help with creating the habitat for their new "guest" to live in. Talk about proper feeding and care of the critter and ask the children to help you with the responsibilities of caring for this living creature. Before your new "guest" is brought into your classroom or learning setting, take time with the children to help them understand how this critter is different from plastic, rubber, or other toy critters they may have played with at home. Help them to understand how to respect and honor their new "guest's" food, handling, habitat, and space needs. You can ask them to draw pictures and create stories about a living creature similar to your new "guest" in which they tell or show how we can all help these creatures to live a healthy life in our setting.

Be aware that some children will show some fear of some creatures. Do not try to force them to handle creatures that scare them. (And it is very important for *you* not to react negatively!) Begin by asking them to observe interesting features of the critter from outside the critter's glassed or caged area. Over time, most children will eventually want to handle the critter once their fears subside and their confidence grows.

When incorporating the use of animals into the doing of science, be sure to continue to remind children that living creatures have similar needs to humans. Like us, they need food, shelter from harm, care, and respect from others. Encourage children to observe living creatures, handle them with gentleness and care, and be responsible for taking good care of them. Also consider inviting park naturalists, veterinarians, or 4-H members to bring animals into the classroom to demonstrate proper handling.

In some of the activities in *A Head Start on Science* you and your children are encouraged to find some sort of critter in your own neighborhood. When you do, make certain that children understand the importance of *returning* that living thing to its own "home" after the activity ends.

Animals provide wonderful opportunities for children to question and wonder as they watch them move, eat, drink, and play. Try to follow the children's questions and allow them to safely explore what it is they wonder about the animals in their care or those they see in the natural environment.

## Resources: Respect for Living Things

"Animals in the classroom." Head Start Guidelines for Animals in the Early Childhood Classroom. *www.head-start.lane.or.us/administration/policy/health/classroom-animals.html*

"Learning to care through kindness: A guide for teachers. Alberta (Canada) Teachers Association. *www.sacsc.ca/PDF%20files/Resources/Humane%20Education.pdf#search=%22respecting%20animals%20in%20the%20classroom%22*

"NSTA position statement on responsible use of live animals and dissection in the science classroom." *www.nsta.org/positionstatement&psid=44*

# Children With Special Needs
# Can Do Science

*All* children can and should do science—starting at a very early age. The science they do should flow from their natural curiosities. Teachers and caregivers of children with special needs may find themselves in pathways that are new to them, with unfamiliar curricula, adaptive technologies, equipment, and other special learning supports. Don't let these new pathways overwhelm or threaten you! They may be new for you, but, as the facilitator of early learning, you need to become familiar and comfortable with all that is available to help support the learning of science by all children. You need not take on these tasks alone, nor all at one time. Let your journey begin with the special needs children currently in your classroom.

## Physical Special Needs

### Children With Allergies or Asthma

Children with allergies and asthma are present in virtually all childhood settings. These children cannot be grouped together under one heading, nor can they be instructionally adjusted for in a single manner. For some, your instructional changes may simply mean eliminating a certain food from use in your activities. For others, the impact may be greater. Allergies to foods, plants, manufactured products, and natural environmental stimuli all need to be considered carefully as you plan for instruction. In general, plan "healthy" science activities that are aimed at all the children BUT be ready to offer alternatives to children who cannot participate in the full original lesson. Choosing alternative foods, working with latex-free gloves, eliminating cleaning products and their odors from the classroom environment, choosing classroom pets with little to no dander—these are some, but not all, of the changes you may need to make to offer a healthy science learning environment.

We know that physically active children typically are healthier children and going outside to play is often part of the daily program. However, children with environmental allergies and asthma are often affected by seasonal changes in the outdoor environment. For example, a science nature hunt or activity in the summer months may work well for all your children, but may need to be adjusted in the fall or spring for any children who are affected by various pollens or molds. Try to be aware of each child's special needs and plan for lesson alternatives accordingly. If you are aware ahead of time, the lesson adjustments needed are usually fairly easy to make.

## Children Who Are Hearing or Sight Challenged

The world of science must not be closed to students who are either hearing or sight challenged. Children with these special needs should be offered ample opportunity to explore based on their curiosities, talents, and abilities. Caregivers and teachers will have to modify lessons to support exploration based on the child's strengths. This may mean enlarging printed text and pictures, using adaptive technologies in the classroom, making sure all lessons take advantage of multiple ways of learning, increasing the number of ways directions are given—verbal, written, images, sign language, Braille—modifying the ways children are asked to interact with one another, adding sign language to skills offered learners in your setting, and discussing how all people are able to learn and contribute in unique ways to our society. The ideas offered in the resource list on page xxviii will help you to make instructional changes based on children's hearing or visual special needs.

## Children Who Have Physical Challenges With Their Limbs

Due to birth defects, disease, or accidents, some young children struggle to use their arms or legs without the aid of adaptive devices such as prostheses, crutches, walkers, or wheelchairs. To assist these students you should first concentrate on modifying the classroom environment to enlarge aisles and traffic pathways to accommodate children who need to use ambulatory devices. Similarly, learning centers, eating areas, and play areas where science activities take place should have tables and areas easily accessible to these children. You may also need to adopt or adapt lesson materials or science tools to make activities possible for those with fine-motor challenges or those using prosthetic limbs. After you have modified the classroom environment and science tools, then you can focus on thinking about doing science outdoors. Once again, choose learning environments that are accessible to all—the terrain, natural barriers, and availability of accessible pathways or vehicles must be taken into consideration when planning outdoor science activities and field trips.

# Cognitive and Emotional Special Needs

Some of your children may have developmental or cognitive impairments, learning disabilities, or sociological or emotional challenges. All of these challenges may negatively affect student attention, engagement, and achievement. But each challenge also brings its own unique set of triggers, trials, and learning implications to the forefront. As teacher or caregiver you need to be aware of your children's diagnosed needs and how each child's family is supporting and coping with these needs and issues. Ultimately you and your colleagues will need to partner with the family to meet the needs of the child.

Science activities can often be door-openers for children coping with learning challenges. The open-endedness, inquiry-based, student-centered environment that is at the heart of rich science learning offers children opportunities to be themselves while exploring and learning science concepts. Teachers who celebrate what children think, what they question, and what they wonder about are wonderful facilitators of all children, especially those with cognitive and socioemotional challenges.

## Cultural and Linguistic Special Needs

As communities around the nation increase in cultural and linguistic diversity, so, too, does the diversity of the children you see each day. Ultimately, research tells us that accepting, respecting, honoring, and celebrating all children's cultures and languages are important first steps in accepting a child fully as a person and as a learner. Science activities offer us great ways to support English language learners as well as to invite full participation into the learning community.

Because hands-on investigations and open-ended activities build on the natural curiosity of children, they help to overcome many language or cultural barriers. Teachers and caregivers can offer the science challenges in multiple languages, use pictures to support conceptual understanding, and support the ways students communicate and interact through language, drawing, and the use of manipulatives. Science should not be thought of as a vocabulary-laden, text-based curricular area, but rather a field of study that is curiosity-based, question-driven, and open-ended. Thinking of science in this way will make it a wonderful common ground on which to bring children of all languages and cultures together as a learning community.

## Resources: Children With Special Needs

"Child care centers and the Americans with Disabilities Act—Frequently asked questions." U.S. Department of Justice. *www.usdoj.gov/crt/ada/childq%26a.htm*

"Coping with crisis: Helping children with special needs—Tips for school personnel and parents." National Association of School Psychologists. *www.nasponline.org/neat/specpop_general.html*

# Introduction

"Early childhood and elementary education disability resource information." *www. disabilityinfo.gov/digov-public/public/DisplayPage.do?parentFolderId=73*

"NSTA position statement on students with disabilities." *www.nsta.org/position statement&psid=41*

Porter, L. 2002. Educating young children with special needs. Thousand Oaks, CA. Sage Publications. *www.sagepub.com/booksProdDesc.nav?contribId=526620&p rodId=Book225572*

"Responding to cultural and linguistic diversity: Recommendations for effective early childhood education—A position statement." National Association for the Education of Young Children. *www.naeyc.org/about/positions/pdf/PSDIV98.PDF#searc h=%22early%20childhood%20cultural%20and%20linguistic%20challenges%22*

Schwartz, I. S., S. L. Odom, and S. R. Sandall. "Including young children with special needs." Redmond, Washington: New Horizons Learning, Childcare Information Exchange. *www.newhorizons.org/spneeds/inclusion/information/shwartz3.htm*

# Safely Doing Science With Young Children

Wonderful science learning happens when young children enthusiastically explore their worlds. As teachers and caregivers of these children, we have the responsibility to provide safe environments for their explorations. Here are some of the safety issues that early childhood educators are likely to encounter and some suggestions for establishing and maintaining safe indoor and outdoor learning environments.

## The Senses

When "doing science," early childhood teachers often encourage activities involving the senses. It is important to think about setting up the classroom and outdoor environment so that children can use their senses to explore safely.

| | |
|---|---|
| Observing/ Seeing: | You will already be aware of the need for safety with respect to children's eyes. In particular, children need to be reminded to use caution when using sticks or sharp objects to probe an object of interest. If available, safety glasses or goggles are appropriate for children to wear at those times. Since these are not usually available to teachers of young children, however, consider using blunt objects for probing. Some teachers use such things as craft sticks, cotton swabs, and unsharpened pencils because they are not sharp and yet are easy for small hands to use to move or lift objects while exploring. However, children should be directly supervised if using these probes because children are apt to stick the probes in their ears and noses (even eyes). A safer probe might be a spatula. Start with a large spatula and work down to a smaller size as you determine your students' dexterity. |
| Touching: | Most of what children will be touching while engaging in science learning will not be dangerous. We often use the sense of touch to discover and to discuss words and concepts such as *smooth, rough, bumpy,* and *patterned*. At times, however, touching objects can be unsafe. For example, it is important to help young children learn the proper way to "touch" hot and sharp objects or elements that might be safety hazards. It is never too early for children to learn the signs and signals that something may be hot. Sensing heat or warmth, seeing a red, white, or blue glow, observing sparks or fire—these are all signs that an object may be *hot* and should NOT |

be touched. You will need to teach children these signs and tell them that they should always be with an adult if hot objects are present in their home, classroom, or outdoor areas.

Teachers and caregivers also need to help children learn about the potential dangers of touching sharp objects. Pins, needles, knives, plants' thorns and needles, saws, and animals' spikes and teeth are all sharp and can easily cut or puncture children's fingers. Helping children recognize sharp objects and their potential dangers is an important first step. Next, limit the number of sharp objects in your learning environment. That would include sharp corners on furniture, playground equipment, and toys. Finally, help the children to understand how to carry sharp objects with their points or sharp edges pointed away from their bodies and to alert an adult immediately if anyone is cut or punctured by a sharp object. Small cuts may only require cleansing (using antibacterial soap) and a Band-Aid, while deeper cuts may require medical attention and stitches. Puncture wounds often require medical attention as the wound can easily become infected.

**Smelling and Tasting:** From birth, children put their hands in their mouths and near their noses as their primary ways of experiencing the world. As you know, this doesn't stop when they become involved in day care or preschool. Much of the excitement of experiencing the everyday world comes through tasting new foods and smelling new smells. Without becoming over-cautious, teachers and caregivers can help children learn some safety tips regarding tasting and smelling in the learning environment. Obviously, young children should learn that they should NEVER put anything in their mouths except foodstuffs or things identified by trusted adults as *foods that are safe to eat*. Furthermore, they need to understand the dangers of putting objects into their noses. When smelling, you should help children learn how to detect odors from a distance of several inches—not by burying their noses into the chosen element to be smelled. **In addition, it is extremely important to check for allergies (e.g., to peanuts or chocolate) among all children in your care before including any foodstuffs in your classroom activities.**

Listening:  One way to experience the details and nuances of the world around us is to use our ears—to sit quietly and *listen*. Assisting children to acquire this skill will help them to become better observers of their environments. An outdoor environment where the children can close their eyes and hear the sounds of nature from the insects, animals, and birds is a perfect place to begin your listening training. If you're in the middle of a city, this still works—except that the sounds will be different! Less desirable would be using tapes or CDs of nature, city, or industry sounds to substitute for this natural experience.

In any case, it is important to remind children to take care of their ears and their hearing throughout their lives. If noises or music are so loud that a sound hurts your ears, the sound level is unsafe and precautions should be taken to keep your ears from being harmed. If possible, turning down the volume of the noise or music should be the first step. If this is not possible, wearing ear plugs to dampen the noise level should be the second choice. In today's world where even young children have music and video hand devices with personal earphones or "earbuds," it is important to educate everyone as to the irreparable harm loud music or noise can cause the human ear. Finally, always remind young children not to put anything into their ears. Cotton swabs and other probe-like objects should not be used in the ears as they can easily damage the ear drum.

## General Caution for All Outside Activities

Extended time outside exposes children to damaging ultraviolet radiation, which is cumulative. Offer parents the option of providing children sunscreen and/or protective clothing to reduce exposure on a regular basis.

Remember that some children have allergies to pollen, grass, and so forth. Parents should be consulted about these possible allergies.

## Electricity

When planning science activities, remember the need to plan for the safe use of electricity. Make sure all unused electrical outlets are covered, all loose cords are handled appropriately, all electrical tools or appliances are unplugged after use, and all electrical appliances are kept away from water and water sources.

## Safety Summary

Being aware of safety hazards and having the resources to plan safe science learning activities are necessary for all those who manage or teach in early childhood learning settings. The reminders and suggestions in the paragraphs above, together with the information found in the section on children with special needs (pp. xxv–xxviii) and the resources listed below, will serve as a fine foundation for planning and implementing safe science activities. In addition, all teachers and caregivers should be aware of the safety procedures, crisis/natural disaster procedures, and parent notification plans in place at their school or caregiver sites. Knowing and following these procedures is vital to the safety of all children.

## Resources: Safety

"First aid and safety." Kids Health. *http://kidshealth.org/parent/firstaid_safe/index.html*

"Food safety quiz for kids." Food and Drug Administration. *www.fda.gov/oc/opacom/kids/html/wash_hands.htm*

"Health, safety and nutrition for young children: Information resource links." *www.headstartinfo.org/infocenter/guides/healthsafetynutrition.htm*

"NSTA position statement on safety and school science instruction." *www.nsta.org/positionstatement&psid=32*

"Why is hand washing important?" Centers for Disease Control and Prevention. *www.cdc.gov/od/oc/media/pressrel/r2k0306c.htm*

Graham, L. 2001. "Farm safety for young children." Iowa State University, University Extension. *www.extension.iastate.edu/Publications/PM1592.pdf#search=%22science%20safety%20with%20young%20children%22*

Kwan, T., and J. Texley. 2002. *Exploring safely: A guide for elementary teachers.* Arlington, VA: NSTA Press.

Texley, J., N. Visconti-Phillips, F. Hess, and K. Roy. 2003. *Safety in the elementary science classroom* (a flipchart). Arlington, VA: NSTA Press.

# SIMPLE GRAPHING
# FOR YOUNG CHILDREN

**Purpose:** Making graphs is one way to document children's investigations. Graphs can help children make sense of their discoveries by giving them a visual representation of their findings. They reinforce the science processes of observing, comparing, classifying, and recording information.

**Procedure:** There are many different ways to make graphs with children. The rule of thumb is, The younger the child, the more concrete the graph should be.

1. The most concrete graphs use real objects. For example, if children were investigating which bird food is most popular with birds, and there were three choices—popcorn, stale bread, and birdseed—children could glue a real piece of food on a graph each time they saw a bird visit a feeder and chose to eat one of the three foods. The graph would look something like this:

**POPCORN**  **BREAD**  **BIRDSEEDS**

2. A variation of the "concrete graphs" described above uses photographs of children to record their choices. For example, if children were choosing their favorite pie from among several (e.g., apple, cherry, pumpkin, and lemon), place pictures of the pies along a horizontal line and then have children "vote" for their favorite by placing their photos above the one they like best. The resulting graph, in which

each child's photo makes up part of a particular bar, depicts how your class has voted on the favorite-pie choices.

In this day of digital cameras, here is an easy way to get a supply of children's photos:

- Take digital "head shots" of each child.

- Take your picture files to a store that prints digital photos and request that a "contact sheet" be made. A contact sheet can also be produced by using a photo software program such as "Photoshop Elements" or "Picassa" (available free online). (You will need access to a printer.) For specific instructions, access the software's "Help" menu and request information about printing "contact sheets."

- You can cut the contact sheet into separate small photos of each of the children, or, to save on printing costs, you can use a copy machine to make 20–30 copies of each sheet. Each contact sheet typically displays 24 pictures. Use a paper cutter to separate the sheets into photos of identical size.

- If you place each child's set of photos in an envelope with his or her name on it, you will have extra photos ready to let the children record their "votes" on any number of issues!

- If you do not have access to a digital camera, get some black-and-white film and take "head shot" pictures as described above. When you take the film for developing and printing, request a "contact sheet" and then proceed as described above.

3. A similar graph could use children's symbols in place of their photos. Younger children will, however, relate more readily to photos than to symbols.

4. A more abstract graph could use children's names. For example, if children made three different kinds of bubble makers, you could make a chart with pictures of the three types. Children who used strawberry baskets would put their names under the picture of the basket (or you could write it for them); those who used pipe cleaners would put their names under the picture of the pipe cleaner; and so forth.

5.  Another type of graph is sometimes done on a sorting mat. This is a piece of poster board or a tray of some sort that is divided in half. After children have experimented with magnets for several days, for example, they could help you put magnetic objects on one side of the graph and those that are not magnetic on the other side. This activity is very concrete, but it will need adult help to decide on the categories (in this case, "magnetic" or "not magnetic").

6.  A "bar" graph helps children to see changes in plants, insects (e.g., silkworms) or animals (e.g., ducks). For example, when measuring plant growth, give the children strips of paper about one inch wide. Tell children the strips will help them keep track of how much their plant has grown. Give children one strip each day and ask them to make their strips the same size as their plant. Have children keep their strips in an envelope. When the plant has grown big enough to send it home, have children glue their strips onto a piece of construction paper. Most will glue them randomly, but some may put them in order of size. Ask questions like "Which strip shows how small your plant was after it was first planted?" "Which shows how big your plant is now?"

# SCIENCE TEACHING BOARDS AND BOXES

All of these teaching aids may be used while doing science activities or can be kept at the science center for the children's use year-round.

### Shape Board

*How to make*: Cut out different shapes from construction paper and glue them on a poster board.

*How to use*: (1) Refer to the board whenever you want to help the children recognize and match the shape of different items. (2) Have children use/sort items on the boards that are similar in shape.

### Color Board

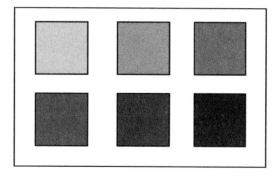

*How to make*: Cut out different-color squares and glue them on the board.

*How to use*: (1) Refer to the color board to match and recognize the colors of different objects. (2) Have children sort different objects on the board that are similar in color.

### Texture Board

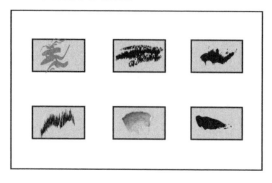

*How to make*: Glue different-texture objects on a board (e.g., cotton = soft; sandpaper = rough; bubble wrap = bumpy; waxed paper = smooth; masking tape = sticky [sticky side up]).

*How to use*: (1) Refer to the board to recognize and match items to various textures. (2) Have children sort different items on the board that are similar in texture.

## Size Box

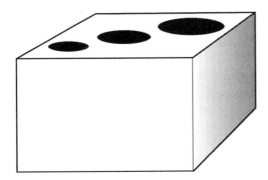

*How to make*: Cut three different-size holes on the lid of a shoe box. Place cardboard "walls" to separate sections inside the shoe box for each size hole. Label holes from smallest to largest—e.g., 1–3.

*How to use*: To help children compare and estimate the size of objects to a given standard, have children predict the smallest hole that a given object will fit into and then try it out.

## Feely Box

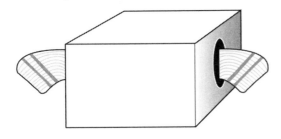

*How to make*: Cut a 3½"–4" hole in both ends of a shoe box. Cut off the top part of two old socks, and tape them hanging out of each hole.

*How to use*: The children should put their hands through the sock top and into the box to feel an object. Two children can use the box at the same time and communicate what each one is touching.

# BASIC MATERIALS LIST

Materials for science activities in an early childhood setting are simple and easy to find. You may be surprised at how many of the suggested materials you already have or have easy access to. Because science happens everywhere in your indoor and outdoor environment, we have listed materials under the areas in which these items might be stored.

|  | Purchased | Found |
|---|---|---|
| **Block Area** | Hard wood unit blocks | Cardboard tubes |
|  | Small cars | Hard wood unit blocks |
|  | Tape |  |
|  | Pipe insulators |  |
|  | Marbles |  |
| **Art Area** | Paint | Water |
|  | Flour | Bowls of various sizes |
|  | Glue | Newsprint |
|  | Food coloring | Coffee filters |
|  | Tissue paper | Spoons |
|  | Salt | Pie pans |
|  | Cornstarch | Strawberry baskets |
|  | Pipe cleaners | Soda-can-holder plastic rings |
|  | Liquid soap | Straws |
|  | Borax | Cardboard tubes from rolls of toilet paper |
|  | Sorting trays | Tubing |
|  | Paintbrushes | Plastic egg cartons |
|  | Paper towels | Colored telephone wire |
|  | Colored paper | String |
|  | Markers, crayons |  |
|  | Feathers |  |
|  | Colored chalk |  |
|  | Clay |  |

| (continued) | Purchased | Found |
| --- | --- | --- |
| **Dramatic Play** | Equal-arm balance<br>Flashlights<br>Different fabrics<br>Measuring cups<br>Terrarium<br>Fish aquarium | Food cans<br>Flowers<br>Different scents<br>Scarves<br>Paper bags<br>Plastic bottles<br>Wooden clothespins<br>Keys<br>Homemade can telephones |
| **Manipulatives** | Magnets<br>Hand lenses<br>Prisms<br>Bottle caps<br>Eyedroppers<br>Marbles | Various size containers |
| **Book Area** | Animal books<br>Critter books<br>Weather books<br>Construction books<br>Machine books<br>Nature books<br>Literature books | Field trip photos<br>Child-made books<br>Newspaper and magazine science photos<br>Museum pamphlets<br>Nature center pamphlets |
| **Music** | Purchased instruments<br>Cassette/CD player<br>Tape recorder<br>Cassettes/CDs<br>Bean bags | Homemade instruments<br>Homemade sound cans<br>Tapes of familiar sounds<br>Scarves |

| (continued) | Purchased | Found |
| --- | --- | --- |
| **Outdoors** | Balls | Trees |
| | Balance beam | Plants |
| | Large wooden blocks | Flowers |
| | Bug boxes | Critters |
| | Swings | Leaves |
| | Slide, climber | Water |
| | Water table | |
| | Sand | |
| | Sandbox | |
| | Camera | |
| | Resealable plastic bags | |
| | Sand and water toys | |
| | Vegetables | |
| | Fruit | |

# THE SENSES

Young children learn about their world through their senses. Babies learn about objects by putting them in their mouths, banging them on the floor, dropping, rolling, shaking, and throwing them. Preschool and primary grade children continue to observe materials and objects to learn about them, although they can begin to be somewhat more systematic in their observations. They also begin to organize their information as they compare and classify objects by their attributes. Is this fruit sweet or tart? How does my skin look when I use a hand lens? Does it look different when I look through the prism? And they can communicate their discoveries in various ways, such as by making a graph or a touch collage, where they separate the rough and smooth textures.

All science activities involve the use of one or more of the senses. Focusing on each sense individually at the beginning of the year helps children become more aware of how the senses are used to learn about their world.

## The Senses: Selected Internet Resources

### Senses in General
- Preschool Activities, Songs, and Resources on Senses—*www.preschoolrainbow.org/ 5senses.htm*

### Shapes and Colors
- Open Directory: Preschool: Shapes and Colors—*http://dmoz.org/Kids_and_Teens/ Pre-school/Shapes_and_Colors*
- Color Songs and Poems—*www.storyplace. org/preschool/activities/musiconact. asp?themeid=15*
- Online Story and Resources About Shapes—*http://pbskids.org/rogers/ parentsteachers/theme/1736.html*

### Taste and Smell
- What Does Purple Smell Like?—*http:// findarticles.com/p/articles/mi_qa3614/ is_199707/ai_n8761391*
- Healthy Food Ideas and Activities for Children, Parents, and Teachers—*www. humec.ksu.edu/fnp/primary.html*

# USEFUL HAND LENSES

**Investigation:** Looking through hand lenses to see how objects change perceived size and visual orientation.

**Process Skill:** Observing

**Materials:** Hand lenses; a variety of objects to look at, such as leaves, rocks, bugs, cloth, shells, and feathers

## Procedure:

*Getting started:*
Put out a variety of hand lenses, one for each child, if possible. If you have a large magnifier, make that available as well. Put out a variety of interesting things for children to look at (see "Materials"). Let children try out their hand lenses. Watch what they do and listen to what they say before asking questions.

*Questions to guide children:*
- What happens when you look through your hand lens?
- What can you see on the (bug) that you couldn't see before?
- How does the hand lens help you see?
- What happens when you move the hand lens farther away from the (bug)?

*What children and adults will do:*
Children will want to look at everything through their hand lens, so be sure to have a large variety of objects. Encourage them to look at each object from a variety of distances.

*Closure:*
Tell children that scientists use hand lenses to help them look at an object carefully and to see very small details they couldn't otherwise see.

## Follow-up Activity:

On another day, do a "walk around" activity, either indoors or outdoors, with a hand lens for each child. Encourage children to look through the magnifier at objects they encounter. Say, "If you want to see it better, look through your hand lens" and, "What can you see now that you couldn't see before?"

## Center Connection:

Always keep a variety of hand lenses in your science center. Encourage children to use them in any part of the classroom or outdoors to help in their investigations. When children are interested in looking at something new, remind them that the hand lens is a tool that will help them to better see the object.

## Literature Connection:

*Is it Larger? Is It Smaller?*
by Tana Hoban, Greenwillow, 1985.

*Look, Look, Look*
by Tana Hoban, Greenwillow, 1985.

## Assessment Outcomes & Possible Indicators*

- **Science A-1** Begins to use senses and a variety of tools and simple measuring devices to gather information, investigate materials and observe processes and relationships.

- **Language Development A-4** For non-English-speaking children, progresses in listening to and understanding English.

- **Language Development B-1** Develops increasing abilities to understand and use language to communicate information, experiences, ideas, opinions, needs, questions and for other varied purposes.

- **Social & Emotional Development B-3** Demonstrates increasing capacity to follow rules and routines and use materials purposefully, safely and respectfully.

*Source: "Head Start Child Outcomes Framework." See Appendix A in this book for the framework.

## What To Look For

| Not Yet | Child does not use hand lens properly or shows no interest. |
|---|---|
| Emerging | Child plays with or handles hand lenses not using it correctly. Child loses interest in activity and is not very talkative. |
| Almost Mastered | Child uses hand lens with adult's help and instruction. Child uses lens on some items and begins to answer a few questions. |
| Fully Mastered | Child uses hand lens correctly. Child looks at objects closely, and eagerly answers most of the adult's questions. Child independently uses hand lens at other times. |

# FAMILY PAGE / PÁGINA PARA LA FAMILIA

## USEFUL HAND LENSES

### Family Science Connection:

**At home** see if family members have some kind of magnifying glass or lens. If so, find three objects to look at under the magnifier and **observe** and **describe** the chosen objects. If a magnifier is not available, find three objects that the family would like to see magnified and see if the **library** has books with pictures that magnify the objects and **compare** the objects at home with the magnified pictures. How do they look different, or do they look just like the real thing but just enlarged?

**Comments or questions** that may add a *sense of wonder* to this activity:

- When you magnified the object, how did it look different?

- What can you see now that you could not see before?

## LENTES ÚTILES

### Ciencia en familia:

**En casa** vea si los **miembros de la familia** tienen una lupa o anteojos de aumento. Si los tienen, **encuentren** tres objetos para verlos con la lupa o anteojos, observarlos y describirlos. Si no tiene disponible ningún lente de aumento, encuentre tres objetos que a la familia le gustaría ver en aumento y vean si la **biblioteca** tiene libros con fotografías de esos objetos en aumento y **compare** los objetos de casa con las fotografías en aumento. ¿Se ven diferentes o se ven como los objetos reales sólo que más grandes?

**Comentarios o preguntas que** pueden *despertar curiosidad* en esta actividad:

- ¿Cuando pusiste el lente sobre el objeto, cómo se veía diferente?

- ¿Qué puedes ver ahora que no podías ver antes?

# LOOKING AT ME

**Investigation:** Looking at skin, nails, hair, and clothes through a hand lens

**Process Skills:** Observing, classifying

**Materials:** Hand lenses (plastic)

## Procedure:

*Getting started:*
Give each child a hand lens and ask the children to look at their hands through the lenses. Give them time to explore before you ask questions. Listen to children's comments to see what they are discovering. Follow their lead. For example, if one child begins looking at the palm of his or her hand, encourage the others to do so also.

*Questions to guide children:*
- What can you see with your hand lens that you couldn't see without it?
- Does your skin look the same on the front of your hand as on the back?
- How did this lens help you?

*What children and adults will do:*
Children will make many discoveries about their hands. On their own they may begin looking at their arms, clothes, or maybe their friends' hair and skin. Follow children's leads, encouraging them to describe what they see.

*Closure:*
If they haven't already, encourage children to look at a friend's or your skin or clothes. Ask, "What do you see that is the same? Different?"

## Follow-up Activities:

Have children use stamp pads to make fingerprints. Then use hand lenses to compare their stamped fingerprints with those on their fingers.

Let children trace each other's bodies on butcher paper, then use appropriate colors to paint the skin tones.

## Center Connection:

Put different things in the science center every week that children can look at with a hand lens. Encourage children to carry their hand lenses with them to look at other objects in the classroom.

## Literature Connection:

*Black Is Brown Is Tan*
by Arnold Adoff, Harper Junior, 1973.

*The Colors of Us*
by Karen Katz, Owlet Paperbacks (reprint ed.), 2002.

*Faces*
by Kati Teague, Renyl Editions, 1989.

*We're Different, We're the Same*
by Bobbi Kates, Random House Books for Young Readers, 1992.

# LOOKING AT ME

## Assessment Outcomes & Possible Indicators*

- **Science A-1** Begins to use senses and a variety of tools and simple measuring devices to gather information, investigate materials and observe processes and relationships.

- **Science B-1** Expands knowledge of and abilities to observe, describe and discuss the natural world, materials, living things and natural processes.

- **Science B-2** Expands knowledge of and respect for their body and the environment.

- **Language Development B-1** Develops increasing abilities to understand and use language to communicate information, experiences, ideas, opinions, needs, questions and for other varied purposes.

- **Social & Emotional Development A-1** Begins to develop and express awareness of self in terms of specific abilities, characteristics and preferences.

*Source: "Head Start Child Outcomes Framework." See Appendix A in this book for the framework.

## What To Look For

| Not Yet | Child does not use hand lens properly or shows no interest. |
|---|---|
| Emerging | Child plays with or handles hand lenses not using it correctly. Child participates but imitates others and is not very talkative or observant. |
| Almost Mastered | Child uses hand lens with adult's help and instruction. Child uses lens to view different body parts and responds to body parts observations. |
| Fully Mastered | Child uses hand lens correctly. Child looks at body parts closely. Child eagerly responds to what is observed and leads most of the discussion. Child shares discoveries with adults and peers, and uses hand lens at other times. |

# FAMILY PAGE / PÁGINA PARA LA FAMILIA

## LOOKING AT ME

### Family Science Connection:

**At home** during a relaxing time (between TV commercials) put two family members' hands together and **observe and describe color, size, shape, and texture differences or similarities.** Do this same observation with other members and other body parts. Talk about physical traits that are most common in the family. Hair color, skin shades, and shape of hands or toes are some traits that can be **classified** as common for your family!

**Comments or questions** that may add a *sense of wonder* to this activity:

- Do your thumbs all have the same shape? Do your fingers?

- What other parts of our bodies look alike? What other family members have the most similar looks?

## MIRÁNDOME A MÍ

### Ciencia en familia:

**En casa** durante un tiempo de descanso (entre los comerciales de televisión) junte las manos de dos miembros de la familia; **observe y describa las diferencias y semejanzas entre los colores, los tamaños, las formas, y los texturas.** Haga esta misma observación con otros miembros de la familia y otras partes del cuerpo. Hable acerca de los rasgos físicos familiares que son más comunes entre la familia. ¡El color de cabello, la tez o el color de la piel, y la forma de las manos o de los dedos de los pies son algunos rasgos que pueden ser **clasificados** como comunes para su familia!

**Comentarios o preguntas** que pueden *despertar curiosidad* en esta actividad:

- ¿Tienen la misma forma todos tus pulgar? ¿Y los dedos?

- ¿Qué otras partes de nuestros cuerpos se parecen mucho? ¿Qué otros miembros de la familia se parecen más entre sí?

# PRISM PLAY

**Investigation:** Discovering that sunlight shining through a prism produces rainbow colors; looking through a prism to see that images change position

**Process Skills:** Observing, communicating

**Materials:** Prisms (one for each child if possible), white paper, nontoxic markers or crayons

## Procedure:

*Getting started:*
Go outside on a sunny day. Let children experiment by looking through their prisms at objects and people. Then have children place pieces of white paper on the ground. Show children how to hold their prisms so that the sunlight shines through the large side of the prism onto the paper. Ask them to move their prisms slightly to see what happens.

*Questions to guide children:*
  • What do you see?
  • What happens when you turn your prism around?

*What children and adults will do:*
Children may need some assistance in discovering exactly how to hold their prisms. They will be excited about seeing the colors of the rainbow. Let them experiment with their prisms. They will notice that sometimes things look upside down. Notice what children say and do and point out their discoveries to the other children.

*Closure:*
Hold one or two of the prisms yourself so that a rainbow shows on the white paper. Give children crayons or markers and ask them to "record" what they see by drawing a rainbow. Once inside, have children try producing a rainbow inside the classroom. Talk briefly about how the light comes through the prism to produce colors.

## Follow-up Activities:

Other ways to make rainbows: (1) On another sunny day when children are making bubbles, see if children notice the rainbows that occur when the sunlight shines through their bubbles. (2) Hang a piece of beveled glass in a window in your classroom and children will notice the rainbow on the wall produced when the sun shines through the glass. You can ask, "Are the rainbows from the bubbles and the rainbows from the glass the same or different? How do we know?"

## Center Connection:

Have prisms in the science center available for children to use.

## Literature Connection:

*A Rainbow of My Own*
by Don Freeman, Viking, 1966.

# PRISM PLAY

## Assessment Outcomes & Possible Indicators*

- **Science A-1** Begins to use senses and a variety of tools and simple measuring devices to gather information, investigate materials and observe processes and relationships.

- **Language Development B-1** Develops increasing abilities to understand and use language to communicate information, experiences, ideas, opinions, needs, questions and for other varied purposes.

- **Creative Arts B-2** Progresses in abilities to create drawings, paintings, models, and other art creations that are more detailed, creative or realistic.

  *Source: "Head Start Child Outcomes Framework." See Appendix A in this book for the framework.

## What To Look For

| Not Yet | Child does not use prism according to directions or shows no interest. |
|---|---|
| Emerging | Child plays with or handles prism, but not correctly; imitates others, repeating what is heard, or is not very talkative or observant. |
| Almost Mastered | Child uses prisms with adult's help and instruction; child finds rainbow colors or sees images change positions. Child tries to describe observations, but doesn't have the correct vocabulary. |
| Fully Mastered | Child uses prisms correctly. Child finds rainbow colors and sees that images change positions; eagerly responds and leads most of the discussion. |

# COLOR WALK

**Investigation:** Looking for objects in the environment that are a particular color

**Process Skills:** Observing, comparing, classifying, communicating

**Materials:** Chart paper, nontoxic markers, a piece of colored paper for each child, a few objects from the environment that are a particular color

## Procedure:

*Getting started:*
Choose a color that will be found often in your environment. Green is a good one to start with, but there may be many other colors depending on the season and your location. (Repeat this on other days with a different color each day.) Tell the children they are going to look for this color as they go on a walk. Hold up several shades of the color you have chosen. Say, "These are all different shades of green, but they are all called green." Give each child a piece of green paper. Go on the color walk. Encourage children to look everywhere for objects that are green.

*Questions to guide children:*
 • What can you find that is green?
 • Do all the greens look the same?
 • How many different things can you find that are green?

*What children and adults will do:*
Children will find many green objects. They may name something that is not green. In that case ask them to look at their paper and ask if it is the same color. Many young children confuse colors and cannot accurately match colors. Don't correct the child but instead point out some of the objects that are green that other children are finding: "Judy found a green car."

*Closure:*
When you return to your classroom, ask children to describe what they saw that was the designated color. Make a chart, labeling it "Our Green Walk." Draw pictures of the objects children remember seeing. Write the words next to the drawings. Write and draw using a marker that is the same color as the objects children were looking for.

## Follow-up Activity:

This activity can be repeated in the classroom; ask parents to send something that is green to school; share on a "green" table.

## Center Connection:

Emphasize the same color for a few days in different ways. Children could make green paint by mixing blue and yellow. Add green food coloring to scrambled eggs.

## Literature Connection:

*Red Is Best*
by Kathy Stinson, Firefly, 1982.

*Color Dance*
by Ann Jonas, Greenwillow, 1989.

*Growing Colors*
by Bruce McMillan, Lothrop, Lee, and Shepard Books, 1988.

*My First Book of Colors*
by Eric Carle, Crowell, 1974.

# COLOR WALK

## Assessment Outcomes & Possible Indicators*

- **Science A-2** Develops increased ability to observe and discuss common properties, differences and comparisons among objects and materials.

- **Science A-4** Develops growing abilities to collect, describe and record information through a variety of means, including discussions, drawings, maps and charts.

- **Language Development B-1** Develops increasing abilities to understand and use language to communicate information, experiences, ideas, opinions, needs, questions and for other varied purposes.

- **Literacy C-2** Develops growing understanding of the different functions of forms of print such as signs, letters, newspapers, lists, messages and menus.

- **Mathematics B-4** Shows growth in matching, sorting, putting in series and regrouping objects according to one or two attributes such as color, shape or size.

- **Mathematics C-3** Begins to make comparisons between several objects based on a single attribute.

*Source: "Head Start Child Outcomes Framework." See Appendix A in this book for the framework.

## What To Look For

| Not Yet | Child does not see or find any objects of the chosen color or shows no interest. |
|---|---|
| Emerging | Child watches others and copies them; near the end of the activity compares a small number of objects, not very talkative. |
| Almost Mastered | Child looks and finds objects that are the same color being discussed; says one or two things about objects and is curious about other objects that are the same color. |
| Fully Mastered | Child looks at and finds many items that are the colors being learned; eagerly responds to what is seen and leads the discussion. Child has a strong curiosity about the subjects and eagerly repeats the process at other times. |

## COLOR WALK

### Family Science Connection:

**At home** during play time, ask your child if he or she can find an object in the house that is of the color he or she likes best. **Talk** about why your child likes that color and find other objects in the house or outside that have that same favorite color. Together **describe** the color of each of the objects that have the **same** color. So if the child picks green as a favorite color and finds a leaf, a sponge, and a toy that are green, talk about how **similar** the greens are to each other. Point out that there are so many shades of green and, yes, each shade can be called green.

**Comments or questions** that may add a *sense of wonder* to this activity:

- What is it that you like about your favorite color?

- Let's count all the things in the house that have your favorite color in them.

## PASEO DE COLORES

### Ciencia en familia:

**En casa** durante la hora de juego, pídale a su niño(a) que encuentre un objeto en la casa que sea de su color favorito. **Hablen** acerca de por qué le gusta ese color y pídale que encuentre otros objetos dentro y fuera de la casa que son del mismo color. Juntos **describan** los tonos de cada uno de los objetos que tienen el **mismo** color. Si el niño escoge el verde como su color favorito y encuentra una hoja, una esponja y un juguete verdes, hablen acerca de cuán **semejantes** son los verdes unos a otros. Explique que existen muchos tonos de verde y cada tono puede ser llamado verde.

**Comentarios o preguntas** que pueden *despertar curiosidad* en esta actividad:

- ¿Qué es lo que te gusta de tu color favorito?

- Contemos todas las cosas en la casa que tienen tu color favorito.

# SHAPE WALK

**Investigation:** Looking for objects in the environment that are the same as or are similar to ("look like") a particular shape

**Process Skills:** Observing, comparing, classifying, communicating

**Materials:** One shape cut out of construction paper for each child, a variety of sizes of the same shape cut out of construction paper, nontoxic glue, crayons, extra construction paper

## Procedure:

*Getting started:*
Choose a shape that will be found often in your environment. A square is a good one to start with, as it is easiest for young children to recognize. (Repeat this on other days with a different shape each day.) Tell the children they are going to look for this shape as they go on a walk. Hold up the shape you have chosen. Give each child a shape cut out of construction paper. Go on the shape walk. Encourage children to look everywhere for objects that are that shape.

*Questions to guide children:*
- What can you find that looks like a square?
- Can you find a bigger square? smaller?
- Are there any squares on the ground?

*What children and adults will do:*
Children will find many objects that match the shape. They may name something that is not that shape. In that case ask them to look at their paper and ask if it is the same shape. Many young children confuse shapes and cannot accurately match them. Don't correct the child but instead point out some of the objects that are the correct shape that other children are finding: "Jimmy found a square window."

*Closure:*
When you return to the classroom, ask children to describe what they saw that was like the designated shape. Give children many different squares (or another shape) cut out of construction paper. They should be of many different sizes but all the same color. Encourage them to make a picture out of their shapes. Have glue and crayons available if they want to use them.

## Follow-up Activity:

Ask children to draw the shapes they found and tell you about them. Then write their words.

## Center Connection:

Put extra cutout shapes in the art area; put shape books in the book area.

## Home Connection:

Ask families to find something in their homes that is one of the basic shapes and send something to school with their child. Make a "square" ("triangle," "circle") bulletin board out of everything that is sent in.

## Literature Connection:

*Color Zoo*
by Lois Ehlert, Lippincott, 1989.

*Triangles and Squares*
by Tana Hoban, MacMillan, 1974.

*Shapes, Shapes, Shapes*
by Tana Hoban, Greenwillow, 1986.

# SHAPE WALK

## Assessment Outcomes & Possible Indicators*

- **Science A-2** Develops increased ability to observe and discuss common properties, differences and comparisons among objects and materials.

- **Science A-4** Develops growing abilities to collect, describe and record information through a variety of means, including discussions, drawings, maps and charts.

- **Language Development B-1** Develops increasing abilities to understand and use language to communicate information, experiences, ideas, opinions, needs, questions and for other varied purposes.

- **Literacy B-1** Demonstrates progress in abilities to retell and dictate stories from books and experiences; to act out stories in dramatic play; and to predict what will happen next in a story.

- **Mathematics B-4** Shows growth in matching, sorting, putting in series and regrouping objects according to one or two attributes such as color, shape or size.

- **Mathematics C-3** Begins to make comparisons between several objects based on a single attribute.

    *Source: "Head Start Child Outcomes Framework." See Appendix A in this book for the framework.

## What To Look For

| Not Yet | Child does not see or find any objects of the designated shape or shows no interest. |
|---|---|
| Emerging | Child finds objects but are not the same shape; not talkative or observant. |
| Almost Mastered | Child sees and compares one or two objects; describes observations and becomes curious about other objects. |
| Fully Mastered | Child finds most items that are the same shapes; eagerly responds to observations and leads most of the discussion; has a strong curiosity and eagerly repeats the process. |

## SHAPE WALK

### Family Science Connection:

Go to the **library** and **find a magazine with lots of pictures**. Together with your child, find shapes within the pictures that your child can name. Find objects that look like circles, squares, triangles, rectangles, and ovals. Next, look around the library and **identify the same shapes** in the room that you found in the magazine. Continue to point out shapes in the environment that the child has learned about in school.

**Comments or questions** that may add a *sense of wonder* to this activity:

- What can we find in the house that looks like a circle, square, rectangle, oval, or triangle?

- Together let's draw a picture with the shapes we have found.

## PASEO DE FIGURAS GEOMÉTRICAS

### Ciencia en familia:

**Vaya a la biblioteca y encuentre una revista con muchas ilustraciones.** Junto con sus niños encuentren figuras geométricas que ellos puedan nombrar. Encuentren objetos que parezcan círculos, cuadrados, triángulos, rectángulos, y óvalos. Luego, miren alrededor de la biblioteca e **identifiquen** las figuras en el salón **iguales** a las de la revista. Continúen señalando figuras en el ambiente que los niños han aprendido en la escuela.

**Comentarios o preguntas que** pueden *despertar curiosidad* en esta actividad:

- ¿Qué podemos encontrar en la casa que parece un círculo, cuadrado, rectángulo, óvalo, o triángulo?

- Hagamos un dibujo con las figuras que hemos encontrado.

# LIGHT TO SEE

**Investigation:** Discovering that your eyes need light to see objects

**Process Skills:** Observing, comparing, communicating

**Materials:** Flashlights

## Procedure:

*Getting started:*
(This activity works best on a cloudy day when not much sunlight is lighting up the room.) Have children sit in a circle on the rug. Ask them what will happen if you turn off the light. Warn children you are going to turn off the lights for a few minutes. Turn off the lights and place some dark-colored objects in the center of the circle. Ask children to describe the objects. (CAUTION: Have children remain seated in the darkened area; moving around could cause them to trip or fall on the dark-colored objects.)

*Questions to guide children:*
 • Can you see the objects clearly?
 • What would help us see them better?
 • What could we do besides turning on the light?

*What children and adults will do:*
Children will be able to see the objects, but not well. Ask children what would help them see the objects better. Follow children's leads when they offer suggestions. They may suggest opening the door. Try that to see if it helps. If they suggest turning on the lights, ask if there is anything else they could try. Give the children flashlights and have them shine their flashlights on the objects. They will want to shine the flashlights on other things in the room as well. Ask children what is needed in order for something to be seen (light).

*Closure:*
Turn the lights on. Let children tell stories of their experiences in the dark. Have them draw pictures of the dark and write down their words.

## Follow-up Activities:

Read stories about activities that take place at night. Let children tell you about their experiences at night.

## Center Connection:

Put lightweight flashlights in the house area for children to use in role-play. Add nighttime props, such as blankets, pajamas, and teddy bears.

## Literature Connection:

*Franklin in the Dark*
by Paulette Bourgeois, Scholastic, 1986.

*Ira Sleeps Over*
by Bernard Waber, Houghton Mifflin, 1972.

*Goodnight Moon*
by Margaret Wise Brown, Harper and Row, 1947.

## Assessment Outcomes & Possible Indicators*

- **Science A-3** Begins to participate in simple investigations to test observations, discuss and draw conclusions and form generalizations.

- **Science B-1** Expands knowledge of and abilities to observe, describe and discuss the natural world, materials, living things and natural processes.

- **Language Development B-1** Develops increasing abilities to understand and use language to communicate information, experiences, ideas, opinions, needs, questions and for other varied purposes.

- **Literacy B-1** Demonstrates progress in abilities to retell and dictate stories from books and experiences; to act out stories in dramatic play; and to predict what will happen next in a story.

- **Literacy D-1** Develops understanding that writing is a way of communicating for a variety of purposes.

- **Creative Arts D-1** Participates in a variety of dramatic play activities that become more extended and complex.

   *Source: "Head Start Child Outcomes Framework." See Appendix A in this book for the framework.

## What To Look For

| | |
|---|---|
| **Not Yet** | Child is unattached or shows no interest in finding out why objects are difficult to see in the dark. |
| **Emerging** | Child sits still and watches, but is not very talkative or observant. |
| **Almost Mastered** | Child looks and is involved; describes what is seen and is curious about other objects in the room. Child uses flashlight to view objects, shows some curiosity, and makes one or two comments. |
| **Fully Mastered** | Child looks at objects in the dark and is very involved. Child uses flashlight correctly; eagerly responds to observations and leads most of the discussion; has a strong curiosity. |

## LIGHT TO SEE

### Family Science Connection:

**At bedtime**, read a story using only a flashlight. After you finish reading the story turn off the flashlight and **discover** if you can see the pages of the story in the dark. Now turn on the flashlight again and **talk** about the need for us as human beings to use light to **see and observe** our surroundings. It's also fun to flash the light in one's own eyes and in another person's eyes to watch the pupils of the eyes close. That's another **observation** about light and how it makes our eyes react without our awareness. Allow the child to continue to **explore** darkness with a flashlight.

**Comments or questions** that may add a *sense of wonder* to this activity:

- Look at the very middle of one of my eyes and see the black part. Is the black part small? Show me on paper how small.

- I'm going to close my eyes and open them and when I open them, look at the black part again and see if that black part changes. What do you think made my eyes change?

## LUZ PARA VER

### Ciencia en familia:

**A la hora de dormir**, lea un cuento usando una linterna. Después de terminar de leer el cuento, apague la linterna y **descubran** si pueden ver las páginas del cuento en la oscuridad. Luego prendan la linterna de nuevo y **hablen** acerca de nuestra necesidad como seres humanos de usar luz para **ver y observar nuestros alrededores**. Es también divertido alumbrar a nuestros ojos y otra los de personas para ver cómo se contraen las pupilas de los ojos. Esta es otra **observación** acerca de la luz y cómo hace que nuestros ojos reaccionen sin que nosotros nos demos cuenta. Permitan que los niños continúen **explorando** la obscuridad con una linterna.

**Comentarios o preguntas** que pueden *despertar curiosidad* en esta actividad:

- Mira al centro de mis ojos y encuentra la parte negra. ¿Es pequeña la parte negra? Muéstrame en papel qué tan pequeña.

- Voy a cerrar mis ojos, y cuando los abra, mira la parte negra de nuevo y ve si la parte negra está creciendo. ¿Qué hizo que mis ojos cambiaran?

# SCAVENGER HUNT

**Investigation:** Using the sense of sight to find matching objects outside

**Process Skills:** Observing, comparing, classifying

**Materials:** Leaves, twigs, rocks, flowers and other materials easily found outside, hand lenses (plastic), paper bags

## Procedure:

*Getting started:*
Ahead of time collect a few items such as leaves, twigs, and rocks from outside. Show them to the children. Ask them to find some objects that look the same as the ones you collected and put them in their bags.

*Questions to guide children:*
- Where are you going to look?
- Do they look exactly alike?
- Are they the same color?
- Are they the same shape?

*What children and adults will do:*
Children will begin to find things that are similar but not exact matches. You can sharpen their observation skills by asking about certain attributes (color, shape, texture).

*Closure:*
Back in the classroom ask children to look at their objects with hand lenses. Ask them to describe how their objects are the same or different.

## Follow-up Activity:

On another day go on a scavenger hunt, looking for living things (e.g., roly-polys). Give children each a cup and a spoon to pick up their treasures. (CAUTION: Prior to scavenger hunt, survey the area for anything unsafe, such as poisonous plants, sharp objects, or trash.)

## Center Connection:

Put some of the things children found outside in the science center with a hand lens so the observations can continue.

## Literature Connection:

*La Vista*
by J. M. Parramón and J. J. Puig, Barron, 1985.

*Seven Blind Mice*
by Ed Young, Philomel Books, 2002.

## Assessment Outcomes & Possible Indicators*

- **Science A-2** Develops increased ability to observe and discuss common properties, differences, and comparisons among objects and materials.

- **Science A-4** Develops growing abilities to collect, describe and record information through a variety of means, including discussions, drawings, maps, and charts.

- **Science B-1** Expands knowledge of and abilities to observe, describe and discuss the natural world, materials, living things, and natural processes.

- **Language Development B-1** Develops increasing abilities to understand and use language to communicate information, experiences, ideas, opinions, needs, questions and for other varied purposes.

- **Mathematics B-4** Shows growth in matching, sorting, putting in series and regrouping objects according to one or two attributes such as color, shape or size.

- **Mathematics C-3** Begins to make comparisons between several objects based on a single attribute.

*Source: "Head Start Child Outcomes Framework." See Appendix A in this book for the framework.

## What To Look For

| Not Yet | Child does not participate in scavenger hunt or shows no interest. |
|---|---|
| Emerging | Child participates but compares one or two objects; is not talkative or observant. |
| Almost Mastered | Child finds things that are the same shape, color, or object; describes how they are similar. |
| Fully Mastered | Child finds most items that are the same shape, color, or object as those that are being compared; eagerly responds to discoveries and leads most of the discussion; uses hand lens correctly; has a strong curiosity about the objects and finds differences and similarities. |

## SCAVENGER HUNT

### Family Science Connection:

Go to the **library** and **look through magazines** together that contain pictures related to nature and weather. You may ask the librarian for assistance.

Now go **home** and **hunt** in your neighborhood for some of the same things you saw in magazines. Here is a list of things you may **discover** near your **home** or at a **park**:

- birds and other animals—different shapes, colors, sizes, sounds, etc.
- trees—different colors, sizes, shapes, textures, etc.
- sky—colors, clouds and their shapes, sun, stars, planes, etc.
- weather—wind, heat, cold, rain, snow, still air, etc.

Together, **describe** the things you see and continue to hunt for objects outside that are **new and different to the senses**.

**Comments or questions** that may add a *sense of wonder* to this activity:

- Which of the things that we found are somewhat alike (same color, size, texture, feel)?

- Let's group the things that look most alike. Maybe all the feathers can be grouped together or all the things that are green.

## LA BÚSQUEDA

### Ciencia en familia:

Vayan a la **biblioteca** y **busquen** juntos las **revistas** que contengan fotografías de la naturaleza y el clima. Podrían pedir ayuda al bibliotecario.

Ahora vayan a **casa** y **busquen** en su vecindario algunas de las cosas que vieron en las revistas. Aquí esta una lista de cosas que ustedes podrían **descubrir** cerca de su **casa** o en el **parque**:

- pájaros u otros animals—diferentes formas, colores, tamaños, sonidos, etc.
- árboles—diferentes colores, tamaños, formas, texturas, etc.
- cielo—colores, nubes y sus formas, sol, estrellas, aviones, etc.
- clima—viento, calor, frío, lluvia, nieve, corriente de aire, etc.

**Describan** juntos las cosas que ven y continúen afuera la búsqueda de objetos que sean **nuevos y diferentes para los sentidos**.

**Comentarios o preguntas** que pueden *despertar curiosidad* en esta actividad:

- ¿Cuáles de las cosas que encontramos se parecen en algo (color, tamaño, textura, etc.)?

- Agrupemos las cosas que se parecen más. Podemos agrupar todas las plumas, o todas las cosas verdes.

# TASTING

**Investigation:** Observing and tasting foods that are salty, sour, sweet, or bitter

**Process Skills:** Observing, comparing, classifying, communicating

**Materials:** Salty tortilla chips, small pickle slices, green apple, lime or lemon slices, dried fruit or canned pineapple, small paper plates. Per child: One small cup of water. (CAUTION: Make sure that the area is sanitized prior to placing food out for consumption.)

## Procedure:

*Getting started:*
Give each child two of the following: salty tortilla chips, dried fruit or canned pineapple, a small piece of pickle, and slice of green apple, lime or lemon. Use only one of each item for the first round of tasting. As children taste each one, ask them to describe how it tastes. If a child uses one of the terms *salty, sweet, sour,* or *bitter*, reinforce those words.

*Questions to guide children:*
  • What foods taste salty? Sweet? Bitter? Sour?
  • What was their favorite taste? Why?
  • Does it taste different when you close your eyes and taste it?
  • What does it taste like?

*What children and adults will do:*
Discuss how our sense of smell has something to do with how well we detect how something tastes. Have the children eat the second piece of food while holding their nose. Does the food taste the same? Was it as easy to detect whether it was sweet, sour, salty, or bitter?

*Closure:*
Make a graph with a drawing of each of the four foods children tasted at the top. Fill in the graph by asking each child, "What was your favorite taste?" Put the child's name under that food. Also use the words *sour, sweet, salty,* and *bitter*: "Andy liked the sour lime."

## Follow-up Activity:

On another day have lemons or limes and sugar available. Ask, "What do you think would happen if we put the sour taste and the sweet taste together?" Try it out. Make limeade or lemonade.

## Center Connection:

Leave the food chart near the art center so children can draw pictures or cut out magazine pictures of different foods to go into the four taste categories.

## Literature Connection:

*El Gusto*
by J. M. Parramón and J. J. Puig, Barron, 1985.

*My Five Senses*
by Margaret Miller, Aladdin, 1998.

*My Five Senses*
by Aliki (Illustrator), Harper Trophy, revised edition, 1989.

# TASTING

- **Science A-1** Begins to use senses and a variety of tools and simple measuring devices to gather information, investigate materials and observe processes and relationships.

- **Science A-2** Develops increased ability to observe and discuss common properties, differences, and comparisons among objects and materials.

- **Science A-4** Develops growing abilities to collect, describe, and record information through a variety of means, including discussions, drawings, maps, and charts.

- **Language Development A-3** Understands an increasingly complex and varied vocabulary.

- **Language Development B-1** Develops increasing abilities to understand and use language to communicate information, experiences, ideas, opinions, needs, questions and for other varied purposes.

- **Mathematics A-5** Begins to use language to compare numbers of objects with terms such as *more, less, greater than, fewer,* and *equal to.*

*Source: "Head Start Child Outcomes Framework." See Appendix A in this book for the framework.

## What To Look For

| Not Yet | Child does not participate or shows no interest. |
|---|---|
| Emerging | Child tastes one or two things and does not identify differences in taste; is not talkative or has incorrect vocabulary. |
| Almost Mastered | Child tastes some things and identifies differences in taste; copies what other children are saying. |
| Fully Mastered | Child tastes all of the food and identifies differences in taste; very talkative; has the correct vocabulary; is eager to try more things. |

# FAMILY PAGE / PÁGINA PARA LA FAMILIA

## TASTING

**Teachers**, please send home a small version of the graph (similar to the one done in class for "Tasting") so the family can try this activity at home.

## Family Science Connection:

**At home** when dinner is being prepared, ask the children to **taste** the various spices that are used to season the dinner. See if the children can **identify if the seasonings are sweet, sour, bitter, or salty**. An older family member can help identify the seasoning by writing the name of the seasoning and a **conclusion** about each seasoning on the graph paper brought home from school. Ask each family member which is their favorite seasoning and why.

**Comments or questions** that may add a *sense of wonder* to this activity:

- Does that seasoning taste sweet? Or sour? Or salty? (Mom or Dad may want to explain about food that is bitter.)

- Which is your favorite seasoning?

## GUSTO

**Maestros**, por favor envíen a casa una versión pequeña de la gráfica (parecida a la que fue hecha en clase para "el Gusto") para que la familia pueda realizar esta actividad en casa.

## Ciencia en familia:

**En casa**, cuando estén preparando la cena, pida a los **niños** que **prueben** los diferentes condimentos que está usando para sazonar la comida. Vea si los niños pueden **identificar si los condimentos son dulces, agrios, amargos, o salados**. Un miembro de la familia que sea mayor puede ayudar a identificar el condimento escribiendo el nombre del condimento y una cosa **interesante** acerca de cada uno de los condimentos en el papel cuadriculado que trajeron de la escuela. Pida a cada miembro de la familia que diga cuál es su condimento favorito y por qué.

**Comentarios o preguntas** que pueden *despertar curiosidad* en esta actividad:

- ¿Sabe dulce el condimento? ¿O agrio? ¿O salado? (Tal vez mamá o papá quieran explicar acerca de la comida amarga.)

- ¿Cuál es tu condimento favorito?

# SMELLY CANS

**Investigation:** Using the sense of smell to observe and identify different scents

**Process Skills:** Observing, comparing, classifying

**Materials:** Five sets of "smelly cans" (film canisters work well). Place one scent on a cotton ball in each film canister in the set. Use scents such as lemon, cinnamon, mustard, relish, mint, or banana. Due to the risk of allergies, do not use nut-based products like peanut butter. Repeat for each of the five sets. Draw a matching picture on an index card to go with each canister. You may want to cover each canister with plastic wrap and tape it to the sides. Poke small holes in the plastic wrap to let the scents out but not reveal the contents. The lids should still fit on the canisters with the plastic wrap on them. (CAUTION: Remind children not to taste or eat the contents of the canisters.)

## Procedure:

*Getting started:*
Discuss how the sense of smell is very important to help identify an object. Have the children play a smell guessing game with you: Have the children close their eyes. Then you open a jar (of pickles, perhaps) under the table. Tell the children to raise their hands when they smell the item—but do not shout out what it is until you count to three. Try the game with another smell.

*Questions to guide children:*
  • How does it smell?
  • What is your favorite smell?
  • What part of you do you use to smell?
  • Can dogs and cats smell? How do you know?

*What children and adults will do:*
Distribute one set of "smelly cans" to each group of two or three children. Tell them to open the cans and describe the smell. Distribute one set of picture cards with each set of cans and ask the children to match the picture card with the correct smell.

*Closure:*
Have children share the matched cans and cards. Have them open their cans to verify their choices.

## Follow-up Activity:

Have children draw a picture of their favorite smell and make a big book called "Our Favorite Smells Book." If possible, smear some of the scents the children choose to draw on a piece of construction paper and glue it onto each picture page. Ask children to tell a story about the smells they chose. Write down their words next to their picture.

## Center Connection:

Place some of the smelly cans at the center with picture cards of each smell. Invite the children to match the smell to the picture. Select cans that have items in them that will not rot over time. (For example, you would not want to use tuna!)

## Literature Connection:

*El Olfato*
by J. M. Parramón and J. J. Puig, Barron, 1985.

*My Five Senses*
by Aliki, Harper Trophy Books, 1989.

*Mis Cinco Sentidos*
by Aliki, Harper Junior, 1989.

# SMELLY CANS

## Assessment Outcomes & Possible Indicators*

- **Science A-1** Begins to use senses and a variety of tools and simple measuring devices to gather information, investigate materials and observe processes and relationships.

- **Science A-2** Develops increased ability to observe and discuss common properties, differences and comparisons among objects and materials.

- **Science A-4** Develops growing abilities to collect, describe and record information through a variety of means, including discussions, drawings, maps and charts.

- **Language Development A-3** Understands an increasingly complex and varied vocabulary.

- **Language Development B-1** Develops increasing abilities to understand and use language to communicate information, experiences, ideas, opinions, needs, questions and for other varied purposes.

- **Literacy D-2** Begins to represent stories and experiences through pictures, dictation, and in play.

  *Source: "Head Start Child Outcomes Framework." See Appendix A in this book for the framework.

## What To Look For

| Not Yet | Child does not participate or shows no interest in identifying the different tastes. |
|---|---|
| Emerging | Child smells one or two things but doesn't identify differences in smell; is not talkative or has incorrect vocabulary. |
| Almost Mastered | Child smells most things and identifies differences in smell; is talkative and has the correct vocabulary but misidentifies some of the smells. |
| Fully Mastered | Child smells all of the scents and identifies the differences in smell; is very talkative, has the correct vocabulary, identifies the smells, and eagerly tries more things. |

# FAMILY PAGE / PÁGINA PARA LA FAMILIA

## INTERESTING SCENTS

### Family Science Connection:

**Take a trip to a store where one can find lots of interesting scents**. A perfume store is a good place to go to find a variety of odors. Try smelling five different fragrances and see if you and your child can **identify the scents. Talk** about which one scent is the strongest and which one has a **very light scent. Classify** them into **strongest to lightest scents**. Then pick the one scent that each of you do not like and **compare** it with your favorite scent. What smells so great about the scent you do like? (CAUTION: Avoid this activity if your child has respiratory allergies that are triggered by perfume vapors or other types of odors.)

**Comments or questions** that may add a *sense of wonder* to this activity:

- What part of our body do we use to smell things?

- The things I like best about the favorite scent I chose are ....

## AROMAS INTERESANTES

### Ciencia en familia:

**Vayan a una tienda en donde puedan encontrar muchos aromas interesantes.** Una tienda de perfumes es un buen lugar para encontrar una variedad de olores. Traten de oler cinco fragancias diferentes y vean si usted y sus niños pueden **identificar los aromas. Hablen** di cuál tiene la fragancia más fuerte y cuál tiene una fragancia. **Clasifiquen** las fragancias de la más fuerte a la más ligera. Luego escojan uno de los aromas que a cada uno de ustedes no les gusta y **compárenlo** con su aroma favorito. ¿Qué es lo que huele tan bien del aroma que le gustó a usted? (PRECAUCIÓN: Evita esta actividad si su hijo tiene alergias respiratorias provocadas por perfumes u otros tipos de olores.)

**Comentarios o preguntas** que pueden *despertar curiosidad* en esta actividad:

- ¿Qué parte del cuerpo usamos para oler?

- Las cosas que me gustan más acerca de la fragancia que escogí son ....

# SMELLING FLOWERS

**Investigation:** Sorting flowers by their aromas

**Process Skills:** Observing, classifying, communicating

**Materials:** Many kinds of flowers, sorting mat (CAUTION: Some children may have respiratory allergies that are triggered by flowers or pollen. Check with parents before doing this activity.)

## Procedure:

*Getting started:*
Put out a variety of flowers. Encourage children to touch and smell the flowers. Give them time to explore the flowers and talk about them before you ask questions.

*Questions to guide children:*
- How does the flower smell?
- Which one smells the nicest? Sweetest?
- Are there any that don't have a smell?
- Do any seem to smell the same?

*What children and adults will do:*
Children will smell and touch the flowers. They may talk about flowers they have in their yards or others they have seen. They will talk about how the flowers look, smell, and feel.

*Closure:*
Have children put their flowers on the sorting mat with all the flowers that smell on one side and those that don't on the other side. Talk about the sense of smell and what we use to smell.

## Follow-up Activities:

Bring herbs for children to smell. Children in one class asked, "What are those leaves? What are they for?" One child commented, "My mom eats this (basil)!" They didn't like the smell of some of the herbs. Make an herb collage to take home. Bring in dried herbs to make into herb tea. Have children choose herbs to put into a piece of netting and make a small potpourri to take home.

## Center Connection:

Put the flowers in the art center. Let children know they can take the flowers apart and use the petals, leaves, and stems to make a flower collage. Encourage them to use hand lenses as they observe.

## Literature Connection:

*Planting a Rainbow*
by Lois Ehlert, Harcourt Brace Jovanovich, 1988.

*Miss Rumphius*
by Barbara Cooney, Viking Penguin, 1982.

# SMELLING FLOWERS

## Assessment Outcomes & Possible Indicators*

- **Science A-1** Begins to use senses and a variety of tools and simple measuring devices to gather information, investigate materials and observe processes and relationships.

- **Science A-2** Develops increased ability to observe and discuss common properties, differences and comparisons among objects and materials.

- **Science A-4** Develops growing abilities to collect, describe and record information through a variety of means, including discussions, drawings, maps and charts.

- **Language Development A-3** Understands an increasingly complex and varied vocabulary.

- **Language Development B-1** Develops increasing abilities to understand and use language to communicate information, experiences, ideas, opinions, needs, questions and for other varied purposes.

   *Source: "Head Start Child Outcomes Framework." See Appendix A in this book for the framework.

## What To Look For

| Not Yet | Child does not participate or shows no interest in smelling the flowers. |
|---|---|
| Emerging | Child smells one or two things but doesn't identify differences in smell; is not talkative or has incorrect vocabulary. |
| Almost Mastered | Child smells and identifies differences; is talkative and can sort into two groups, but isn't fully involved during the activity. |
| Fully Mastered | Child smells all of the scents and identifies the differences; is very talkative, sorts all items, and eagerly sorts the flowers with different attributes, such as smell. |

## SMELLING FLOWERS

### Family Science Connection:

**As a family, visit a nursery or arboretum** and take time to **smell** the various **flowers. Describe** what the different flowers smell like. Maybe the fragrance reminds you of certain foods or past experiences. Carefully look inside each flower to **observe** what it looks like. Together describe what the flower looks like as you continue to **explore** each flower.

**Comments or questions** that may add a *sense of wonder* to this activity:

- Wow, what does the smell from that flower remind you of?

- Let's see how many different flower smells we can count.

## OLIENDO FLORES

### Ciencia en familia:

**Visiten como familia un vivero, tienda de plantas, o arboreto** y tomen tiempo para **oler** diferentes **flores. Describa** a qué huelen las diferentes flores. Pueden ser aromas que le recuerden ciertas comidas o experiencias antiguas. Vean con cuidado dentro de cada flor para **observar** su apariencia. **Describan** juntos la apariencia de cada flor mientras continúan **explorando** cada flor.

**Comentarios o preguntas** que pueden *despertar curiosidad* en esta actividad:

- ¡Mmmm! ¿Qué te recuerda el olor de esa flor?

- Veamos cuántos olores de flores podemos contar.

# SOUND: SHAKE, RATTLE, AND ROLL

**Investigation:** Exploring, comparing, and identifying sounds

**Process Skills:** Observing, comparing, classifying

**Materials:** Five sound sets. Each set should have 12 plastic film canisters (six clear and six black). Place items in each clear canister (and repeat for black canisters) such as: two pennies, one teaspoon of rice, two pea-sized wads of paper, three small paper clips (plastic), one marble, two jingle bells, a few dried beans, or whatever items you have on hand that make different pitched sounds.

## Procedure:

*Getting started:*
Have the children close their eyes and focus on their sense of sound to identify this sound: Scratch on the tabletop with your fingernails. While their eyes are closed, have the children point to the source of the sound. Then have them open their eyes to see if they were correct. Try several different sounds and let the children guess with their eyes closed. Select a few children to make the sounds for the group. Next, distribute one set of the clear sound canisters to each group of two to three children. Allow time for the children to experience and identify the sounds.

*Questions to guide children:*
  • What does it sound like?
  • Which one makes the highest sounds? Loudest sounds? Softest sounds?

*What children and adults will do:*
After the children spend time observing and listening to the set of clear sound canisters, ask them to put them in a row in front of their group. Distribute another set of black sound canisters to each group and have them listen to each one and then match it to the correct clear canister. Have them put the matching canisters next to one another when finished.

*Closure:*
(1) Have one of the children choose a canister and shake it. All the children should try to find the canister in their set that matches. (2) Discuss briefly how important sound is to gather information about what's happening around you.

## Follow-up Activity:

Make a tape recording of familiar sounds from around the classroom. Play it on another day and have the children try to identify the sounds.

## Center Connection:

Place the sound canisters at the science center for all the children to experience. Have the children take home one empty clear and one empty black canister, and ask them to put the same mystery item in each canister and bring them back to school for another activity or to put them in the center.

## Literature Connection:

*Thump, Thump, Tat-a-Tat-Tat*
by Gene Baer, Harper Junior, 1989.

*El Oído*
by J. M. Parramón and J. J. Puig, Barron, 1985.

# SOUND: SHAKE, RATTLE, AND ROLL

- **Science A-1** Begins to use senses and a variety of tools and simple measuring devices to gather information, investigate materials and observe processes and relationships.

- **Science A-2** Develops increased ability to observe and discuss common properties, differences and comparisons among objects and materials.

- **Language Development A-4** For non-English-speaking children, progresses in listening to and understanding English.

- **Language Development B-1** Develops increasing abilities to understand and use language to communicate information, experiences, ideas, opinions, needs, questions and for other varied purposes.

*Source: "Head Start Child Outcomes Framework." See Appendix A in this book for the framework.

## What To Look For

| Not Yet | Child does not participate or shows no interest in identifying sounds. |
|---|---|
| Emerging | Child hears the sounds but does not identify where they are coming from or what they are; is not talkative or doesn't match similar sounds. |
| Almost Mastered | Child hears the sounds and identifies where they are coming from or what they are; child is talkative and matches one or two sounds. |
| Fully Mastered | Child hears the sounds and identifies where they are coming from and what they are; child is very talkative and matches all of the sounds with one another. |

## SOUND: SHAKE, RATTLE, AND ROLL

### Family Science Connection:

Ask your child to find **objects in the home that will make sounds**. Some objects to pick that would make great sounds to guess are beans in a bag, cereal in the box, a baby's rattle, a barking dog, a bell, or water running from the faucet. Have the child lead an older family member around the house making sure that that person's eyes are closed. Have the child make the sound of that object and then have the person guess what object made the sound. **Talk** about how important it is to **listen** to different sounds and how each sound the children made was easy or hard to identify. After five sounds are **identified**, switch places and let the children be the ones who guess.

**Comments or questions** that may add a *sense of wonder* to this activity:

- You picked some great sounds to have me guess! Which sound did you like the best? Was that sound loud or soft?

- Did the sounds you picked remind you of other sounds, and what are those sounds? Maybe the cereal box sounded like the baby's rattle.

## RUIDOS Y SONIDOS

### Ciencia en familia:

Pida a los niños más pequeños en casa que encuentren **objetos que hacen ruido**. Algunos objetos que pueden tomar que hacen excelentes sonidos para adivinar son frijoles en bolsa, cereal en caja, la sonaja de un bebé, un perro ladrando, una campana, o agua saliendo de la llave. Pida a los niños que lleven a la persona mayor por la casa asegurándose que los ojos de esa persona estén cerrados. Pida a los niños que hagan el sonido de ese objeto y luego pidan a la persona que adivine qué objeto produjo ese sonido. **Hablen** acerca de lo importante que es **escuchar** los diferentes sonidos y por qué cada sonido que hicieron los niños fue fácil o difícil de adivinar. Después de haber **identificado** cinco sonidos, cambien de lugar y pidan a los niños que sean ellos los que adivinen.

**Comentarios o preguntas** que pueden *despertar curiosidad* en esta actividad:

- ¡Has escogido un excelente sonido para identificar! ¿Qué sonido te gustó mas? ¿Era el sonido fuerte o suave?

- Los sonidos que has escogido, ¿te recuerdan de otros sonidos? ¿Cuáles? Tal vez la caja de cereal sonaba como la sonaja de un bebé.

# A SOUND WALK

**Investigation:** Walking around the school grounds or surrounding neighborhood to listen for different sounds

**Process Skills:** Observing, classifying, comparing, communicating

**Materials:** Tape recorder (optional), several classroom objects that make sounds, such as a musical instrument, stapler, or crumpled paper

## Procedure:

*Getting started:*
In a box, have several things that make sounds. Ask the children to close their eyes and identify the sounds as you touch them. Then tell the children they are going on a "sound walk" to listen for different sounds outside. Plan your walk away from busy streets, as traffic noise will prevent children from hearing other sounds.

*Questions to guide children:*
  • What is that loud noise?
  • Can you hear more than one sound?
  • What kinds of sounds are you making with your feet?

*What children and adults will do:*
Ask children to walk without talking for a while until they hear some sounds. They will then start talking and pointing in the direction of the sounds they hear. From time to time you may want to quiet children so that they can listen for a "new" sound. To focus children you may want to give each a 3 × 5 card with a picture of something they are likely to encounter that makes a noise (bird, plane, car, dog). They can listen specifically for that sound, then listen for other sounds. Record sounds if you wish.

*Closure:*
Back in the classroom make a list on chart paper of all the sounds children were able to identify. Write each word with a simple drawing next to it.

## Follow-up Activities:

On another day, walk in a different direction or a different neighborhood to see if the sounds are different. Take a walk after a rain to hear how the water has created new sounds (tires in puddles, wind blowing raindrops off roofs).

## Center Connection:

Put the tape recording of the sounds you heard on your walk or pre-recorded sound tapes (available from educational materials companies) in your listening center.

## Literature Connection:

*What's That Noise?*
by M. Lemieux, Morrow, 1985.

*Noisy Nora*
by R. Wells, Dial, 1973.

*The Listening Walk*
by Paul Showers, Harper Trophy, 1993.

*Listen to the Rain*
by Bill Martin and John Archambault, Holt, 1988.

# A SOUND WALK

- **Science A-2** Develops increased ability to observe and discuss common properties, differences and comparisons among objects and materials.

- **Language Development B-1** Develops increasing abilities to understand and use language to communicate information, experiences, ideas, opinions, needs, questions and for other varied purposes.

- **Literacy B-1** Demonstrates progress in abilities to retell and dictate stories from books and experiences; to act out stories in dramatic play; and to predict what will happen next in a story.

- **Literacy D-1** Develops understanding that writing is a way of communicating for a variety of purposes.

  *Source: "Head Start Child Outcomes Framework." See Appendix A in this book for the framework.

## What To Look For

| Not Yet | Child does not identify any sounds heard or shows no interest. |
|---|---|
| Emerging | Child hears and identifies one or two sounds, but is not talkative or observant. |
| Almost Mastered | Child hears and identifies some of the sounds; child matches a picture to the sound heard and is curious about other sounds that are in the area. |
| Fully Mastered | Child hears and identifies most sounds; eagerly responds to sounds heard and leads most of the discussion; has a strong curiosity about the sounds heard and matches all of the sounds to pictures. |

## A SOUND WALK

### Family Science Connection:

Have two or three members of the family sit quietly for about five minutes without the TV on and **listen for sounds**. At the end of this short time, think about and try to **identify** all of the sounds heard. **Count all the different sounds** that were heard and **talk** together about each sound. See if the sounds can be categorized. A car honking and a dog barking might be considered low-pitched sounds, whereas a baby crying or a cat meowing might be considered high-pitched sounds. Try doing this same activity outside and **compare** the outdoor experience with the indoor experience.

**Comments or questions** that may add a *sense of wonder* to this activity:

- Name the sounds that were easiest to recognize.

- Imitate the sounds that you identified.

## UN PASEO DE SONIDOS

### Ciencia en familia:

Pídale a dos o tres miembros de la familia que se sienten calladamente por unos cinco minutos en la sala con la televisión apagada y que traten de **escuchar sonidos**. Después de este breve tiempo, piensen acerca de todos los sonidos que escucharon y traten de **identificarlos**. **Cuenten los diferentes sonidos** que oyeon y **platiquen** acerca de cada uno de éstos. Vean si pueden organizar los sonidos por categorías. La bocina de un auto y el ladrido de un perro se pueden considerar sonidos de tono bajo, mientras que el llanto de un niño o el maullido de un gato se pueden considerar sonidos de tono alto. Traten de hacer la misma actividad afuera y **comparen** la experiencia interior con la experiencia exterior.

**Comentarios o preguntas** que pueden *despertar curiosidad* en esta actividad.

- Nombra los sonidos que fueron más fáciles de reconocer.

- Imita los sonidos que tú identificaste.

# VIBRATIONS

**Investigation:** Exploring sound and its vibrations

**Process Skills:** Observing, comparing, classifying

**Materials:** Rulers (plastic), small objects, rubber bands (CAUTION: Some children are allergic to rubber-based products.)

## Procedure:

*Getting started:*
Tell children they are going to make some sounds using rulers. Have children work together in pairs. One child should put a ruler on the table, letting one end of the ruler hang over the edge of the table. While standing, that child should hold the edge of the ruler tightly on the table. The other child plucks the end of the ruler that hangs over the edge. Listen to what happens. Try it several times. Reverse roles.

*Questions to guide children:*
- What is the ruler doing?
- What does it sound like?
- Can you make a different sound?
- Do we sound like a band?

*What children and adults will do:*
Some children will have difficulty holding the ruler tightly enough. You may have to demonstrate and help some of the children. You might have two children hold the ruler together while another child does the plucking.

*Closure:*
Let each child demonstrate the sound he or she was able to make. Talk about the differences. Ask children their ideas of what made the sounds change.

## Follow-up Activity:

Make a mini-ukulele by wrapping a rubber band around a ruler. Put a small object (counting bear, pencil, small block) under the rubber band. Pluck the rubber band and note the sound it makes. Do this with different objects under the rubber band and see if it makes a different noise each time.

## Center Connection:

Place different objects such as tuning forks and other sound makers in the science center for all the children to experience. Bring a real guitar or ukulele to school for children to try out.

## Literature Connection:

*Thump, Thump, Tat-a-Tat-Tat*
by Gene Baer, Harper Junior, 1989.

*El Oido*
by J. M. Parramón and J. J. Puig, Barron, 1985.

## Assessment Outcomes & Possible Indicators*

- **Science A-1** Begins to use senses and a variety of tools and simple measuring devices to gather information, investigate materials and observe processes and relationships.

- **Science A-2** Develops increased ability to observe and discuss common properties, differences and comparisons among objects and materials.

- **Science B-4** Shows increased awareness and beginning understanding of changes in materials and cause-effect relationships.

- **Language Development B-1** Develops increasing abilities to understand and use language to communicate information, experiences, ideas, opinions, needs, questions and for other varied purposes.

- **Social & Emotional Development C-1** Increases abilities to sustain interactions with peers by helping, sharing and discussion.

  *Source: Head Start "Child Outcomes Assessment Framework." See Appendix in this book for the framework.

## What To Look For

| | |
|---|---|
| **Not Yet** | Child does not participate or shows no interest in making sounds with a ruler. |
| **Emerging** | Child plays with ruler, is not talkative or involved. |
| **Almost Mastered** | Child plays with ruler and makes sounds with adult's help; is talkative and has the correct responses; seems distracted. |
| **Fully Mastered** | Child plays with ruler and makes sounds by working with other children; is talkative and has the correct responses; is fully involved during the activity, and is eager to try more things. |

# NOISE MAKERS

**Investigation:** Using recycled materials to make sounds

**Process Skills:** Observing, comparing

**Materials:** Paper cups, damp paper towels, paper clips (plastic), string

## Procedure:

*Getting started:*
(The day before, have children throw all their cups and paper towels into a separate bag. Save this bag.) The next day explain to children that they will be using their cup from breakfast (or lunch) to make something. Instead of throwing their cups away they should each rinse theirs and save it. After washing their hands, they should also save their damp paper towels.

*Questions to guide children:*
- What do you think is making that sound?
- Can you make the sound last longer?
- Is there another way you can make the sound?
- What does that noise sound like?

*What children and adults will do:*
Children will each bring a used cup and damp paper towel to the table. Adults need to fasten a paper clip to the center of the cup bottom and tie a string about 2 feet long to the paper clip. Children then take a damp paper towel and rub along the string. The result is a very realistic duck sound! Children will want to continue this activity all day long.

*Closure:*
Have children look at the bag of cups and paper towels from the day before. Talk about how much we use and throw away each day. Ask them what they were able to save today to use in another way (the cup and paper towel). Have them walk to the next activity like a duck!

## Follow-up Activity:

Take out some of the classroom instruments. Have children try out one kind of instrument at a time, then tell what kind of sound it makes. Ask them, "Do you know something else that makes that sound?"

## Center Connection:

Let children take their duck horns outside.

## Literature Connection:

*Farm Noises*
by Jane Miller, Simon and Schuster, 1988.

*Whistle for Willie*
by Ezra Jack Keats, Viking, 1964.

*The Bremen Town Musicians*
by I. Plume, Doubleday, 1980.

# NOISE MAKERS

- **Science A-1** Begins to use senses and a variety of tools and simple measuring devices to gather information, investigate materials and observe processes and relationships.

- **Language Development B-1** Develops increasing abilities to understand and use language to communicate information, experiences, ideas, opinions, needs, questions and for other varied purposes.

- **Creative Arts A-2** Experiments with a variety of musical instruments.

*Source: "Head Start Child Outcomes Framework." See Appendix A in this book for the framework.

## What To Look For

| Not Yet | Child does not participate or shows no interest in making noise with string and a paper towel. |
|---|---|
| Emerging | Child makes sounds but needs help from an adult; is not talkative or doesn't work independently. |
| Almost Mastered | Child makes sounds without help; is talkative and answers some adult's questions. |
| Fully Mastered | Child makes sounds and continues independently; child is very talkative and changes sounds in some kind of way (e.g., louder, longer). |

## NOISE MAKERS

### Family Science Connection:

**Check out a book about the sounds animals make** and read it together. As you read about the different sounds, see if your child can make the sound for each animal. Some sounds may be hard to make, so **experiment** with different materials like a soda bottle, a paper cup, or sandpaper and see if you can make the **different animal sounds** using your materials and imagination.

**Comments or questions** that may add a *sense of wonder* to this activity:

- Let me hear you make the sounds of your favorite animals.

- What animal sounds are hard to imitate?

## CREACIÓN DE SONIDOS

### Ciencia en familia:

**Saquen de la biblioteca un libro acerca de los sonidos que hacen los animales** y léanlo juntos. Mientras lean acerca de los diferentes sonidos, vean si pueden hacer el sonido de cada uno de los animales. Algunos sonidos son difíciles de hacer, así que **experimenten** con diferentes materiales como una botella de refresco, un vaso de papel, o papel de lija, y vean si pueden hacer los **diferentes sonidos de animales** usando estos materiales y su imaginación.

**Comentarios o preguntas** que pueden *despertar curiosidad* en esta actividad:

- Déjame oírte hacer los sonidos de tus animales favoritos.

- ¿Cuáles sonidos de animales son difíciles de imitar?

# A TOUCH COLLAGE

**Investigation:** Identifying various materials by touch

**Process Skills:** Observing, comparing

**Materials:** Glue (nontoxic); cardboard or heavy paper such as tagboard; any variety of textured materials such as sand, gravel, beans, sticks, fabric, cotton, or foam

## Procedure:

*Getting started:*
Put all the materials on the table. Encourage children to pick up and touch various materials. Ask them to choose some of the materials to glue onto their piece of cardboard (or tagboard).

*Questions to guide children:*
  • How does that piece feel?
  • Is your collage like your friend's?
  • Why did you choose this item?

*What children and adults will do:*
Some children will work quickly to glue a few items to make a collage. Others will work carefully to create patterns or even a picture. Some will layer their items. Talk to them about the textures they are using. Ask them questions about their work. As they finish, encourage them to look carefully at their own collage. Tell them, "Later today, I will want to see if you can find your own collage." Put children's names on the back of the collages so they won't easily identify them by their names.

*Closure:*
Just before going home, put children's collages on tables (in groups of five to six). Have children walk around and find their own. Ask questions like, "How did you know that one was yours?" You may have to help some children by giving them hints such as, "I remember you used one piece of shiny red material. Let's see if we can find one that has shiny red material on it."

## Center Connection:

Put any leftover materials in the art area. Add things such as leaves and flower petals when they are available.

## Literature Connection:

*The Quilt Story*
by Tony Johnston, Putnam, 1985.

*The Keeping Quilt*
by Patricia Polacco, Simon and Schuster, 1988.

# A TOUCH COLLAGE

- **Science A-1** Begins to use senses and a variety of tools and simple measuring devices to gather information, investigate materials and observe processes and relationships.

- **Language Development A-3** Understands an increasingly complex and varied vocabulary.

- **Language Development B-1** Develops increasing abilities to understand and use language to communicate information, experiences, ideas, opinions, needs, questions and for other varied purposes.

- **Literacy B-1** Demonstrates progress in abilities to retell and dictate stories from books and experiences; to act out stories in dramatic play; and to predict what will happen next in a story.

- **Creative Arts B-1** Gains ability in using different art media and materials in a variety of ways for creative expression and representation.

*Source: "Head Start Child Outcomes Framework." See Appendix A in this book for the framework.

## What To Look For

| Not Yet | Child is unengaged or shows no interest in touching materials and making a collage. |
|---|---|
| Emerging | Child touches some items and describes them, but is not talkative and only adds one or two items to collage. |
| Almost Mastered | Child touches most items and is involved; describes what is felt and is curious about other objects; is talkative and adds some of the items to the collage. |
| Fully Mastered | Child touches all of the items and is involved; describes what is felt and is curious about other objects; is very talkative and adds all of the items to collage. |

# FAMILY PAGE / PÁGINA PARA LA FAMILIA

## A TOUCH COLLAGE

### Family Science Connection:

At **home** have you and your child **find small pieces of leftover material** to glue onto recycled cardboard. Try using a variety of textured items to glue as you make a touch collage. Macaroni, crayon shavings, fabric, popsicle sticks, or scrap paper are a few things you may want to use in your collage. Before you start gluing, **feel** each item and identify it by texture, weight, size, and color. When your child is finished gluing and everything is dry, together **count** how many objects are on the touch collage.

**Comments or questions** that may add a *sense of wonder* to this activity:

- Name the items on the collage that feel rough, soft, bumpy, and smooth.

- Tell me what you like best about your touch collage.

## COLLAGE DEL TACTO

### Ciencia en familia:

En **casa** usted y su niño(a) **encuentren pequeños pedazos de sobrantes de tela** para pegarlos con goma en un cartón. Traten de usar objetos con diversas texturas para pegarlos juntos para hacer un collage del tacto. Podrían usar macarrones, colores de cera rallados, telas, palitos de paleta, o papel desechado para hacer un collage. Antes de empezar a pegar, **toquen** cada objeto e identifíquenlo según su textura, peso, medida, y color. Cuando su niño(a) termine de pegar y todo esté seco, **cuenten** juntos cuántos objetos hay en el collage del tacto.

**Comentarios o preguntas** que pueden *despertar curiosidad* en esta actividad:

- Nombra los objetos en el collage que se sienten rasposos, suaves, abollados, o lisos.

- Dime qué fue lo que más te gustó de tu collage del tacto.

# The Senses

# MATCHING BY TOUCH

**Investigation:** Using the sense of touch to match materials or objects

**Process Skills:** Feeling, classifying

**Materials:** Matching sets of materials that differ in texture and/or shape, feeling box (a box with holes large enough to reach into cut in each end)

## Procedure:

*Getting started:*
Have one feeling box for each group of two to three children. Put one set of materials in each box. Give each child a matching set of materials. Give children a few minutes to explore the materials in front of them.

*Questions to guide children:*
- What does it feel like?
- Is it soft? bumpy? cold?
- Can you find one that's not the same?

*What children and adults will do:*
Children choose a material or object, then take turns reaching into the feeling box to find its match. A variation: One child is the leader and chooses an object on the table that the other children have to find in the feeling box.

*Closure:*
Ask children to put all the items that are the same in one pile on the table. Talk about how they were able to find matching items without looking (but by using the sense of touch).

## Follow-up Activities:

After playing this game several times with different objects, children can make their own sets by choosing matching sets of objects from materials in the room (play food, crayons, Legos—anything that has a match and will fit in the box). On another day, give children ice cubes in a baggy to hold. After identifying this as cold, ask them to find something that feels warm.

## Center Connection:

Put the feeling box in the science area and change what is in the box every few days. Let children make a texture collage from materials added to the art area.

## Literature Connection:

*El Tacto*
by J. M. Parramón and J. J. Puig, Barron, 1985.

*Is It Rough? Is It Smooth? Is It Shiny?*
by Tana Hoban, Greenwillow, 1984.

# MATCHING BY TOUCH

- **Science A-1** Begins to use senses and a variety of tools and simple measuring devices to gather information, investigate materials and observe processes and relationships.

- **Language Development A-3** Understands an increasingly complex and varied vocabulary.

- **Language Development B-1** Develops increasing abilities to understand and use language to communicate information, experiences, ideas, opinions, needs, questions and for other varied purposes.

- **Mathematics B-3** Begins to be able to determine whether or not two shapes are the same size and shape.

   *Source: "Head Start Child Outcomes Framework." See Appendix A in this book for the framework.

## What To Look For

| Not Yet | Child does not participate or shows no interest in identifying objects in the box. |
|---|---|
| Emerging | Child feels one or two items but does not identify what it is, or describes it (lacks vocabulary); is not talkative or doesn't match similar textures. |
| Almost Mastered | Child feels some of the items, identifies some of them, and describes some (has vocabulary); is talkative and matches similar textures. |
| Fully Mastered | Child feels all of the items, identifies them, and describes them (has vocabulary); is very talkative and matches similar textures. |

# FAMILY PAGE / PÁGINA PARA LA FAMILIA

## MATCHING BY TOUCH

### Family Science Connection:

**Mom, Dad, or older brothers or sisters** can find various **matching textured objects** around the house. Now with three or four of these objects covered, ask the younger child to **feel** them and see if he or she can identify the object, **describe** it, and feel if there is another match to it under the towel. Objects that you might use include crayons, fruit, small books, and socks.

**Comments or questions** that may add a *sense of wonder* to this activity:

- Do the objects you are feeling seem smooth, bumpy, soft, or hard?

- Can you find one object that feels the same as another object?

## PARES AL TACTO

### Ciencia en familia:

**Mamá, papá, hermanos o hermanas mayores** pueden encontrar en casa **objetos** que hagan pareja según su textura. Ahora, con tres o cuatro de estos objetos cubiertos pídale al niño que los **sienta** y trate de adivinar qué objeto es; que lo **describa** y sienta si hay otro objeto debajo de la toalla que haga pareja con este. Se pueden usar crayones, fruta, pequeños libros, calcetines, etc.

**Comentarios o preguntas** que pueden *despertar curiosidad* en esta actividad:

- Los objetos que estás tocando, ¿se sienten, suaves, rasposos o duros?

- ¿Puedes encontrar un objeto que se sienta igual a otro objeto?

# WEATHER

Weather is something with which children come in contact every day. It affects what they wear and sometimes what they can or cannot do ("No playing outside today!") Weather is quite often fascinating to observe—for example, clouds, hailstorms, wind, lightning, and cloud shadows.

Because weather can be easily observed and the changes in weather simply recorded, it is an ideal science topic for young children. Little or no materials are needed. The children themselves, their clothing and the objects around them are all that are needed to determine whether it is warm or cold, windy or still, sunny or cloudy. Observing the weather can help children learn time concepts even as they notice shadows on the playground one day but none the next.

Weather is always with us, so observing weather can be a spur-of-the-moment activity with no planning involved, or it can be the topic of a small-group activity that leads to many different investigations.

## Weather: Selected Internet Resources

### Shadows
- Shadows and Light: Kids Research Center—Information for Kids, Science—*www.gigglepotz.com/krc_shadows.htm*
- Groundhog Day and Shadow Activities—*http://childfun.com/index.php*

### Seasons
- Winter Theme Ideas, Songs, and Activities—*www.preschoolrainbow.org/preschool-winter.htm*
- Interactive Online Winter-Themed Games—*www.primarygames.com/seasons/winter/games.htm*
- Seasonal Ideas for Teachers—*www.theteacherscorner.net/seasonal/index.htm*

### Weather
- Weather Resources and Activities for Teachers, Parents, and Children—*http://weathereye.kgan.com/*

# A WIND WALK

**Investigation:** Discovering that wind makes objects move and a strong wind produces sounds

**Process Skills:** Observing, communicating

**Materials:** None

## Procedure:

*Getting started:*
On a windy day, take the children for a walk around the school grounds. Ask children to look for things that are moving. Watch what the children do and listen to what they say. (CAUTION: On windy days, sand and dirt can be blown into the eyes and cause damage. Also, children with allergies to particulates, pollen, etc., may be placed in harm's way. Always check first with parents.)

*Questions to guide children:*
- What do you see that is moving?
- Stand still. Is anything on you moving?
- Is something in the sky moving?
- What is making everything move?

*What children and adults will do:*
Children enjoy being out in the wind. As they notice things moving, change their focus from time to time by pointing out things on the ground, above their eye level, or in a different direction from the one in which they are looking. Repeat what some children say so other children can notice the same objects moving.

*Closure:*
Gather children inside. Ask them what things they saw moving outside. Draw pictures on a chart of the objects they talk about and label it "Our Wind Walk."

## Follow-up Activity:

On another day, put out leaves, pieces of paper, cotton, and other small objects of varying weights on a table. Provide children with straws and ask them if they can pretend to be the wind and move some of the objects. Ask them which things are easiest to move and why they think so.

## Center Connection:

Put some of the same objects and straws in the science area.

## Literature Connection:

*Mirandy and Brother Wind*
by Patricia McKissack, Knopf, 1988.

*Gilberto and the Wind*
by Marie Hall Ets, Penguin, 1978.

# A WIND WALK

- **Science A-2** Develops increased ability to observe and discuss common properties, differences and comparisons among objects and materials.

- **Language Development B-1** Develops increasing abilities to understand and use language to communicate information, experiences, ideas, opinions, needs, questions and for other varied purposes.

- **Literacy D-1** Develops understanding that writing is a way of communicating for a variety of purposes.

- **Approaches to Learning A-1** Chooses to participate in an increasing variety of tasks and activities.

*Source: "Head Start Child Outcomes Framework." See Appendix A in this book for the framework.

## What To Look For

| Not Yet | Child shows no interest in how objects are moved by wind. |
|---|---|
| Emerging | Child observes movement of objects, shows some interest when guided by an adult. |
| Almost Mastered | Child discusses movement of objects and makes comparisons with the help of an adult. |
| Fully Mastered | Child independently compares objects moved by wind and describes the common properties and differences. |

## A WIND WALK

### Family Science Connection:

**Around the house,** find things that the family can **blow** on and make move. **Blow** on a **feather, a paper napkin or tissue, a pencil on the table,** or whatever the family finds that can be **moved**. After blowing on these objects, **describe** what the family saw, felt, or heard. (CAUTION: Children should not get their eyes close to moving or flying objects.)

**Comments or questions** that may add a *sense of wonder* to this activity:

- What object was the easiest to move when blown upon? Did it weigh the least or the most?

- If we blow harder on an object will it move faster or slower?

## EXPLORACIÓN DEL VIENTO

### Ciencia en familia:

Encuentre objetos **en la casa** a los que la familia puede **soplar** y hacer mover. **Sople** a una pluma, **una servilleta de papel abierta, un pañuelo de papel, un lápiz sobre la mesa,** o cualquier cosa que la familia encuentre que pueda **despertar los sentidos**. Después de soplar en estos objetos, **describan** lo que vio, sintió, y oyó la familia. (PRECAUCIÓN: Los niños no deben poner los ojos cerca de objectos que se mueven o vuelan.)

**Comentarios o preguntas** que pueden *despertar curiosidad* en esta actividad:

- ¿Cuál fue el objeto más fácil de soplar? ¿Pesaba más o menos que todos?

- Si le soplamos más fuerte a un objeto, ¿se moverá más rápido o más despacio?

# A WINDY DAY

**Investigation:** Discovering what makes objects move

**Process Skills:** Observing, comparing

**Materials:** Small sticks, straws, or tongue depressors with cloth or tissue streamers attached

## Procedure:

*Getting started:*
Go outside on a windy day. Give each child a small stick with a streamer attached. Let them experiment with their streamers. Watch children and listen to what they say. Challenge children to walk in different directions and notice what happens to their streamers. (CAUTION: On windy days, sand and dirt can be blown into the eyes and cause damage. Also, children with allergies to particulates, pollen, etc., may be placed in harm's way. Always check first with parents.)

*Questions to guide children:*
- When does your streamer move?
- What seems to push the streamer?
- Can you see the wind? Hear the wind?
- Can you find a place where your streamer doesn't move?

*What children and adults will do:*
Children will stand, then run with their streamers. They won't want to talk about what they are doing right away. Let them have the experience of moving with their streamers before asking questions. Encourage them to move in different directions and to hold their streamers in different ways to see what happens.

*Closure:*
Gather up the streamers and go inside. Sit in a circle and ask children to tell about what happened with their streamers and the wind. Ask some of the questions listed above, phrasing them in the past tense: "When did your streamer move?" "What happened when you turned around?"

## Follow-up Activity:

Make the streamers available outdoors on windy days and occasionally on a day with no wind to help children make further discoveries. Tie streamers to tricycles. Take out scarves on a windy day.

## Literature Connection:

*Catch the Wind! All About Kites*
by Gail Gibbons, Little, Brown, 1989.

*The Wind Blew*
by Pat Hutchins, Macmillan, 1974.

# A WINDY DAY

- **Science B-1** Expands knowledge of and abilities to observe, describe and discuss the natural world, materials, living things and natural processes.

- **Language Development B-2** Progresses in abilities to initiate and respond appropriately in conversation and discussions with peers and adults.

- **Approaches to Learning A-3** Approaches tasks and activities with increased flexibility, imagination and inventiveness.

  *Source: "Head Start Child Outcomes Framework." See Appendix A in this book for the framework.

# What To Look For

| Not Yet | Child does not participate in experimenting with a streamer. |
|---|---|
| Emerging | Child participates reluctantly, but does not fully get involved in trying different moves with the streamer. |
| Almost Mastered | Child shows interest in experimenting with the streamer and describes and asks questions about the activity. |
| Fully Mastered | Child participates fully and independently experiments with streamer, makes connections to other activities involving wind, and initiates discussions. |

# FAMILY PAGE / PÁGINA PARA LA FAMILIA

## A WINDY DAY

### Family Science Connection:

**At home,** have a family member blow up several balloons and attach them to a ribbon or string. Outside, encourage the children to run in **different** directions holding their attached balloons. Let them see how high in the air their balloons will go. (CAUTION: If your child is allergic to rubber products, use only non-latex-type balloons.)

Next attach the balloons to the outside cover of an indoor fan. Have an **adult** turn the fan on low and see how the balloons move. **Talk** about how **different strengths of wind** can make things fly. You can also try this activity with other objects such as streamers. (CAUTION: This activity should only be done under the direct supervision of an adult. Be careful that children do not stick their fingers or other objects into the fan blade.)

**Comments or questions** that may add a *sense of wonder* to this activity:

- When you are standing in place, is the wind helping to make your balloon go up in the air?
- Will running with your balloon make it go up higher in the air than if you are just standing in place?

## UN DÍA CON VIENTO

### Ciencia en familia:

**En casa**, pida a un miembro de la familia que infle varios globos y los ate con un listón o un hilo. Afuera, anime a los niños a que corran en **diferentes** direcciones agarrando sus globos. Deje que vean qué tan alto pueden subir los globos. (PRECAUCIÓN: Si su hijo es alérgico a la goma, usa solamente globos que no son de látex.)

Luego amarre los globos al frente de un abanico eléctrico. Asegúrese que un **adulto controle** la velocidad del abanico. Colóquela en Abaja y vean cómo se elevan los globos. **Hablen** acerca de cómo las **diferentes fuerzas del viento** pueden hacer que las cosas vuelen. Puede también intentar esta actividad atando otros objetos con listones. (PRECAUCIÓN: Solo se debe hacer esta actividad bajo la supervisión de un adulto. Tenga cuidado que los niños no pongan los dedos u otros objetos en las aletas del ventilador.)

**Comentarios o preguntas** que pueden *despertar curiosidad* en esta actividad:

- Cuando estás parado en un lugar, ¿ayuda el viento a que tu globo se eleve?

- ¿Se elevan más tu globo si corres que si te quedas parado en un solo lugar?

# AIR THAT MOVES

**Investigation:** Discovering what makes objects move

**Process Skill:** Observing

**Materials:** Electric fans, paper to make hand fans, streamers from "A Windy Day"

## Procedure:

*Getting started:*
(Do this activity after the "Wind Walk" and "A Windy Day.") Ask children to describe again their experiences on the wind walk they took. What kinds of things moved and when? Ask if they think they could get their streamers to move inside without the wind.

*Questions to guide children:*
  · When does your streamer move?
  · What seems to push it?
  · Can you make your streamer move in a different direction?
  · Can we keep our streamers very still? How?

*What children and adults will do:*
Some children will take their streamers and wave them or run with them. Ask if they can think of another way to move their streamers. Bring out an electric fan and let children hold their streamers in front of it (not so close that the streamer can become tangled in it). Ask if there is another way to move their streamers. Give children paper and show them how to fold it to make a fan. (CAUTION: This activity should only be done under the direct supervision of an adult. Be careful that children do not stick their fingers or other objects into the fan blade.)

*Closure:*
When all the children have finished making their fans, have them work in pairs, one with a streamer and the other with a hand fan to try to move the other's streamer. Let them take turns for as long as they stay interested.

## Follow-up Activities:

(1) Have balls available—some of which are inflated and some which are not. Have children try bouncing both. Ask children what the deflated balls need. Have children help you inflate them. (2) See if any of the children can whistle. Read *Whistle for Willie*, then have children try whistling. Have children put their hands in front of their mouths as they whistle. (3) Make the streamers and fans available outdoors on windy days and occasionally on a day with no wind to help children make further discoveries.

## Literature Connection:

*The Ball That Wouldn't Bounce*
by Mel Cebulash, Scholastic, 1972.

*Hot Air Henry*
by Mary Calhoun, William Morrow, 1981.

*Whistle for Willie*
by Ezra Jack Keats, Viking Press, 1963.

*Outside, Inside*
by Carolyn Crimi, Simon & Schuster, 1995.

## Assessment Outcomes & Possible Indicators*

- **Science A-5** Begins to describe and discuss predictions, explanations and generalizations based on past experiences.

- **Literacy B-1** Demonstrates progress in abilities to retell and dictate stories from books and experiences; to act out stories in dramatic play; and to predict what will happen next in a story.

- **Social & Emotional Development C-1** Increases abilities to sustain interactions with peers by helping, sharing and discussion.

  *Source: "Head Start Child Outcomes Framework." See Appendix A in this book for the framework.

## What To Look For

| Not Yet | Child does not participate in trying to make the streamer move. |
|---|---|
| Emerging | Child participates briefly and watches as an adult conducts the activity. |
| Almost Mastered | Child places streamer near the fan and describes what happens, participates in adult-led discussion. |
| Fully Mastered | Child makes a fan and attempts to move another child's streamer with the fan; discusses the outcome independently. |

# AIR THAT MOVES

## Family Science Connection:

**Together** with your child, **gather a few items** around the house that will wave or fly though the outdoor air. You might try running with various objects like a scarf, cloth napkin, baby's bedsheet, pillowcase, or bath towel to experiment and observe which objects fly easiest in the air. After you have spent some time **identifying** these objects, **talk** together about what makes some objects wave or fly. **Compare** the objects by weight.

**Comments or questions** that may add a *sense of wonder* to this activity:

- Show me how your object moves best through the air.

- Let's see how many different ways you can get different objects to float in the air.

# EL AIRE QUE MUEVE

## Ciencia en familia:

**Junto** con su niño(a) **tomen algunos objetos** de su casa que puedan ondular o volar en el viento. Pueden tratar de correr con varios objetos como una pañoleta, una servilleta de tela, una sábana de bebé, una funda, o una toalla de baño para experimentar y observar cuáles objetos vuelan más fácilmente con el viento. Después de haber **identificado** estos objetos por un tiempo, **platiquen** acerca de qué es lo que hacer ondular o volar a los objetos. **Comparen** los objetos según su peso.

**Comentarios o preguntas** que pueden *despertar curiosidad* en esta actividad:

- Muéstrame cómo se mueve mejor por el aire tu objeto.

- Veamos de cuántas maneras diferentes puedes hacer que tus objetos floten en el aire.

# PARACHUTES

**Investigation:** To play with a parachute in order to make discoveries about air

**Process Skills:** Observing, communicating

**Materials:** A parachute with hand-holds along the edge, playground ball

## Procedure:

*Getting started:*
If the children have not played with a parachute before, let them just enjoy it for several days before you begin asking questions or guiding the discoveries in any way. When you feel they are ready, begin introducing different activities:
  • Letting go of the parachute to see what happens.
  • Moving the parachute up and down, then dropping it to the ground to "capture" the air in the middle.
  • Bouncing a ball on the parachute.
  • One child at a time running under the parachute from one side to the other.

*Questions to guide children:*
  • What happened when you let go?
  • I wonder what is holding the parachute up in the air.

*What children and adults will do:*
This is always a favorite activity and can be a large-group activity if you have a large parachute. Let the children's reactions and suggestions guide you. They may want to try "hiding" under the parachute. Let them try it but limit the number who can "hide" at the same time.

*Closure:*
Let children talk about their parachute experiences. Have them draw a picture of their favorite parachute activity.

## Follow-up Activity:

Make the parachute available on a regular basis so children can repeat their experiences.

# PARACHUTES

- **Science A-5** Begins to describe and discuss predictions, explanations and generalizations based on past experiences.

- **Creative Arts B-2** Progresses in abilities to create drawings, paintings, models, and other art creations that are more detailed, creative or realistic.

- **Approaches to Learning A-3** Approaches tasks and activities with increased flexibility, imagination and inventiveness.

- **Physical Health & Development B-1** Shows increasing levels of proficiency, control and balance in walking, climbing, running, jumping, hopping, skipping, marching and galloping.

*Source: "Head Start Child Outcomes Framework." See Appendix A in this book for the framework.

## What To Look For

| Not Yet | Child shows no interest in the parachute. |
|---|---|
| Emerging | Child holds the parachute, but does not move around. |
| Almost Mastered | Child moves when told to do so by an adult; describes the activity and asks some questions. |
| Fully Mastered | Child shows great interest; comes up with other ideas of how to use the parachute; discusses discoveries and asks related questions. |

# MY SHADOW

**Investigation:** Seeing one's own shadow and observing how it changes

**Process Skills:** Observing, comparing, communicating

**Materials:** Chalk of different colors

## Procedure:

*Getting started:*
Take children outside on a sunny day. Ask children to look at the ground next to where they are standing to see what they can see. As soon as someone notices his or her shadow, introduce the word *shadow*. Encourage children to move around to see what happens to the shadows. Give children time to experiment. Observe what they do and listen to what they say.

*Questions to guide children:*
  · What does your shadow look like?
  · Can you make your shadow smaller? Bigger?
  · Can you find a place where you don't have a shadow?
  · What happens to your shadows when two people stand close together?

*What children and adults will do:*
Children will move about to see what happens to their shadows. They will look at each other's. Challenge children to change the shape of their shadows and to make them "disappear" and "reappear."

*Closure:*
Trace around children's feet with chalk as they stand in the sun. Trace their shadows as they stand still. (Or children could trace each other's). Put each child's name on each shadow outline. Point out

where the sun is now. Tell children they will be "checking" on their shadow several times during the day to see what happens. Go inside, then return to the shadows after about an hour. Have children stand on their footprints to see if anything happened. Ask children to describe what happened. Point out the Sun's new position. You could trace the new shadow with different color chalk and repeat the experiment later in the day.

## Follow-up Activity:

To help children begin to make a connection between the position of the Sun and their shadows, use a flashlight as our "Sun" and a doll or stick figure as "me." Observe the shadow changes as the "Sun" is moved about relative to "me." Do this in the room on several different days, especially when children have expressed interest in shadows.

## Center Connection:

During outdoor time, encourage children to look at their shadows on different days to see the differences. Add music and streamers to create new shadows. Play "catch a shadow." Children stand in a circle; one child calls out a friend's name then tries to step on the friend's shadow.

## Literature Connection:

*My Shadow*
by Robert Louis Stevenson, LC Publishing, 1991.

*Me and My Shadow*
by Arthur Durros, Scholastic, 1990.

*The Biggest Shadow in the Zoo*
by Jack Kent, Parents Magazine Press, 1981.

*Sun Up, Sun Down*
by Gail Gibbons, Voyager Books, 1987.

*What Is the Sun?*
by Reeve Lindbergh, Candlewick Press, 1994.

# MY SHADOW

- **Science A-4** Develops growing abilities to collect, describe and record information through a variety of means, including discussions, drawings, maps and charts.

- **Language Development B-1** Develops increasing abilities to understand and use language to communicate information, experiences, ideas, opinions, needs, questions and for other varied purposes.

- **Physical Health & Development B-1** Shows increasing levels of proficiency, control and balance in walking, climbing, running, jumping, hopping, skipping, marching and galloping.

*Source: "Head Start Child Outcomes Framework." See Appendix A in this book for the framework.

## What To Look For

| Not Yet | Child does not participate in attempting to make or change shadows. |
|---|---|
| Emerging | Child stands in place and allows an adult to pose him or her but does not experiment with changing the shadow. |
| Almost Mastered | Child moves about, allows an adult to trace his or her feet, and asks one or two questions. |
| Fully Mastered | Child moves about while describing changes in shadows, traces nearby peer's feet, allows adults or peers to trace his or her feet and discusses the activity in detail. |

## MY SHADOW

### Family Science Connection:

On a sunny day go outside and **look for your shadow**. As you move around, **observe how your shadow changes**. See whose shadow is larger: mom's, dad's, brother's, sister's, or yours. **Experiment** to see if one person's shadow can hide in another person's shadow. Try making your shadow shorter, thinner, wider, and taller. Try making your shadow dance!

**Comments or questions** that may add a *sense of wonder* to this activity:

- Can you make your shadow wiggle, stay still, or run?

- Can you make your shadow grow taller or shrink?

## MI SOMBRA

### Ciencia en familia:

En un día soleado **vayan afuera y vean sus sombras. Observen cómo se mueve su sombra** cuando ustedes se mueven. Vean cuál sombra es la más larga, la de mamá, de papá, del hermano, o la suya. **Experimenten** para ver si la sombra de una persona se puede esconder detrás de la sombra de otra persona. Traten de hacer su sombra más corta, delgada, ancha, y más alta. ¡Traten de hacer que su sombra baile!

**Comentarios o preguntas** que pueden *despertar curiosidad* en esta actividad:

- ¿Puedes hacer que tu sombra se menee, se esté quieta o que corra?

- ¿Puedes hacer que tu sombra crezca o se encoja?

# SHADOWS ON MY PLAYGROUND

**Investigation:** Observing shadows of objects to see how different objects make shadows of different shapes and sizes

**Process Skills:** Observing, comparing, communicating

**Materials:** Chalk of different colors

## Procedure:

*Getting started:*
(Do this after the "My Shadow" activity.) Take children outside on a sunny day. Have them look around for shadows. As children find them, ask them to describe the shadows and find what is making them. (CAUTION: Remind students not to look directly at the Sun.)

*Questions to guide children:*
- What seems to be making that shadow?
- How is the object different from its shadow?
- What shape is the shadow?
- Can you find a smaller shadow? Bigger?
- If the object moves, what happens to the shadow?
- Is it warmer (colder) in the sunny places or the shadows?

*What children and adults will do:*
Children will move about finding many shadows of different shapes and sizes. After a few minutes ask each child to choose his or her favorite shadow (one that is of a stationary object, not one that is moving). Give children chalk and ask them to trace the shadow.

*Closure:*
As a group, talk about the different shadows. Point out where the Sun is, and tell them that as the Sun shines on an object it causes a shadow. Go inside, then return to the shadows in about an hour or so. Look at the chalk outlines, and ask children to describe what they see. Point out where the Sun is now and that it has changed positions. (Children should be cautioned not to look directly at the Sun.) When the sun is in a new position the shadows change too.

## Follow-up Activity:

On any sunny day, encourage children to observe and describe shadows. Have children draw pictures of shadows and describe them. Put them all together for a class shadow book.

## Literature Connection:

*Bear Shadow*
by Frank Asch, Simon and Shuster, 1985.

*Shadows and Reflections*
by Tana Hoban, Greenwillow Books, New York, 1990.

*Grandmother and the Runaway Shadow*
by Liz Rosenberg, Harcourt, 1996.

# SHADOWS ON MY PLAYGROUND

- **Science A-2** Develops increased ability to observe and discuss common properties, differences and comparisons among objects and materials.

- **Science B-1** Expands knowledge of and abilities to observe, describe and discuss the natural world, materials, living things and natural processes.

- **Mathematics B-3** Begins to be able to determine whether or not two shapes are the same size and shape.

- **Creative Arts B-2** Progresses in abilities to create drawings, paintings, models, and other art creations that are more detailed, creative or realistic.

  *Source: "Head Start Child Outcomes Framework." See Appendix A in this book for the framework.

## What To Look For

| | |
|---|---|
| **Not Yet** | Child shows no interest in shadows. |
| **Emerging** | Child is interested in his or her own shadow but does not compare it to others. |
| **Almost Mastered** | Child shows interest, recognizes similarities and differences of the various shadows; participates in some of the discussion; asks few questions. |
| **Fully Mastered** | Child independently observes the various shadows, clearly discusses the findings, and goes on to explore shadows of other objects. |

## SHADOWS ON MY PLAYGROUND

### Family Science Connection:

**Go to the library** and ask for a **book about shadows**. Have mom or dad read to the children about shadows. Talk about how shadows are made by the Sun and an object or person that stands in the light of the Sun. Try going outside and find each family member's shadow. Have one person **chalk out each person's shadow** and where that person was standing at that time. Come back outside in an hour and see how your **shadows have changed** by standing in the same place. **Compare the chalk** mark to what the shadow looks like now. Is it bigger, smaller, wider, or thinner?

**Comments or questions** that may add a *sense of wonder* to this activity:

- I wonder what made our shadows change to look differently than they did an hour ago.

- How did your shadow change from an hour ago? Did it get bigger or smaller? Did it grow wider or thinner? What else changed about it?

## SOMBRAS, NADA MÁS

### Ciencia en familia:

**Vayan a la biblioteca** y pidan un **libro acerca de las sombras**. Que mamá o papá le lea a los niños acerca de las sombras. **Hablen** acerca de cómo se forman las sombras por el Sol y un objeto o persona enfrente la luz del Sol. Vayan afuera y vean la sombra de cada miembro de la familia. Pídale a un miembro de la familia que **dibuje con gis la sombra de cada persona** y donde la persona estaba parada en ese momento. Regresen después de una hora y vean **cómo ha cambiado su sombra**, parándose en el mismo lugar. **Comparen la marca de gis** y cómo se ve la sombra ahora. ¿Es más grande, más pequeña, más ancha, o más angosta?

**Comentarios o preguntas** que pueden *despertar curiosidad* en esta actividad:

- Me pregunto qué hace cambiar a nuestras sombras para verse diferente de como hace una hora.

- ¿Cómo cambió tu sombra de como era hace una hora? ¿Se hizo más grande o más pequeña? ¿Se hizo más ancha o más delgada? ¿Qué más cambió?

# WHERE DID THE SHADOWS GO?

**Investigation:** Discovering that on cloudy days there is sometimes not enough sun to cause shadows

**Process Skills:** Observing, comparing, communicating

**Materials:** None

## Procedure:

*Getting started:*
(Do this activity after the "My Shadow" and "Shadows on My Playground" activities.) On a cloudy day, remind children of the experiences they have already had with shadows. Ask them to describe some of the shadows they remember. Tell children they are going to go outside and look for shadows again.

*Questions to guide children:*
- What do you see on the ground? In the sky?
- Can you find any shadows?
- How does the sky look different today than it did the other day when we looked for shadows?
- Where do the shadows go at night?

*What children and adults will do:*
Children will look for shadows and probably be surprised not to find them. If the clouds are intermittent, the shadows may come and go, but on an overcast day there will be none. Encourage children to continue looking and to describe any they find. Discuss the differences in how the sky looks today from the other day you looked for shadows.

*Closure:*
Tell children that every day they should look for shadows and also look to see whether it is a sunny or cloudy day. Keep a chart for a week, asking children each day if it is sunny or cloudy. Then ask if they think it will be a day for shadows. Have them go outside to check their predictions.

## Follow-up Activity:

On a cloudy day, go outside and look at the clouds. Ask children to describe what they see. Have children make clouds by gluing cotton on blue or gray construction paper. Encourage them to name or describe their clouds. Watch for days when there are clouds moving. Encourage children to look for shadows in the shady and sunny areas of the yard.

## Literature Connection:

*It Looked Like Spilt Milk*
by Charles G. Shaw, Harper and Row, 1947.

*The Cloud Book*
by Tomie de Paulo, Holiday House, 1975.

*Little Cloud*
by Eric Carle, Philomel Books, 1996.

## Assessment Outcomes & Possible Indicators*

- **Science A-4** Develops growing abilities to collect, describe and record information through a variety of means, including discussions, drawings, maps and charts.

- **Science A-5** Begins to describe and discuss predictions, explanations and generalizations based on past experiences.

- **Language Development B-1** Develops increasing abilities to understand and use language to communicate information, experiences, ideas, opinions, needs, questions and for other varied purposes.

- **Creative Arts B-1** Gains ability in using different art media and materials in a variety of ways for creative expression and representation.

*Source: "Head Start Child Outcomes Framework." See Appendix A in this book for the framework.

## What To Look For

| Not Yet | Child is not interested in finding out whether or not there are shadows on any particular day. |
|---|---|
| Emerging | Child shows little interest in, or understanding of, the lack of shadows on a cloudy day; asks few questions. |
| Almost Mastered | Child is interested in the clouds; asks some questions about the lack of shadows and is able to participate in the discussion. |
| Fully Mastered | Child is greatly interested, asks several questions, and is able to connect this activity with other experiences on cloudy days. |

## WHERE DID THE SHADOWS GO?

This activity should follow the other two shadow lessons to be most effective.

### Family Science Connection:

**This activity should be done on a cloudy or rainy day.**

Talk about the day you went looking for shadows and found them as the Sun was shining. Ask your children if they think today would be a day to find shadows; why or why not? Now go outside and see if you can find your shadow. Did you **predict correctly about finding your shadow on a cloudy day?** Try looking for shadows for the rest of the week and remember that shadows are best found on a sunny day!

**Comments or questions** that may add a *sense of wonder* to this activity:

· Where is the Sun today?

· Do you think we will find our shadows today? Let's go look.

## ¿ADÓNDE SE FUERON LAS SOMBRAS?

Esta lección deberá seguir a las otras dos lecciones acerca de las sombras para que pueda ser más efectiva.

### Ciencia en familia:

**Esta actividad debe hacerse en un día nublado o lluvioso.**

Hablen acerca del día que fueron en busca de sus sombras y las encontraron cuando el Sol estaba brillando. Pregúntenle a sus niños si ellos piensan que este día encontrarán sus sombras. ¿Por qué o por qué no? Ahora salgan y vean si pueden encontrar sus sombras. ¿Fue **correcta tu predicción acerca de que si encontrarías tu sombra en un día nublado?** Traten de encontrar sus sombras por el resto de la semana y ¡recuerden que la mejor manera de encontrar sombras es en un día soleado!

**Comentarios o preguntas** que pueden *despertar curiosidad* en esta actividad:

· ¿Dónde está el sol el día de hoy?

· ¿Crees que encontraremos nuestras sombras hoy? ¡Vamos a buscarlas!

# WHAT IS THE WEATHER LIKE TODAY?

**Investigation:** Going outside to determine whether it is sunny, cloudy, rainy, windy, foggy, snowy, cold, or hot

**Process Skills:** Observing, classifying, comparing, communicating

**Materials:** 2-foot lengths of string with a feather taped to each string

## Procedure:

*Getting started:*
(Do this activity after the "A Wind Walk" and "My Shadow" activities). Ask children if they know what the weather is like today. Have all the children go outside to determine the temperature and to note if the weather is sunny or cloudy, rainy or dry, and windy or still.

*Questions to guide children:*
- Is today's weather the same as yesterday's?
- Is it windy? How can you tell?
- What is making your feather blow?

*What children and adults will do:*
While children are outside, ask about the different weather conditions. To determine whether or not it is sunny, have children look for shadows. Have children hold the string with the feather attached to it to look for movement and determine whether or not the wind is blowing. Children can also look at what they are wearing to decide whether or not they dressed appropriately for the weather.

*Closure:*
Back inside the classroom, record children's findings on a weather chart. The typical weather chart has only one arrow for one response. Add arrows with brads, or make your own, so that children can come up with multiple responses. For example, it could be sunny, cold, and windy all at the same time.

## Follow-up Activities:

This is a good activity to do each day to help children become better observers of their own environment. You could also keep track of one aspect of the weather—for example, how many sunny days there are during the year. During outdoor time, children could choose to take the string outside to check on the wind, or look for shadows to see if it is still sunny.

## Literature Connection:

*Sun Up, Sun Down*
by Gail Gibbons, Harcourt Brace Jovanovich, 1983.

*Gilberto and the Wind*
by Marie Hall Ets, Penguin, 1978.

*The Snowy Day*
by Ezra Jack Keats, Penguin, 1976.

*Rain*
by Robert Kalan, Mulberry, 1978.

*What Will the Weather Be Like Today?*
by Paul Rogers, Greenwillow, 1990.

*Umbrella*
by Taro Yashima, Scott Foresman (Pearson K–12), 1985.

## Assessment Outcomes & Possible Indicators*

- **Science A-4** Develops growing abilities to collect, describe and record information through a variety of means, including discussions, drawings, maps and charts.

- **Science B-1** Expands knowledge of and abilities to observe, describe and discuss the natural world, materials, living things and natural processes.

- **Language Development B-2** Progresses in abilities to initiate and respond appropriately in conversation and discussions with peers and adults.

  *Source: "Head Start Child Outcomes Framework." See Appendix A in this book for the framework.

## What To Look For

| Not Yet | Child does not participate in describing the weather. |
|---|---|
| Emerging | Child looks for movement with the help of an adult; adds to discussion only when being asked questions directly. |
| Almost Mastered | Child looks for movement, checks for different weather conditions and checks his or her clothing; asks a few questions and describes some findings. |
| Fully Mastered | Child participates fully, checks the weather, compares it to the previous day's weather, and initiates discussion with others. |

## WHAT IS THE WEATHER LIKE TODAY?

### Family Science Connection:

Each morning for the next five days have your young children look outside to see and feel what the weather looks like. **Ask** them to tell you if it is sunny or cloudy, windy or still, rainy or dry. Then with your guidance, ask them what clothes they should wear that are appropriate for the weather. **Talk** about how the weather can make us feel hot or cold. **Chart each day** by writing: *sunny, rainy, windy, cloudy, dry*, or *still* on a sheet of paper and keep it on the refrigerator. On the last day of your observations, **count up the number of days that were sunny**. A great book to go along with this activity is *What Will the Weather Be Like Today?* by Paul Rogers.

**Comments or questions** that may add a *sense of wonder* to this activity:

- Is today's weather the same as yesterday's?

- What is your favorite weather? Tell me what you like about your favorite weather.

## ¿CÓMO ESTÁ EL CLIMA HOY?

### Ciencia en familia:

Cada mañana por los siguientes cinco días pidan a sus niños pequeños que vean hacia afuera para ver y sentir el clima. **Pídanles** que les digan si está soleado o nublado, con viento o calmado, lluvioso o seco. Pregunten qué tipo de ropa deberían usar que sean apropiadas para ese clima. **Hablen** de cómo es que el clima puede hacer que sintamos frío o calor. **Hagan una gráfica** y escriban columnas por *soleado, lluvioso, con viento, nublado, seco*, o *tranquilo* y marquen en cada día el clima correspondiente y conserven la gráfica en el refrigerador. En el último día de sus observaciones, **cuenten el número de días en que estuvo el clima soleado**. Un buen libro que va muy bien con esta actividad es, *What Will the Weather be Like Today?* por Paul Rogers.

**Comentarios o preguntas** que pueden *despertar curiosidad* en esta actividad:

- ¿Es el clima de hoy igual que el de ayer?

- ¿Cuál es tu clima favorito? Dime qué es lo que te gusta más de tu clima favorito.

# SNOW TRACKS AND TRACES

**Investigation:**   Investigating tracks in the snow

**Process Skills:**   Observing and comparing

**Materials:**   Freshly fallen snow (CAUTION: Try to ensure there are no slip/trip hazards like foreign objects or ice under the snow on which children can fall and get hurt.)

## Procedure:

*Getting started:*
Go outside with the children and choose one child to make tracks in the snow by continually jumping forward. Look at the tracks from the jumping and see how the prints from each boot are side by side. Have the same child walk through the snow and see how the tracks from walking are different from the tracks from jumping forward. Encourage the children to make all kinds of different tracks. Have the children cover their eyes and invite one child to make some tracks in special ways (e.g., by crawling on his or her hands and knees). Challenge the rest of the children to look at the special tracks and make tracks like those special tracks.

*Questions to guide children:*
  • What different kinds of snow prints can you make?
  • What's the difference between these snow prints?
  • How can you make snow prints that look like these?

*What children and adults will do:*
The focus of this activity is on helping children begin to see that tracks and traces can tell stories about things that have not been seen. Even though you do not see how a track was made, you can still get some clues about how it was made. Ask the children how tracks can tell stories. Ask the children if their tracks will stay in the snow for very long. See if the children have ever seen other kinds of tracks (tire tracks in the mud, tracks left by worms on a sidewalk).

## Follow-up Activity:

Take a couple of objects (a pail, a coffee can [CAUTION: Make sure there are not sharp edges on the can], a cup with a handle, a large plastic toy) outside with you and when the children are not looking (eyes covered) place the objects in the snow in different ways to make different snow prints. Challenge the children to use the objects to make snow prints just like yours.

## Art Connection:

Children can move objects (marbles and other objects) over a painted piece of paper and make tracks in the wet paint.

## Literature Connection:

*The First Snowfall*
by Anne Harlow and Harlow Rockwell, Macmillan, 1987.

*Amy Loves the Snow*
by Julia Hoban, HarperTrophy, 1993.

*Snowballs*
by Lois Ehlert, Harcourt, 2001.

## Assessment Outcomes & Possible Indicators*

- **Science A-2** Develops increased ability to observe and discuss common properties, differences and comparisons among objects and materials.

- **Science B-3** Develops growing awareness of ideas and language related to attributes of time and temperature.

- **Science B-4** Shows increased awareness and beginning understanding of changes in materials and cause-effect relationships.

- **Mathematics A-5** Begins to use language to compare numbers of objects with terms such as more, less, greater than, fewer, equal to.

*Source: "Head Start Child Outcomes Framework." See Appendix A in this book for the framework.

## What To Look For

| Not Yet | Child does not participate in making tracks in the snow. |
|---|---|
| Emerging | Child participates reluctantly, with the encouragement of an adult. |
| Almost Mastered | Child makes tracks by walking in the snow and asks some questions. |
| Fully Mastered | Child makes tracks by walking, crawling, jumping, and running; asks several questions, observes similarities and differences of tracks made with different objects, and initiates discussion of these findings. |

## SNOW TRACKS AND TRACES

### Family Science Connection:

After a freshly fallen snow, go out into the snow with your child. **Look** for some prints in the snow and ask, "What happened here?" Have your child hide his or her eyes while you make some tracks in the snow (jumping or hopping or crawling). **Ask your child to look at the tracks** you have made and see if he or she can make tracks that look like yours. If this is too difficult for your child, have your child watch as you make a new set of tracks. Then ask if the new tracks were made in the same way as the old tracks. While you cover your eyes, have your child make tracks in funny ways and then try to make tracks like those tracks. Just have fun making all sorts of tracks and prints in the snow.

**Comments or questions** that may add a *sense of wonder* to this activity:

- I wonder what different kinds of snow prints you can make.

- What's the difference between these snow prints and those snow prints over there?

- How can you make snow prints that look like these?

- Prints can help us tell stories about things we have not seen.

## HUELLAS Y RASTROS EN LA NIEVE

### Ciencia en familia:

Después de una nevada reciente, salga a la nieve con su hijo(a). **Busquen** huellas en la nieve y pregunte: "¿Qué pasó aquí?" Pídale a su hijo(a) que se tape los ojos mientras usted deja sus huellas en la nieve (brincando, saltando o a gatas). **Pídale a su hijo(a) que vea las huellas** que usted ha hecho para ver si puede hacer huellas como las suyas. Si es muy difícil para su hijo(a), permítale ver cuando hace huellas nuevas. Pregúntele si se hicieron igual que las primeras. Después cúbrase usted los ojos mientras su hijo(a) hace huellas chistosas y luego trate de hacer huellas como las que él(ella) hizo. Simplemente diviértanse haciendo huellas e impresiones en la nieve.

**Comentarios o preguntas** que pueden *despertar curiosidad* en esta actividad:

- Me pregunto cuántas clases diferentes de impresiones puedes hacer en la nieve.

- ¿Cuál es la diferencia entre estas huellas y las huellas de allá?

- ¿Cómo puedes hacer huellas como estas?

- Las huellas nos pueden ayudar a contar cosas que no hemos visto.

# SNOW ON THE GO

**Investigation:** Exploring the properties of snow and how snow changes into liquid water.

**Process Skills:** Observing and comparing

**Materials:** Snow piled high in the water or sensory table, plastic cups

## Procedure:

*Getting started:*
Pile a few (two to four) buckets of freshly fallen snow into the water or sensory table. Have the children pack snow into plastic cups so the cups are full of snow. Ask the children what will happen to the snow in their cups. If they suggest that the snow will turn into water, ask them if a full cup of snow will make a full cup of water. Set the cups of snow aside and allow the children an opportunity to explore the snow in the water table. (CAUTION: When using water, make sure that all electrical receptacles in the classroom are protected by a ground fault circuit interrupter [GFCI].)

*Questions to guide children:*
  · What can we say about snow?
  · Where did the snow go that was in the water or sensory table?
  · What is snow made out of?

*What children and adults will do:*
The children will likely predict that a full cup of snow will turn into a full cup of water. Don't try to explain why snow takes up more space than the liquid water that comes from it. Children will not necessarily understand that snow is made of solid water. Nevertheless, it is interesting to find out what children think snow is made of.

*Closure:*
If the children have placed their cups of snow in different places around the room, they may have noticed that snow in some cups took longer to melt than snow in other cups. Find out if the children have observed this and ask them why snow melted faster here than over there.

## Follow-up Activities:

How many cups of snow does it take to make one cup of water? To answer this question, see how many cups of melt water (water from melted snow) it takes to make one cup of water. Most of the focus has been on the melting snow. Switch the focus to how we might keep snow from melting. Ask the children, "What could we do to keep snow from melting?" Outside, challenge children to make some snow sculptures and shapes. Encourage them to observe how snow changes as the temperature changes.

## Literature Connection:

*The Snowy Day*
by Ezra Jack Keats, Puffin Books, 1962.

## Assessment Outcomes & Possible Indicators*

- **Science A-2** Develops increased ability to observe and discuss common properties, differences and comparisons among objects and materials.

- **Science B-3** Develops growing awareness of ideas and language related to attributes of time and temperature.

- **Science B-4** Shows increased awareness and beginning understanding of changes in materials and cause-effect relationships.

- **Mathematics A-5** Begins to use language to compare numbers of objects with terms such as more, less, greater than, fewer, equal to.

*Source: "Head Start Child Outcomes Framework." See Appendix A in this book for the framework.

## What To Look For

| Not Yet | Child is not interested. |
|---|---|
| Emerging | Child shows some interest, packs snow into cup, attempts to make a prediction, and asks one or two questions. |
| Almost Mastered | Child is interested in the outcome of the experiment, asks some questions, makes predictions and discusses the outcome. |
| Fully Mastered | Child is highly interested, makes predictions based on past experiences, fills other containers with snow in order to make comparisons, and initiates discussions about the experiment. |

## SNOW ON THE GO

### Family Science Connection:

After or during a fresh snowfall, **go outside with your child and look at snow up close**. See how it sparkles in the sunlight and how it is made of tiny pieces (flakes). If snow is falling, help your child catch snow on his or her sleeve or glove and **watch** what happens to the snow. Also, you and your child might try catching some falling snow on your tongues. Mark an area of undisturbed snow and come back to that same place at other times to see how the snow has changed. Take some snow indoors and watch what happens to the snow.

**Comments or questions** that may add a *sense of wonder* to this activity:

- It's wonderful to think that the snow on the ground is made up of all these little pieces of snow (flakes). There must be many, many, many flakes of snow on the ground.

- See how the flakes sparkle and see all the little "arms" on each flake of snow. How fragile snowflakes must be!

- I wonder where snow comes from. What is snow made of?

## LA NIEVE QUE SE MUEVE

### Ciencia en familia:

Después de una nevada reciente o cuando esté cayendo, **salga con su hijo(a) y vea la nieve de cerca**. Vean cómo brilla con el sol y cómo está formada de pequeñas partes (copos). Si la nieve está cayendo, ayúdele a su hijo(a) a atrapar nieve en su manga o guante y **observen** lo que le pasa a la nieve. También pueden intentar atrapar nieve del cielo con la lengua. Marquen un área con nieve sin tocar y regresen al mismo lugar en diferentes ocasiones para ver cómo cambió la nieve. Lleven un poco de nieve adentro y observen lo que le pasa a la nieve.

**Comentarios o preguntas** que pueden *despertar curiosidad* en esta actividad:

- Es maravilloso pensar que la nieve en el piso está formada de pedacitos de nieve (copos). Deben haber muchísimos copos de nieve en el suelo.

- Mira cómo brillan los copos y mira los "abracitos" que tiene cada uno. Cuán frágiles deben ser los copos de nieve.

- Me pregunto de dónde viene la nieve. ¿De qué se compone la nieve?

# KEEPING WARM: COATS

**Investigation:** Discovering how coats keep things warm

**Process Skills:** Observing and comparing

**Materials:** Two or more empty 12- or 20-ounce plastic soda bottles with screw tops, hot water in a carafe or thermos, funnel, newspaper and other material to use as coats, and rubber bands to hold the coats close to the bottles.

## Procedure:

*Getting started:*
Have a couple of children bring over their coats for all to see. Ask, "What can we say about these coats?" Explore the various parts of coats (button, zippers, hoods, and elastic around the cuffs) and wonder along with the children about what the coat and its parts do for us. Tell the children, "We are going to do an investigation with soda bottle 'people' to find out what coats do for us."

*Questions to guide children:*
· When do we wear coats?
· Why do we wear coats?
· Which soda bottle "person" (the one without the coat or the one with the coat) will keep the warmest?

*What children and adults will do:*
After talking with children to find out what they know and think about coats, introduce them to the two soda bottle "people." Use a funnel and carefully pour very warm water (hot, but not scalding) into each of the bottles. (CAUTION: Keep children at a safe distance while pouring water to prevent them from being splashed.) Put on the caps and dry off each bottle. Touch the outside of the bottles to feel how warm (hot) they are. If the bottles are not too hot, invite the children to feel how hot those bottles are. (CAUTION: This touching should be done only under direct adult supervision.)

Next, fold a double page of newspaper lengthwise. This should make a strip that is four pages thick, half a single page wide, and a whole page long. Wrap the strip around one of the bottles. Repeat this with at least two more strips and hold all strips in place around one of the bottles with rubber bands. You have now created a coat (at least 12 sheets thick) for one of the soda bottle people. The other soda bottle person does not have a coat. Ask the children which bottle will stay the warmest. Go off for a while (at least 30 minutes) and come back to touch the bottles to see which is the warmest. You will have to slide the coat down on the one bottle so you can feel how warm the bottle is.

Touch should tell you and the children which bottle is the warmest. You might pour some of the water over children's fingers so they can feel the difference in warmth. After the first test, slide the coat up over the bottle. Repeat the test every 30 minutes.

*Closure:*
Children should see that the newspaper coat kept the soda bottle person warmer. Connect the newspaper coats with real coats that we wear. Coats keep us warmer.

## Follow-up Activity:

Children can also explore a number of different things we use to keep us warm (gloves, hats, scarves).

## Literature Connection:

*The Jacket I Wear in the Snow*
by Shirley Neitzel, Greenwillow, 1989.

*Thomas' Snowsuit*
by Robert Munsch, FireFly Books, 1989.

## Assessment Outcomes & Possible Indicators*

- **Science A-5** Begins to describe and discuss predictions, explanations and generalizations based on past experiences.

- **Science B-3** Develops growing awareness of ideas and language related to attributes of time and temperature.

- **Science B-4** Shows increased awareness and beginning understanding of changes in materials and cause-effect relationships.

- **Physical Health & Development C-4** Builds awareness and ability to follow basic health and safety rules such as fire safety, traffic and pedestrian safety, and responding appropriately to potentially harmful objects, substances and activities.

*Source: "Head Start Child Outcomes Framework." See Appendix A in this book for the framework.

## What To Look For

| Not Yet | Child does not participate in talking about coats or touching the bottles. |
|---|---|
| Emerging | Child watches as others touch the bottles, asks one or two questions, and listens attentively. |
| Almost Mastered | Child touches bottles, asks questions, joins in discussions, and makes some connections to what coats do. |
| Fully Mastered | Child touches bottles, makes comparisons, and openly discusses findings. |

## KEEPING WARM: COATS

### Family Science Connection:

**Explore** the closets and chests for things that keep us warm. **Look for items** (jackets, sweaters, hats, scarves, and gloves) that keep us warm while we are outside. Also, look for items (blankets, robes) that keep us warm while we are inside. If you have a furry pet, look at its coat.

**Comments or questions** that may add a *sense of wonder* to this activity:

- I wonder which of these coats (or hats, or sweaters) would keep us the warmest.

- If I am cold in bed, should I add more blankets to the bed or take blankets off the bed?

- Feel our dog's (or cat's, or rabbit's) coat. Isn't it interesting that some animals have their coats on all of the time? What would happen to you if you had to keep your coat on all of the time?

## CONSERVANDO EL CALOR: ABRIGO

### Ciencia en familia:

**Exploren** los armarios y arcones, y busquen cosas que nos ayudan a conservar el calor. **Busquen artículos** (chamarras, suéteres, sombreros, bufandas y guantes) que nos ayudan a conservar el calor cuando estamos afuera. También busquen artículos (cobijas, batas) que nos ayudan a conservar el calor cuando estamos adentro. Si tienen una mascota mechuda, observen su pelaje.

**Comentarios o preguntas** que pueden despertar curiosidad en esta actividad:

- Me pregunto cuáles de estos abrigos (o sombreros, o suéteres) nos ayudarán a conservar el calor mejor.

- Si tengo frío en la cama, ¿debería poner más cobijas o quitar cobijas de la cama?

- Siente el pelaje de nuestro perro (o gato, o conejo). ¿No es interesante que algunos animales tienen su abrigo puesto siempre? ¿Qué pasaría si tuvieras que traer siempre tu abrigo puesto?

## Section 3:

# PHYSICAL SCIENCE

Young children are fascinated by what things are made of, how they move and why, and how they can make things happen. Children often have the most questions about their physical world—"How does the magnet stick to the refrigerator?" "Why is this rock so heavy?" Adults are often unsure of how to answer these questions and therefore avoid activities involving physical science concepts.

The following activities can be enjoyed by both children and adults. Don't be afraid to show your surprise and delight when you discover something new—"Will a magnet work through a table? Your hand? Through water?" As adults rediscover their own sense of wonder, children's delight in discovering facts about their world will be enhanced.

These activities require adults to give children long periods of uninterrupted time in order to make discoveries on their own. Ramps and roller coasters will occupy some children for days and weeks as they try out all sorts of configurations with various items to roll. Similarly children will want to collect many different rocks and try out many experiments with them. Encourage children to use their own ideas when working with materials.

## Physical Science: Selected Internet Resources

### Songs
- Physical Science Songs—*http://physics. bgsu.edu/~vanhook/physicssongs*

### Blocks
- Stages of Development Related to Block Building—*www.communityplaythings. com/c/Resources/Articles/BlockPlay/ Buildingachildsmind.htm*

### Wheels and Rolling
- Online Interactive Story About Wheels— *www.storyplace.org/preschool/activities/ countthewheels.asp*

# WHAT'S MAGNETIC?

**Investigation:**   Exploring what's magnetic

**Process Skills:**   Observing, comparing, classifying, communicating

**Materials:**   One magnet per child, assorted items for testing, sorting mat, a "Science Wonder Box" (a cardboard box for holding the items for testing) (CAUTION: If metal magnets are used, make sure that they are clean—no rust, oil, filings—with no sharp edges. Also, select magnets that can be easily handled by this age group.)

## Procedure:

*Getting started:*
Hand out identical magnets to each child. Give the children time to explore the magnets, then ask, "What can you tell me about them?" Place the "Science Wonder Box" in the center of the table and open the top. Tie a magnet onto a piece of string and lower it into the science box until several different items are attached to the magnet. Pull it out and ask what happened. Listen to the children's comments.

*Questions to guide children:*
  • What do you know about magnets?
  • Why doesn't it pick up leaves?
  • What can magnets pick up?

*What children and adults will do:*
Give each child a magnet and ask them to test some of the objects on the table to find out which ones are attracted to magnets. Give them plenty of time to explore freely first. Then ask them to make a little pile of the magnetic objects to share them later. You may also want to give the children a sorting mat.

*Closure:*
After the children have explored the objects at the table, ask them to share their magnetic objects. Ask what the objects that attached to the magnet had in common (all metals). Have children try to pick up an aluminum can with their magnets. Encourage them to discover that not all metals are attracted to the magnet.

## Follow-up Activity:
On another day put water in a pan. Ask children if they think their magnet will "work" in the water. Have them drop objects into the water, then try to pick up the objects with a magnet. (CAUTION: Make sure that only ground fault circuit interrupter [GFCI]–protected electrical receptacles are in the room where water is being used to prevent an electrical accident with the water.)

## Center Connection:
Place all of the objects plus some new ones in the science center. You can tie strings onto the magnets to attach them to the center table if needed.

## Literature Connection:

*Mickey's Magnet*
by Franklyn Branley and Eleanor Vaughan, Crowell, 1956. Reissued 1976.

*Magnets: Pulling Together, Pushing Apart*
by Natalie Rosinsky, Picture Window Books, 2002.

*Magnets (All Aboard Science Reader)*
by Anne Schreiber, Grosset & Dunlop, 2003.

## Assessment Outcomes & Possible Indicators*

- **Science A-1** Begins to use senses and a variety of tools and simple measuring devices to gather information, investigate materials and observe processes and relationships.

- **Science A-4** Develops growing abilities to collect, describe and record information through a variety of means, including discussions, drawings, maps and charts.

- **Language Development A-3** Understands an increasingly complex and varied vocabulary.

- **Mathematics C-3** Begins to make comparisons between several objects based on a single attribute.

*Source: "Head Start Child Outcomes Framework." See Appendix A in this book for the framework.

## What To Look For

| Not Yet | Child shows no interest or curiosity about magnets. |
|---|---|
| Emerging | Child watches other children using magnets; eventually tries out a magnet but loses interest quickly. |
| Almost Mastered | Child experiments with magnets and describes what is happening either in a group or independently. May ask one or two questions about magnets. |
| Fully Mastered | Child chooses to experiment with magnets and make connections between properties of items magnets attract; asks many questions about magnets. |

## WHAT'S MAGNETIC?

### Family Science Connection:

When the family goes to **the park, bring a magnet to explore** the things that might be **magnetic**. Have the children in your family **talk** about the objects in the playground area that they think might be **attracted to magnets** and see if they are. If the magnet sticks to the object then you can say that that object is "magnetic." See if the family can **compare** those things that are magnetic with those things that are not. (CAUTION: Magnets will attract sharp pieces of metal, razor blades, pins, etc.)

**Comments or questions** that may add a *sense of wonder* to this activity:

- Let's name the things in the park that we found that are magnetized.

- What are the things in the park that did not stick to the magnet?

## ¿QUÉ ES MAGNÉTICO?

### Ciencia en familia:

**Lleve un imán al parque para explorar** las cosas que puedan ser **magnéticas**. Pídale a los niños de su familia que **hablen** acerca de los objetos en el área de juego que ellos piensen que puedan estar **magnetizados** y vean si lo están. Si el imán se pega al objeto, entonces pueden decir que el objeto está magnetizado. Vean si su familia puede **comparar** aquellas cosas que están magnetizadas con aquellas que no lo están. (PRECAUCIÓN: Imanes atraerán pedazos afilados de metal, hojas de afeitar, alfileres, etc.)

**Comentarios o preguntas** que pueden *despertar curiosidad en esta* actividad:

- Nombremos las cosas que encontramos en el parque que eran magnéticas.

- ¿Cuáles fueron las cosas en el parque que no se pegaron al imán?

# Physical Science

# MAGNETIC SCAVENGER HUNT

**Investigation:** Finding magnetic items in the classroom

**Process Skills:** Observing, classifying, communicating

**Materials:** One magnet per child

## Procedure:

*Getting started:*
Ask the children if they can remember what the magnetic items they found last time had in common (all were metals). Ask the children to give you a few examples of items that are magnetic—that is, that attract or stick to a magnet.

*Questions guide children:*
- What items do you think are magnetic in the classroom?
- How can you find out?
- Will your magnet pick this _____ up?

*What children and adults will do:*
Give each child a magnet. Have the children go around the room and find objects that will attract or stick to their magnet. (CAUTION: Children should not go near the computer or near pins, paper clips, or other sharp objects with their magnets.)

*Closure:*
Have each child walk to one of the things that he or she discovered was magnetic. Let each child tell a story about what he or she discovered. Summarize the children's discoveries (all were metals but not all metals are magnetic—a soda can is aluminum and not magnetic; most keys are not magnetic; coins are not magnetic).

## Follow-up Activity:

Take children outside to discover what's magnetic on the playground. Have children experiment with putting their magnets into the sandbox to see what happens.

## Center Connection:
Place all of the objects plus some new ones in the science center. You can tie strings onto the magnets to attach them to the center table if needed. Children should feel free to continue exploring the classroom with a magnet as long as they stay away from the computers.

## Literature Connection:

*Magnets for Tommy*
by Russell Hoban, Harper Junior, 1962.

*Mickey's Magnet*
by Franklyn Branley and Eleanor Vaughan, Crowell, 1956. Reissued 1976.

*Magnets: Pulling Together, Pushing Apart*
by Natalie Rosinsky, Picture Window Books, 2002.

*Magnets (All Aboard Science Reader)*
by Anne Schreiber, Grosset & Dunlop, 2003.

# MAGNETIC SCAVENGER HUNT

## Assessment Outcomes & Possible Indicators*

- **Science A-3** Begins to participate in simple investigations to test observations, discuss and draw conclusions and form generalizations.

- **Language Development B-1** Develops increasing abilities to understand and use language to communicate information, experiences, ideas, opinions, needs, questions and for other varied purposes.

- **Mathematics C-3** Begins to make comparisons between several objects based on a single attribute.

- **Approaches to Learning C-3** Progresses in abilities to classify, compare and contrast objects, events and experiments.

  *Source: "Head Start Child Outcomes Framework." See Appendix A in this book for the framework.

## What To Look For

| Not Yet | Child does not participate in scavenger hunt. |
|---|---|
| Emerging | Child participates but only tries out the magnet on a few items. |
| Almost Mastered | Child shows interest in the scavenger hunt and experiments with many items in the classroom; describes and asks some questions about findings. |
| Fully Mastered | Child shows great interest in the scavenger hunt and continues independently to seek out other magnetic items both inside and out of the classroom; shares discoveries with adults and peers and asks questions. |

## MAGNETIC SCAVENGER HUNT

### Family Science Connection:

**At a family gathering, bring a magnet** and have the children see if any objects that the adults have in their pockets or purses are **attracted to magnets.** (CAUTION: Keep magnets away from credit cards. A magnet can "demagnetize" the strip on the back of the credit card, making the credit card unusable.) Continue the experience the children had from the classroom magnetic scavenger hunt to see who found the most magnetized objects. Put all of the magnetized objects the children found on a table so everyone can play with the magnetized objects. **Decide** which objects are most powerfully attracted to the magnet and have a **family discussion** about possible reasons this is so.

**Comments or questions** that may add a *sense of wonder* to this activity:

- What did the teacher share with you at school about magnets?

- Let's put the objects that have the strongest pull to the magnet in a pile and those that have the weakest pull in another pile. Do more things want to stick to the magnets?

## BÚSQUEDA DE IMANES

### Ciencia en familia:

**En una reunión familiar traiga un imán** y pide que los niños encuentren objetos **magnetizados** que los adultos tengan en sus bolsillos o bolsos. (PRECAUCIÓN: Mantenga imanes lejos de tarjetas de crédito. Un imán puede demagnetizer la banda en la parte atrás de la tarjeta, inutilizandola.) Continúe la experiencia que los niños tuvieron en clasede la búsqueda de imanes para ver quién encuentra más objetos magnetizados pequeños. Ponga todos los objetos magnetizados que los niños encontraron sobre una mesa para que todos puedan **jugar** con ellos. **Decida** cuáles objetos son atraídos más fuertemente por el imán y **hablen en familia** acerca de las posibles razones de que esto suceda.

**Comentarios o preguntas** que pueden *despertar curiosidad en esta* actividad:

- ¿Qué fue lo que tu maestra les enseñó en la escuela acerca de los imanes?

- Pongamos los objetos que tienen mayor atracción con el imán en un montón, y los que tienen menor atracción en otro. ¿Se pegan al imán la mayoría de las cosas?

# MAGNETIC FORCE THROUGH OBJECTS

**Investigation:** Exploring what objects a magnetic force can go through

**Process skills:** Observing, comparing, classifying, communicating

**Materials:** Two magnets per child; small and large paper clips (plastic coated); empty, clear, plastic cups; Styrofoam cups; two or three books; a few paper plates; different objects to test to see if the magnetic force will pass through them

## Procedure:

*Getting started:*
Place a small box (with two to three magnets inside) in the center of the table. Slowly move it about ½" over a pile of paper clips and watch the paper clips attach to the bottom of the box. Ask the children, "How did that happen? What do you think is in the box?" Listen to several of their suggestions and then open the box so they can see the magnet inside and that it is not MAGIC but magnets!

*Questions to guide children:*
- What do you know about magnets?
- Will the magnets push or pull each other around?
- Will the magnets attract through different objects (cup, paper plate, a piece of paper, a tabletop, pages in a book, shirt, socks)?
- Could the magnet work through my hand?

*What children and adults will do:*
Place all of the different objects in the center of the table for easy access. Ask children to find out what items the magnetic force will go through. Demonstrate how to move a paper clip around with a magnet while going through different objects (e.g., a piece of paper or a book). The magnetic force will go through some of these, but not all. Have the children experiment by placing a magnet on one side of the object and trying to move the paper clip on the other.

*Closure:*
Have each child share what he or she discovered about what objects a magnetic force goes through.

## Follow-up Activity:

This activity could be done again with different objects and trying to see what objects a magnetic force will pass through. Try putting objects in a clear plastic cup partially filled with water. See if the magnet placed on the outside of the cup will move the objects.

## Center Connection:

Place all of the objects at the science center for further investigation.

## Literature Connections:

*Mickey's Magnet*
by Franklyn Branley and Eleanor Vaughan, Crowell, 1956. Reissued 1976.

*Magnets: Pulling Together, Pushing Apart*
by Natalie Rosinsky, Picture Window Books, 2002.

*Magnets (All Aboard Science Reader)*
by Anne Schreiber, Grosset & Dunlop, 2003.

# MAGNETIC FORCE THROUGH OBJECTS

- **Science A-1** Begins to use senses and a variety of tools and simple measuring devices to gather information, investigate materials and observe processes and relationships.

- **Science A-5** Begins to describe and discuss predictions, explanations and generalizations based on past experiences.

- **Language Development B-1** Develops increasing abilities to understand and use language to communicate information, experiences, ideas, opinions, needs, questions and for other varied purposes.

- **Approaches to Learning A-1** Chooses to participate in an increasing variety of tasks and activities.

   *Source: "Head Start Child Outcomes Framework." See Appendix A in this book for the framework.

## What To Look For

| | |
|---|---|
| **Not Yet** | Child shows no interest in experimenting with the magnet. |
| **Emerging** | Child participates in the activity but loses interest after trying out the magnet on one or two of the objects. |
| **Almost Mastered** | Child tries out magnet on all of the objects provided and describes what is happening; may ask one or two questions about the process. |
| **Fully Mastered** | Child participates fully in the activity then continues to try out objects other than those provided (e.g., other classroom objects, parts of the body); shares discoveries with adults and peers and asks questions. |

## MAGNETIC FORCE THROUGH OBJECTS

### Family Science Connection:

Find an old **shoe box** and put a large paper clip in it. (CAUTION: Ends of paper clips can be sharp and can cut skin.) **Exploring** to see if it is magnetic, put a **magnet** to the paper clip and see if it sticks. Now try putting other items in the box, one at a time, and observe how the item sticks or doesn't stick to the magnet. Now **experiment** with other items putting the magnet *under* the box with the item inside. **Observe** if the magnet can still move the item. Try **experimenting with different objects** to see if the magnet can move the objects with the box in its way.

## FUERZA MAGNÉTICA A TRAVÉS DE OBJETOS

### Ciencia en familia:

Encuentren una **caja vieja de zapatos** y pongan dentro un clip grande para papeles. (PRECAUCIÓN: Las puntas de un clip pueden ser afilados y cortar la piel.) **Exploren** para saber si es magnético, pónganle un imán para ver si se adhiere. Ahora traten de poner otros objetos en la caja (uno a la vez) y **observen** si la fuerza del imán todavía puede mover el objeto. Ahora experimentan con otros objetos dentro de la caja y con el imán *debajo*. **Observen** si la fuerza del imán todaría puede mover el objeto. Traten de **experimentar con diferentes objetos** para ver si el imán puede mover los objetos con la caja de por medio.

# MAGNETIC MAZES

**Investigation:** Using a magnet to push or pull a paper clip through a maze (CAUTION: Ends of paper clips can be sharp and can cut skin.)

**Process Skills:** Observing

**Materials:** Per child: One photocopied or pre-drawn maze, one magnet, one small paper clip, one crayon

## Procedure:

*Getting started:*
Ask the children if they know how to move a paper clip on top of the paper by using a magnet. Have the children demonstrate their suggestions. Discuss how a magnet can PULL or PUSH an object that is magnetic. *A magnet can be attracted or repelled by another magnet, and can push or pull a "magnetic" object.*

*Questions to guide children:*
• What can your magnet do?
• Will the magnet work through the table?
• Will your magnet pull the paper clip?

*What children and adults will do:*
Give each child a copy of the "Magnet Maze" sheet, a small paper clip, and a magnet. You may want to show the children how to tape a magnet on the end of a ruler so the magnet may be moved easily under the paper. After the children have mastered the maze they may turn the paper over and draw a maze of their own.

*Closure:*
Discuss how the magnet pushed or pulled the paper clip through the maze. Have the children quickly share the mazes that they made.

## Follow-up Activities:

Have children design their own mazes or magnetic games. Draw a simple map of your classroom indicating the various play areas, such as blocks, library, and art. As children are deciding what they want to do during choice time, ask them to use a magnet to move a small magnet shape on the map to the area of the room they want to work in.

## Center Connection:

Place several different maze drawings on pieces of lightweight cardboard at the science center. (You may want to make little dog or cat cutouts and clip them onto magnets so the child can move the "animal" through the maze.)

## Literature Connections:

*Mickey's Magnet*
by Franklyn Branley and Eleanor Vaughan, Crowell, 1956. Reissued 1976.

*Magnets: Pulling Together, Pushing Apart*
by Natalie Rosinsky, Picture Window Books, 2002.

*Magnets (All Aboard Science Reader)*
by Anne Schreiber, Grosset & Dunlop, 2003.

# MAGNETIC MAZES

- **Science A-1** Begins to use senses and a variety of tools and simple measuring devices to gather information, investigate materials and observe processes and relationships.

- **Language Development A-2** Shows progress in understanding and following simple and multiple-step directions.

- **Mathematics B-5** Builds an increasing understanding of directionality, order and positions of objects, and words such as up, down, over, under, top, bottom, inside, outside, in front and behind.

- **Physical Health & Development A-1** Develops growing strength, dexterity and control needed to use tools such as scissors, paper punch, stapler and hammer.

*Source: "Head Start Child Outcomes Framework." See Appendix A in this book for the framework.

## What To Look For

| | |
|---|---|
| **Not Yet** | Child does not participate in the maze activity. |
| **Emerging** | Child watches others navigate the maze with a magnet and paper clip; near the end of the activity tries it out for a short time. |
| **Almost Mastered** | Child participates fully in the maze activity and is mostly successful in navigating the maze with a magnet and paper clip; describes what is happening. |
| **Fully Mastered** | After successfully completing the maze, draws another maze and continues experimenting, describing what is happening and asking questions. |

# Physical Science

# THE MAGNET CONTEST: WHICH MAGNET IS STRONGER?

**Investigation:** Experimenting to find out which magnet is the strongest

**Process Skills:** Observing, comparing

**Materials:** Different types of magnets (try to provide at least one larger magnet that is weaker than a smaller one), a pile of paper clips

**Procedure:**

*Getting started:*
Give each child one magnet. Ask, "What do you think a stronger magnet would look like?" Wait for their ideas, then ask, "How could we find out if one magnet is stronger than another?" Put out a pile of paper clips for each to experiment with.

*Questions to guide children:*
- Which magnet is strongest? How do you know?
- How close does your magnet have to get to a paper clip in order to pick it up?
- Is a larger magnet always stronger than a smaller one?

*What children and adults will do:*
Children will begin picking up paper clips with their magnets. They will see that some magnets can pick up more paper clips than others. They may also notice that they have to move some magnets closer to the paper clip than others in order to attract the paper clip. Encourage them to discuss their ideas.

*Closure:*
Ask children to share their strongest magnet and how they know it is the strongest. Ask one or two to demonstrate what their magnets pick up. Either count with the children or weigh the paper clips to compare which magnet picked up more.

## Center Connection:

Place one or two of the setups in the science center so the children may continue testing the strength of different magnets.

## Literature Connection:

*Mickey's Magnet*
by Franklyn Branley and Eleanor Vaughan, Crowell, 1956. Reissued 1976.

*Magnets: Pulling Together, Pushing Apart*
by Natalie Rosinsky, Picture Window Books, 2002.

*Magnets (All Aboard Science Reader)*
by Anne Schreiber, Grosset & Dunlop, 2003.

# THE MAGNETIC CONTEST:
# WHICH MAGNET IS STRONGER?

- **Science A-3** Begins to participate in simple investigations to test observations, discuss and draw conclusions and form generalizations.

- **Mathematics A-5** Begins to use language to compare numbers of objects with terms such as more, less, greater than, fewer, equal to.

- **Approaches to Learning C-2** Grows in recognizing and solving problems through active explorations, including trial and error, and interactions and discussions with peers and adults.

  *Source: "Head Start Child Outcomes Framework." See Appendix A in this book for the framework.

## What To Look For

| Not Yet | Child shows no interest in attempting to determine which magnet is stronger. |
|---|---|
| Emerging | Child watches others experimenting with different magnets; eventually uses one magnet to pick up paper clips but does not experiment with others to compare magnetic power. |
| Almost Mastered | Child experiments with several different magnets; shares some observations with adult and peers. |
| Fully Mastered | Child eagerly tries out all the different magnets; counts the number of paper clips each picks up; asks questions about the differences observed. |

# MY FAVORITE ROCK

**Investigation:** Collecting rocks

**Process Skills:** Observing, comparing, communicating

**Materials:** Bags, boxes, or aluminum pans

## Procedure:

*Getting started:*
Take the children on a rock hunt. Pick a location where there are rocks, or scatter some yourself ahead of time. Give each child a bag. Encourage the children to look for rocks they find interesting to put in their bags. Let them spend time looking for rocks before you ask questions. Listen to what they say. (CAUTION: Some pieces of sharp trash glass can look like rocks and can cut skin.)

*Questions and comments to guide children:*
- What can you tell me about your rock?
- What makes it like (unlike) your friend's rock?
- What do you like about your rocks?
- Let's look for some different-colored rocks.
- Can you find a rock that's bigger than yours? Smoother? A different color? A different shape?

*What children and adults will do:*
The children will find all kinds of rocks. As they talk about their rocks, repeat some of their language. Ask questions that follow their trains of thought. For example, if they seem to be most interested in how heavy the rocks are, your questions should encourage them to compare the weights of different rocks.

*Closure:*
Back in the classroom, have children put their rocks in front of them. Have each child choose one rock to show to the others. Ask children to describe what they like about their rocks. Say, "This is your pet rock. In a few minutes, we are going to put them together in a pile. Do you think you can find yours?" Go ahead and try it. If children have trouble, ask questions about their rocks to help them find their own rocks. Have children put all the rocks into a box or pan for further investigation.

## Cultural Variations:
If you can't find interesting rocks where you are, this activity works well with leaves (CAUTION: Make sure leaves are preselected without any exposure to poisonous plants.), shells (CAUTION: Some shells have sharp edges and can cut skin.), seedpods, twigs, or other natural materials. You can also use food—apples, oranges, pinion nuts, or whatever you have in abundance. (CAUTION: Remember that some students may be allergic to food products such as nuts.)

## Center Connection:

Put the pan of rocks in the science area along with hand lenses and an equal-arm balance.

## Art Connection:

Put out play dough and various rocks. Let children experiment with using their rocks to make prints in the dough or using rocks to decorate their play dough creations.

## Literature Connection:

*Everybody Needs a Rock*
by Byrd Baylor, Macmillan, 1985.

# MY FAVORITE ROCK

- **Science A-2** Develops increased ability to observe and discuss common properties, differences and comparisons among objects and materials.

- **Creative Arts B-1** Gains ability in using different art media and materials in a variety of ways for creative expression and representation.

- **Approaches to Learning C-3** Progresses in abilities to classify, compare and contrast objects, events and experiments.

*Source: "Head Start Child Outcomes Framework." See Appendix A in this book for the framework.

## What To Look For

| Not Yet | Child shows no interest in looking for rocks; does not choose a favorite rock. |
|---|---|
| Emerging | Child watches others look for rocks before attempting to locate some; collects a few rocks but does not describe their differences. |
| Almost Mastered | Child collects many different rocks and chooses a favorite rock; describes some of the differences such as color and shape. |
| Fully Mastered | Child collects many rocks, chooses a favorite rock, and describes in detail many of the differences; asks questions such as why some rocks are heavier than others. |

# FAMILY PAGE / PAGINA PARA LA FAMILIA

## MY FAVORITE ROCK

### Family Science Connection:

**In the neighborhood**, go on a **rock hunt** and find as many **different** rocks as possible to **collect** and **take home**. **At dinner** have each family member pick their favorite rock that was collected and put it near their plate. As a **family discussion**, ask each member to **describe** their favorite rock and tell why they like it. (CAUTION: Rocks taken from lawns may contain pesticides or fungicides put there by the owners of the lawns. Make sure that rocks are washed with soap and water before being placed on the dinner table near food.)

**Comments or questions** that may add a *sense of wonder* to this activity:

· What do you like about your rock?

· Can you find another rock on the table that is bigger than your rock? Smoother? A different color? Different shape or smell?

## MI PIEDRA FAVORITA

### Ciencia en familia:

**En el vecindario**, vayan en una **exploración** de piedras y busquen **diferentes** piedras para **recolectarlas** y **llevarlas a casa**. **Durante la cena** pida a cada miembro de la familia que escoja su piedra favorita y que la coloque cerca de su plato. Como **discusión familiar**, pida a cada miembro de la familia que **describa** su piedra favorita y diga por qué le gusta. (PRECAUCIÓN: Piedras tomadas de jardínes pueden contener pesticidas o funguicidas puestos ahí por los dueños de los parques. Asegurese que las piedras sean lavadas con jabón y agua antes de colocarse en la mesa cerca de la comida.)

**Comentarios o preguntas** que pueden *despertar curiosidad* en esta actividad:

· ¿Qué es lo que te gusta de tu piedra?

· ¿Puedes encontrar otra piedra en la mesa que sea más grande que tu piedra? ¿Más lisa? ¿De diferente color? ¿De diferente forma u olor?

# ALL KINDS OF ROCKS

**Investigation:** Exploring rocks

**Process Skills:** Observing, comparing, classifying, communicating

**Materials:** Rocks children have collected, sorting trays or mats, equal-arm balance, hand lenses

## Procedure:

*Getting started:*
Put out the box of rocks and let children explore. Listen to what they say and watch what they do before you ask questions. Encourage children to use hand lenses.

*Questions and comments to guide children:*
- Do you see any rocks that are the same?
- How are they the same?
- My rock feels smooth.
- Does your rock have a smell?
- Which one is the heaviest? How can you tell?
- What can you see if you look through the hand lens?

*What children and adults will do:*
Encourage children to use the sorting mats and trays to put similar rocks together or to match the rock to a shape or color. If children don't think of it themselves, suggest using the balance.

*Closure:*
Ask children, "What did you find out about your rocks?" Let each child choose one favorite rock to take home.

## Follow-up Activities:

Take the rocks and a tub of water outside. Ask the children to look carefully at each rock, then to see what happens when it gets wet (some change color). On another day, provide different grades of sandpaper, and let children try to polish their rocks using the sandpaper. (CAUTION: Certain types of sandpaper can be rough enough to cause skin abrasions if improperly handled.)

## Center Connection:

Put rocks, hand lenses, equal-arm balance, and sorting mats and trays in the science center for children to use on their own.

## Art Connection:

Let children choose several rocks of different sizes and textures to make rock prints by dipping each rock in tempera paint then pressing firmly on paper.

## Literature Connection:

*Sylvester and the Magic Pebble*
by William Steig, Simon and Schuster, 1988.

## Assessment Outcomes & Possible Indicators*

- **Science A-2** Develops increased ability to observe and discuss common properties, differences and comparisons among objects and materials.

- **Creative Arts B-1** Gains ability in using different art media and materials in a variety of ways for creative expression and representation.

- **Approaches to Learning A-2** Develops increased ability to make independent choices.

- **Approaches to Learning C-3** Progresses in abilities to classify, compare and contrast objects, events and experiments.

*Source: "Head Start Child Outcomes Framework." See Appendix A in this book for the framework.

## What To Look For

| Not Yet | Child shows no interest in exploring the different rocks. |
|---|---|
| Emerging | Child watches others explore the rocks before beginning to examine them. |
| Almost Mastered | Child picks up many rocks, examines and describes them; uses hand lens or balance scale to compare rocks; is not interested in using the sorting mat. |
| Fully Mastered | Child eagerly explores each rock, using hand lens and balance scale to compare; describes rocks to adults and peers using a variety of descriptive words and attempts to group similar rocks on the sorting mat. |

## ALL KINDS OF ROCKS

### Family Science Connection:

As a continuation to the activity "My Favorite Rock," have the **family collect** rocks for a **rock garden. Find your collection in the neighborhood** and **compare the various sizes, shapes, weights, smells, and looks of each rock.** (CAUTION: Be aware that some rocks taken from lawns may contain pesticides or fungicides put there by the owners of the lawns. Also, be careful not to pick up trash glass, metal-can tops, etc., which can cut children.)

Now put the collected rock garden outside and continue, over the course of the seasons, to observe any changes that might occur from the climate. Share your observations as a family.

- What do you like best about your rocks?

- As you look at your rock garden each day, week, and month, how are the rocks changing? Notice how your rock looks. Is its shape changing? Is it still the same color, feel, temperature?

## TODA CLASE DE ROCAS

### Ciencia en familia:

Como continuación de la actividad "Mi Piedra Favorita," pídale a la **familia** que **colecte** rocas para un **jardín de rocas**. Encuentre las rocas para su **colección en el vecindario** y compare la **variedad de medidas, formas, pesos, olores, y apariencia de cada roca.** (PRECAUCIÓN: Tome en cuenta que algunas rocas sacadas de jardines pueden tener pesticidas o funguicidas puestos ahí por los dueños del parque. También tenga cuidado de levanter vidrio, tapas de latas de metal, etc., que pueden cortar a los niños.)

Ahora forme el jardín de rocas recolectadas y continúe, durante las estaciones del año, **observando** cualquier **cambio** que pueda ocurrir debido al clima. Compartan como familia sus observaciones.

- ¿Qué es lo que te gustó más acerca de tus rocas?

- Al mirar tu jardín de rocas todos los días, cada semana, y al paso de los meses, ¿cómo han cambiado las rocas? ¿Tienen todavía los mismos colores, texturas, temperaturas?

# BALANCE

**Investigation:** Comparing objects using a balance

**Process Skills:** Observing, comparing, communicating

**Materials:** Several equal-arm balances, a variety of small objects to compare, some uniform objects such as inch blocks, pennies, cotton balls, beans

## Procedure:

*Getting started:*
Introduce children to the balance by putting objects of equal weights on the two sides of the scale. Give children time to explore by putting different objects on the balance. Watch what they do and listen to what they say before you begin to guide their further exploration.

*Questions and comments to guide children:*
- Which one is the heaviest?
- How can you tell?
- Which of these two things weighs the most?
- How can we tell?
- How many pennies does this rock weigh?
- I wonder what will happen if we add another penny.

*What children and adults will do:*
Two or more children can work with one balance, taking turns choosing things to weigh or compare. Encourage children to add or subtract weight from one side and to predict what will happen when they do.

*Closure:*
Choose several of the more popular items to weigh and have the children count how many pennies or inch blocks it takes to balance each. Make an object graph by placing that number of blocks or pennies next to each of the items that were weighed.

## Follow-up Activity:

Keep your eye out for a large construction project in your neighborhood. Take the children to see the crane operating. (CAUTION: Observe only from outside the fenced construction area.) Most seaports also use cranes to load and unload cargo bins. Children can pretend to be a crane by lifting one arm straight out from their bodies. Place something fairly heavy in each child's hand so he or she can experience the effect on balance.

## Center Connection:

Always keep a balance in the science center so children can weigh or compare new objects. Encourage children to use a balance with many different materials and on many occasions so that it becomes a tool they use all the time, not just during special activities.

## Literature Connection:

*Why Does It Fall Over?* Projects About Balance by Jim Pipe, Copper Beech Books, 2002.

*You Can Use a Balance* by Linda Bullock, Children's Press, 2004.

# BALANCE

- **Science A-1** Begins to use senses and a variety of tools and simple measuring devices to gather information, investigate materials and observe processes and relationships.

- **Science A-3** Begins to participate in simple investigations to test observations, discuss and draw conclusions and form generalizations.

- **Mathematics A-1** Demonstrates increasing interest and awareness of numbers and counting as a means for solving problems and determining quantity.

- **Mathematics A-3** Develops increasing ability to count in sequence to 10 and beyond.

*Source: "Head Start Child Outcomes Framework." See Appendix A in this book for the framework.

## What To Look For

| Not Yet | Child shows no interest in using the balance to compare objects. |
|---|---|
| Emerging | Child places different objects on the balance scale; with assistance from adult, begins to make simple comparisons. |
| Almost Mastered | Child independently uses the balance scale to make comparisons between objects; experiments with a variety of types and numbers of objects to test ideas. |
| Fully Mastered | Child experiments with a wide variety of objects to compare weights; discusses findings and asks questions about discoveries; tests ideas by varying the number and sizes of objects. |

## BALANCE

### Family Science Connection:

Find objects around your house that have about the same weights—for example, a feather and a tissue, a can of food and a book, a stuffed animal, and a pillow. Talk about weight by using these objects to feel and see weight. Talk about heavy- and lightweight and see if the family can classify the objects in an order of heavy- to lightweight.

**Comments or questions** that may add a *sense of wonder* to this activity:

· I wonder which object weighs the most. Which is the lightest weight?

· Let's put the objects in three piles: a heavyweight pile, a lightweight pile, and a middleweight pile.

## EQUILIBRIO

### Ciencia en familia:

Encuentre objetos en tu casa que tengan pesos parecidos—por ejemplo, una pluma (de ave) y un pañuelo de papel, una lata de comida y un libro, un muñeco de peluche y una almohada. Hablen acerca del peso usando estos objetos para sentir y ver el peso. Hablen acerca de lo que es pesado y liviano y vean si su familia puede clasificar los objetos del más pesado al más liviano.

**Comentarios o preguntas** que pueden *despertar curiosidad* en esta actividad:

· Me pregunto qué objeto pesa más. ¿Cuál es el más liviano?

· Pongamos los objetos en tres grupos: uno de objetos pesados, uno de objetos livianos, y otro de objetos de peso mediano.

# Physical Science

# BALANCING ME

**Investigation:** Discovering how an object or a person can use gravity to help retain balance

**Process Skills:** Observing, comparing

**Materials:** Balance beam, peg-type wooden clothespins, 24 inches of wire for each clothespin toy (CAUTION: Wire can have sharp edges that can cut skin or pierce eyes.), large metal washers or old keys for weights

**Procedure:**

*Getting started:*
Have children try to balance a clothespin upright on the end of a finger. Then have them stand on one foot and try to balance. Ask children what makes it easier to balance (putting their hands out straight). Next, have them walk across a balance beam. (CAUTION: Do this only with adult supervision; some children may have balancing problems and may fall.)

*Questions to guide children:*
- Can you walk with your hands together in front of you?
- Can you walk with your hands on your head?
- What happens if you put your arms out to the side?
- Which way is easier?

*What children and adults will do:*
Some children will have an easier time than others walking on the beam and balancing on one foot. Encourage children to discover what makes it easier. Then have children sit on the floor while you make a clothespin toy. Wrap wire around the base of the clothespin so there is an equal amount of wire left on each side. Ask children if they can think of how the wire could help the clothespin balance the way their arms helped them. Bend the wire to attach a washer or key to each side. Put the clothespin on a child's finger and bend the wire to adjust it until it balances.

*Closure:*
Have all the children try it with some toys you have made ahead of time. Keep reminding them to compare how the toy balances with how their own arms helped them balance.

**Center Connection:**

Put several clothespin toys in the science center for further exploration. Put out the balance beam during outdoor time. (CAUTION: Adult supervision required.)

**Literature Connection:**

*Balancing*
by Terry J. Jennings, Gloucester, 1989.

*Tug-of-War: All About Balance*
by Kirsten Hall and Bev Luedecke, Scholastic, 2005.

# Assessment Outcomes & Possible Indicators*

- **Science B-2** Expands knowledge of and respect for their body and the environment.

- **Science B-4** Shows increased awareness and beginning understanding of changes in materials and cause-effect relationships.

- **Language Development A-2** Shows progress in understanding and following simple and multiple-step directions.

- **Physical Health & Development B-1** Shows increasing levels of proficiency, control and balance in walking, climbing, running, jumping, hopping, skipping, marching and galloping.

*Source: "Head Start Child Outcomes Framework." See Appendix A in this book for the framework.

# What To Look For

| Not Yet | Child participates but shows no interest in the subject of balance. |
|---|---|
| Emerging | Child participates but imitates others rather than attempting to vary positions in order to solve balance problems. |
| Almost Mastered | Child follows directions of the adult, then experiments independently by changing positions; offers suggestions of how to balance the clothespin. |
| Fully Mastered | Child tries out many positions to see how balance is affected; discusses findings; experiments with the clothespin and asks questions related to balance. |

## BALANCING ME

### Family Science Connection:

In the neighborhood, at the park, or on a walk, look for places the children can balance themselves. These places could include a wall to walk along, the edge of the curb (CAUTION: Watch for street traffic.), or cracks in the sidewalk. With the handheld help of a parent or older child, have the younger children feel their own balance. Ask the children to feel if they can let go of the helping hand. Talk about what balance feels like with their body.

**Comments or questions** that may add a *sense of wonder* to this activity:

- Try different ways to place your hands as you walk and balance.

- What makes it so easy to walk with your favorite hand position?

## EQUILIBRÁNDOME

### Ciencia en familia:

En el vecindario, en el parquet, o de paseo busquen lugares donde los niños puedan equilibrarse por sí mismos. Esos lugares podrían ser una barda para caminar, un borde (PRECAUCIÓN: Esté atento al tráfico en la calle.), grietas en la banqueta, o en una toma de agua. Con la mano sostenida del padre o de un niño mayor, deje que el niño sienta su propio equilibrio. Pregúntele al niño si se siente capaz de soltar la mano de quien lo está ayudando. Hable acerca de cómo se siente con el equilibrio de su cuerpo.

**Comentarios o preguntas** que pueden *despertar curiosidad* en esta actividad:

- Trata diferentes formas de poner tus manos cuando camines, guardando el equilibrio. ¿En cuál posición de las manos parece ser la más fácil para guardar el equilibrio?

- ¿Qué es lo que hace que sea fácil caminar con las manos en tu posición favorita?

# TOWERS

**Investigation:** Experimenting with blocks of different shapes to see how they can be balanced

**Process Skills:** Observing, comparing, classifying, communicating

**Materials:** Wooden blocks of various shapes and sizes

## Procedure:

*Getting started:*
Let each child find a spot on the floor where he or she can build. Let children choose at least 15 blocks of various shapes and sizes, with extra blocks in the middle of the floor. Ask, "What can you do with your blocks?" Watch for a while before you ask any further questions.

*Questions to guide children:*
- Can you build a tall tower?
- How can you make it taller?
- Why do you think that block fell?
- Could you build the tower a different way?
- What would happen if you put a different block (a cylinder, for example) on the bottom?

*What children and adults will do:*
Children will begin stacking their blocks individually. If some want to work together, that's OK. Point out what different children are doing while asking a few questions.

*Closure:*
Ask children, "How can we decide which tower is tallest?" Follow up on their ideas. They may decide to compare the towers by standing next to them. You could also introduce the idea of measuring with a piece of adding-machine tape or a long stick if you have one. Encourage children to talk about how they built their towers. See if children can put the blocks away one at a time without knocking them down.

## Follow-up Activity:

Add more blocks to the block center to encourage more elaborate building that requires more balancing.

## Center Connection:

Encourage those children who never choose the block area to build again during their center or work time. Talk to children about their work with blocks as they build.

## Literature Connection:

*City Seen From A to Z*
by Rachel Isadora, Greenwillow, 1983.

*The Village of Round and Square Houses*
by Ann Grifalconi, Little, Brown, 1986.

*How Tall, How Short, How Faraway?*
by David A. Adler, Holiday House, 1999.

*A Day With a Bricklayer*
by Mark Thomas, Children's Press, 2001.

# TOWERS

- **Science A-3** Begins to participate in simple investigations to test observations, discuss and draw conclusions and form generalizations.

- **Mathematics B-3** Begins to be able to determine whether or not two shapes are the same size and shape.

- **Mathematics C-4** Shows progress in using standard and non-standard measures for length and area of objects.

- **Approaches to Learning A-3** Approaches tasks and activities with increased flexibility, imagination and inventiveness.

- **Physical Health & Development A-2** Grows in hand-eye coordination in building with blocks, putting together puzzles, reproducing shapes and patterns, stringing beads and using scissors.

  *Source: "Head Start Child Outcomes Framework." See Appendix A in this book for the framework.

## What To Look For

| Not Yet | Child shows no interest in building a tower; places them side by side on the floor instead. |
|---|---|
| Emerging | Child watches others build towers; participates by adding to others' structures only. |
| Almost Mastered | Child builds a tower. Rebuilds after it falls down; does some experimenting with different sizes and shapes of blocks but generally builds the same structure over and over. |
| Fully Mastered | Child builds many towers, continually changing the sizes and shapes of blocks to see which ones produce the tallest tower; asks to compare sizes of various towers. |

## TOWERS

### Family Science Connection:

Find **objects** around the house that **are placed in stacks.** One example is a bunk bed. Another example could be a stack of clothes for the wash. Blocks are another example of a stack or tower of something. Are there objects in the house that could be stacked to the height of the shortest child in the family? See if the family could balance items to such a height.

**Comments or questions** that may add a *sense of wonder* to this activity:

- Let's look around the house and find things to stack up to how tall you are (your child).

- Wow, look how high our tower is! What else could we add to it to make it even taller?

## TORRES

### Ciencia en familia:

Encuentre **objetos** a su alrededor que están **uno sobre otro**. Un ejemplo es las camas literas. Otro ejemplo podría ser un montón de ropa sucia. Los bloques son otro ejemplo de torre o montón de algo. ¿Hay objetos en casa que podrían ser amontonados a la altura del niño más pequeño de la familia? Vea si la familia puede poner en un montón objetos a esta altura.

**Comentarios o preguntas** que pueden *despertar curiosidad* en esta actividad:

- Busquemos en la casa cosas que podamos amontonar a tu estatura (su niño).

- ¡Caramba, mira qué tan alta está nuestra torre! ¿Qué otra cosa podemos agregar para hacerla más alta?

# BUILDING WITH BLOCKS

**Investigation:** Using patterns in block building

**Process Skills:** Observing, classifying, communicating

**Materials:** Unit blocks of many shapes and sizes

## Procedure:

*Getting started:*
Sit in the block area with a small group of children. Make sure there is enough space and plenty of blocks so each child can participate fully. Challenge children to build something with their blocks. Give children time to build for a while before asking any questions.

*Questions and comments to guide children:*
- How did you get those blocks to balance?
- I see you are using the long blocks for your bridge.
- Can you build it higher?

*What children and adults will do:*
Observe the patterns children use as they build (e.g., two horizontal and a bridge; two blocks parallel then two more parallel but in opposite direction). Talk to children about the blocks they are using. If a building falls, ask, "How could you build it so it won't fall?"

*Closure:*
Encourage children to take their buildings down one block at a time ("How can you take your building down so it doesn't fall?") Then ask them to put the blocks away, matching the labels on the shelves.

## Follow-up Activity:
Encourage children who don't usually choose blocks to build with blocks. Add materials they like to the block area to make it more inviting.

## Center Connection:
Add different types of blocks to the blocks. Take blocks outside for children to use. Enlarge your block area if children seem to need more room. Add work gloves, hard hats, overalls, work boots, safety goggles, a tool belt, and tools to the block area so children can pretend to be construction workers.

## Literature Connection:

*Building a House*
by Byron Barton, Greenwillow Books, 1981.

*I Can Build a House! (I Can Do It All By Myself)*
by Shiego Watnabe, Philomel, 1983.

*Block City*
by Robert Louis Stevenson, Dutton, 1988.

*Let's Try It Out With Towers and Bridges: Hands-On Early-Learning Activities*
by Seymour Simon, Nicole Fauteux, and Doug Cushman, Simon & Schuster, 2003.

# BUILDING WITH BLOCKS

- **Science A-2** Develops increased ability to observe and discuss common properties, differences and comparisons among objects and materials.

- **Mathematics B-5** Builds an increasing understanding of directionality, order and positions of objects, and words such as up, down, over, under, top, bottom, inside, outside, in front and behind.

- **Creative Arts D-2** Shows growing creativity and imagination in using material and in assuming different roles in dramatic play situations.

- **Physical Health & Development A-2** Grows in hand-eye coordination in building with blocks, putting together puzzles, reproducing shapes and patterns, stringing beads and using scissors.

  *Source: "Head Start Child Outcomes Framework." See Appendix A in this book for the framework.

## What To Look For

| Not Yet | Child shows no interest in building with blocks. |
|---|---|
| Emerging | Child watches others build with blocks for a while before joining in; builds mostly two-dimensional structures. |
| Almost Mastered | Child builds, using a variety of blocks; describes structure(s); responds to adults' questions and comments by changing or adding to the structure. |
| Fully Mastered | Child eagerly builds complex structure(s); shows creativity and imagination in building and describing the structure; may work together with peers. |

## BUILDING WITH BLOCKS

### Family Science Connection:

Find items around your house that can be used in place of blocks to stack. Use household items that are safe for children to play with, such as books, boxes, recycled plastic containers (cleaned), hats, and boxed or canned foods that are lightweight.

**Take a walk** and find buildings that look like they are stacked up like blocks—for example, parking garages, tall downtown buildings, or libraries.

**Comments or questions** that may add a *sense of wonder* to this activity:

- Let's find 10 buildings that look like stacked-up blocks!

- How high can we get these things to sit on one another (balance)?

## CONSTRUCCIÓN CON BLOQUES

### Ciencia en familia:

Encuentre artículos en tu casa que puedan usarse en lugar de bloques para apilar. Use utensilios de casa que sean seguros para que jueguen los niños, como libros, cajas, recipientes de plásticos reciclados (limpios), sombreros, y comida en cajas o enlatadas que sean de bajo peso.

**Den un paseo** y encuentren edificios que parezcan estar en torre o apilados como bloques—por ejemplo, los estacionamientos, edificios altos en el centro de la ciudad, o bibliotecas.

**Comentarios o preguntas** que pueden *despertar curiosidad* en esta actividad:

- ¡Busquemos 10 edificios que parezcan bloques apilados!

- ¿Qué tan alto podemos poner estas cosas equilibrándolas unas encima de otras?

# WILL IT ROLL?

**Investigation:** Discovering which objects will roll

**Process Skills:** Observing, classifying, communicating

**Materials:** Objects of different shapes (e.g., ball, can, cereal box, matchbox, crayon, paper towel tube, funnel cone) or blocks of various geometric shapes, or a combination of both

## Procedure:

*Getting started:*
Put objects on the floor with children seated in a circle around them; ask each child to choose an object and try to push it across the floor. Have children experiment with several of the objects. (CAUTION: Objects that roll can be slip/fall hazards.) Listen to what they say about what is happening.

*Questions and comments to guide children:*
- What happened when you pushed the ___?
- Why do you think the ____ rolled?
- Can you show me all the ones that roll?
- That one doesn't seem to roll.
- Do you think the ____ will roll?

*What children and adults will do:*
Children will experiment with all the objects. They will compare what their objects are doing with what their classmates' objects are doing. They will notice what rolls easiest and farthest.

*Closure:*
Use a sorting map to help children record which objects roll and which do not. Ask them to explain why some roll and some do not. Listen carefully to their answers.

## Center Connection:

Add different objects to the block area, encouraging children to use them as vehicles. See which ones they use and which they discard.

## Literature Connection:

*Things That Go*
by Anne Rockwell, E. P. Dutton, 1986.

*Truck Song*
by Diane Siebert, Harper and Row, 1984.

*What Does a Wheel Do?*
by Jim Pipe, Copper Beech Books, 2002.

# WILL IT ROLL?

- **Science A-5** Begins to describe and discuss predictions, explanations and generalizations based on past experiences.

- **Language Development B-1** Develops increasing abilities to understand and use language to communicate information, experiences, ideas, opinions, needs, questions and for other varied purposes.

- **Mathematics B-1** Begins to recognize, describe, compare and name common shapes, their parts and attributes.

- **Approaches to Learning C-3** Progresses in abilities to classify, compare and contrast objects, events and experiments.

   *Source: "Head Start Child Outcomes Framework." See Appendix A in this book for the framework.

## What To Look For

| Not Yet | Child does not attempt to roll various objects. |
|---|---|
| Emerging | Child watches others attempt to roll objects; eventually participates but does not respond to adults' questions or comments. |
| Almost Mastered | Child experiments with many different objects; begins to predict which will roll; discusses finding with adults and peers. |
| Fully Mastered | Child experiments with all the different objects; predicts which will roll; explains why some roll and others do not and asks questions; separates objects that roll from those that do not. |

## WILL IT ROLL?

### Family Science Connection:

**At home** find objects that the child thinks can roll easily and have the child, with other **members of the family**, roll these chosen objects.

**At the park** find objects that might roll and create a game to see which family member finds the best object for rolling on grass at the park. A family member just might be the best object that rolls on the grass!

**Comments or questions** that may add a *sense of wonder* to this activity:

- Why do you think the fastest rolling object rolled so fast?

- Show me all the objects that did not roll. Why do you think they did not roll?

## ¿RODARÁ?

### Ciencia en familia:

**En casa** encuentre objetos que el niño piense que puedan rodar fácilmente y haga que el niño, con otros **miembros de la familia,** rueden los objetos que escogieron. Trate de rodar esos mismos objetos en varias superficies de la casa. Compartan juntos lo que descubrió el niño acerca de los objetos que ruedan mejor en cada superficie.

**En el parque** encuentre objetos que puedan rodar e invente un juego en el cual los miembros de la familia encuentren el objeto que ruede mejor en el césped del parque. ¡Incluso el mismo cuerpo de alguien de la familia podría ser el que rodase mejor!

**Comentarios o preguntas** que pueden *despertar curiosidad* en esta actividad:

- ¿Por qué piensas que el objeto que rodó más rápido pudo hacerlo?

- Muéstrame todos los objetos que no pudieron rodar. ¿Por qué piensas que no pudieron rodar?

# RAMPS

**Investigation:** Changing the angle of a ramp to affect the distance that an object will roll

**Process Skills:** Observing, comparing, communicating

**Materials:** Paper towel rolls (cut in half lengthwise), table tennis balls, marbles, small cars, blocks, tape

## Procedure:

*Getting started:*
Show children how to make a ramp by taping the top of a paper towel tube to a block. Let children experiment by rolling various objects down their ramps. Watch what children do and listen to what they say before you ask questions.

*Questions and comments to guide children:*
- Which object went the farthest?
- Why do you think the _____ went farther than the _____?
- How could you make your ball go farther?
- I wonder what will happen if I put another block under the ramp like this.

*What children and adults will do:*
Children will experiment with all three objects (table tennis balls, marbles, small cars) and may find other objects to try. After a while, encourage children to vary the steepness of the ramp. Ask them to tell you what happened when they did.

*Closure:*
Hold a final "race" by having all the children let go of their objects at the same time to see which travels the farthest. (The tops of the ramps need to be lined up first.) Use adding-machine tape or measuring sticks to compare distances.

## Follow-up Activity:

Outside, put long boards, large blocks, and balls together so children can experiment further with ramps.

## Center Connection:

Add pieces of pressboard or plywood to the block area so children can use them for ramps.

## Literature Connection:

*Train Song*
by Diane Siebert, Thomas Y. Crowell, 1990.

*Wheels*
by Venice Shone, Scholastic, 1990.

*What Is a Plane?*
by Lloyd G. Douglas, Children's Press, 2002.

# RAMPS

- **Science A-3** Begins to participate in simple investigations to test observations, discuss and draw conclusions and form generalizations.

- **Science B-3** Develops growing awareness of ideas and language related to attributes of time and temperature.

- **Language Development B-1** Develops increasing abilities to understand and use language to communicate information, experiences, ideas, opinions, needs, questions and for other varied purposes.

- **Approaches to Learning C-2** Grows in recognizing and solving problems through active explorations, including trial and error, and interactions and discussions with peers and adults.

  *Source: "Head Start Child Outcomes Framework." See Appendix A in this book for the framework.

## What To Look For

| Not Yet | Child shows no interest in experimenting with ramps. |
|---|---|
| Emerging | Child watches as others experiment with ramps; tries out a ramp several times but does not use all items. |
| Almost Mastered | Child experiments with all three objects to see which rolls fastest, but does not try changing the angle of the ramp; discusses findings with adults and peers. |
| Fully Mastered | Child experiments with all three objects, then tries changing the angle and height of the ramp to see if it affects the speed; repeats activity at another time without adult direction. |

## RAMPS

### Family Science Connection:

**In the house or yard, build** a ramp with things from around the house. Use chairs, tables, wood boards, towel rolls, or toys and see how creative you can be and still get objects to roll down this homemade ramp. **Talk** about the favorite objects that were rolled down the ramp and **compare** why these objects were most fun to watch.

**Comments or questions** that may add a *sense of wonder* to this activity:

- What objects rolled the fastest? What objects rolled the slowest?

- What objects were the most fun to watch as they rolled down the ramp? Why?

## RAMPAS

### Ciencia en familia:

**En casa o en el patio, construyan** una rampa con cosas que tengan en casa. Usen sillas, mesas, tablas de madera, rollos de toallas, o juguetes y vea cuán creativos pueden ser y hacer que rueden objetos hacia abajo en esta rampa hecha en casa. **Hablen** acerca de los objetos favoritos que rodaron sobre la rampa y **comparen** por qué esos objetos fueron los que más les gustó observar.

**Comentarios o preguntas** que pueden *despertar curiosidad* en esta actividad:

- ¿Qué objetos rodaron más rápido? ¿Qué objetos rodaron más despacio?

- ¿Qué objetos fueron los más divertidos de observar cuando rodaban hacia abajo de la rampa? ¿Por qué?

# ROLLER COASTERS

**Investigation:** Observing how gravity
affects marbles as they roll

**Process Skills:** Observing, comparing

**Materials:** Masking tape, pipe
insulators (¾" or larger),
various size marbles

## Procedure:

*Getting started:*
(Do this activity after "Will It Roll?" and
"Ramps.") Cut pipe insulators in half lengthwise. Demonstrate how to connect the pipe insulators with masking tape. Next, show how to
connect the tracks to create loops, ramps, and
curves. Encourage children to drop marbles on
the tracks to discover how gravity affects the
marbles' roll. Give children time to explore on
their own before asking questions.

*Questions to guide children:*
  - What do you think will happen if we
    change this loop (ramp, curve)?
  - Can you make the marble go faster?
    Farther?
  - What will happen if we add another
    curve at the bottom? At the top?

*What children and adults will do:*
Children will first use the structures that
adults have set up. After they have enjoyed using those structures for a while, encourage children to change some of the component pieces
or to start from the beginning and create their
own. The marbles will roll an amazingly long
distance so you may want to put up some barriers around the perimeter.

*Closure:*
Tell children the materials will be in the block
area so they can continue to try out their ideas.

## Center Connection:

Put materials in either the block area or another area where there is space to build. Take the
materials outside if you have a carpet or blan-
ket on which to place them so marbles don't
get lost.

## Literature Connection:

*Roller Coaster*
by Maria Frazee, Voyager Books, 2006.

# ROLLER COASTERS

## Assessment Outcomes & Possible Indicators*

- **Science A-5** Begins to describe and discuss predictions, explanations and generalizations based on past experiences.

- **Mathematics B-5** Builds an increasing understanding of directionality, order and positions of objects, and words such as up, down, over, under, top, bottom, inside, outside, in front and behind.

- **Social & Emotional Development C-1** Increases abilities to sustain interactions with peers by helping, sharing and discussion.

- **Approaches to Learning C-2** Grows in recognizing and solving problems through active explorations, including trial and error, and interactions and discussions with peers and adults.

*Source: "Head Start Child Outcomes Framework." See Appendix A in this book for the framework.

## What To Look For

| Not Yet | Child shows no interest in helping to build a roller coaster. |
|---|---|
| Emerging | Child watches others build a roller coaster; participates by rolling a marble and retrieving marbles but does not help in building it. |
| Almost Mastered | Child eagerly participates in helping to build a roller coaster; assists in taping several lengths together; tries out different configurations; discusses findings. |
| Fully Mastered | Child builds at least part of the roller coaster without help; works with others to complete a complex structure; experiments by changing the height and angle of various selections; asks questions about the project; asks for the activity to be repeated. |

# FAMILY PAGE / PÁGINA PARA LA FAMILIA

## ROLLER COASTERS

### Family Science Connection:

**Collect** several **cardboard paper towel and toilet paper centers.** Together with **family members create a roller coaster track** using the cardboard centers. **Experiment** by making the track curve, loop and drop from a great height. Next, roll marbles and/or round objects through the track. **Play** with your newly created roller coaster by **changing the track, adding to it, and timing how fast the marbles move** within the track.

**Comments or questions** that may add a *sense of wonder* to this activity:

- What do you think will roll the fastest on the roller coaster: a marble, a toy car, or a pencil?

- What ended up rolling the fastest and what do you think made it win?

## MONTAÑAS RUSAS

### Ciencia en familia:

**Guarden varios centros de cartón de las toallas de papel y papel sanitario.** Junto con miembros de la familia hagan un riel de la montaña rusa usando los centros de cartón. **Experimenten** haciendo el riel curvo dando varias vueltas, y caídas de altura. Luego dejen rodar canicas u objetos redondos dentro del riel. **Jueguen** con su montaña rusa **cambiando de rieles, agregando más rieles, tomando el tiempo que toman las canicas para pasar** por el riel.

**Comentarios o preguntas** que pueden *despertar curiosidad* en esta actividad:

- ¿Qué piensas que rodará más rápido en la montaña rusa, una canica, un carro de juguete, o un lápiz?

- ¿Qué fue lo que rodó más rápido y qué piensas que le hizo ganar?

# MARBLE PAINTING

**Investigation:** Observing that marbles roll down inclined planes

**Process Skills:** Observing, comparing

**Materials:** Box lids lined with paper or aluminum foil pans, marbles, bowls of paint (CAUTION: Use only nontoxic paint designed for children's activities.)

## Procedure:

*Getting started:*
Drop a marble into a bowl of paint, then into a box lid. Ask, "What do you think will happen if I move this box lid around?" Listen to what the children say as you tilt the box lid in different directions. Let children get started on their own paintings.

*Questions and comments to guide children:*
- How can you make your marble move?
- Tony is making a straight line. Hoa's is wiggly.
- How can you make your marble move from one side to the other?
- How did you make that line?
- I think I'll try adding another color.

*What children and adults will do:*
Children will choose a color and begin their painting. They will talk about what they are doing, then change colors as often as they want to.

*Closure:*
Let children choose where they want to hang their marble paintings.

## Follow-up Activity:

On another day give children box lids and marbles without paint. Put a sticker in the middle of the paper lining the lid. Challenge them to move their marbles around without touching the sticker.

## Center Connection:

Put box lids, marbles, and paint in the art center for those who want to continue marble painting. Put out other things that roll that children can use to paint with (corks, small cars, Ping-Pong balls). Have them use some heavier items (lemons) then lighter items (Ping-Pong balls). Ask them to describe the difference in how they worked in the paint.

## Literature Connection:

*Marbles (Games Around the World)*
by Elizabeth Dana Jaffe, Compass Point Books, 2001.

*Painting With Picasso*
by Julie Merberg and Suzanne Bober, Chronicle Books, 2006.

# MARBLE PAINTING

- **Science A-3** Begins to participate in simple investigations to test observations, discuss and draw conclusions and form generalizations.

- **Approaches to Learning A-1** Chooses to participate in an increasing variety of tasks and activities.

- **Approaches to Learning A-3** Approaches tasks and activities with increased flexibility, imagination and inventiveness.

- **Creative Arts B-1** Gains ability in using different art media and materials in a variety of ways for creative expression and representation.

*Source: "Head Start Child Outcomes Framework." See Appendix A in this book for the framework.

## What To Look For

| Not Yet | Child shows no interest in participating in marble painting. |
|---|---|
| Emerging | Child watches others marble paint; eventually tries it out using only one color. |
| Almost Mastered | Child participates in marble painting by choosing to use several colors and discussing what is happening with adults and peers. |
| Fully Mastered | Child eagerly participates in marble painting by choosing to use several colors, discussing what is happening and asking questions; asks on another day to repeat the activity. |

## MARBLE PAINTING

### Family Science Connection:

**At home** find an **old gift or shoe box** and put one ingredient in the box that the family thinks would be fun to **experiment** with. (Some possible ingredients include sugar, flour, salt, pancake syrup, mustard, and jelly. Use only ingredients that are safe if swallowed.) Now put the marble in the box too and **observe** and **describe** how easily the marble moves or is hindered from moving. Try two different ingredients and again observe and describe how the marble moves. Also **talk** with the **child about this experience** that was done at school. What ingredients did the children use there? How **fast** or **slow** did the marble roll with what was used at school? Ask the child to **compare** what happened at school with what happened at home.

**Comments or questions** that may add a *sense of wonder* to this activity:

- What do you think will happen when we put the marble and the flour in the box?

- What ingredient might allow the marble to roll faster? Slower?

## PINTANDO CON CANICAS

### Ciencia en familia:

**En casa** encuentre una **caja vieja de zapatos y ponga** un ingrediente en la caja que piensa la familia que sería divertido **experimentar.** (Algunos ingredientes posibles son azúcar, harina, sal, miel para panqueques, mostaza, y mermelada. PRECAUCIÓN: Solamente usa ingredientes que son seguros al tragar) Ahora ponga la canica en la caja también y observe y describa con qué facilidad se mueve o se impide su movimiento. Pruebe con dos ingredientes diferentes y otra vez **observe y describa** cómo se mueve la canica. **También hable con el niño sobre esta experiencia** que ha sido hecha en la escuela. ¿Qué ingredientes usaron los niños allá? ¿Con qué rapidez o lentitud rodaron las canicas que se usaron en la escuela? Pida al niño que **compare** lo que pasó en la escuela con lo que pasó en casa.

**Comentarios o preguntas** que pueden despertar curiosidad en esta actividad:

- ¿Qué piensas que sucederá cuando pongamos la canica y harina en una caja?

- ¿Qué ingredientes harán que la canica ruede más rápido? ¿Más despacio?

# BUBBLES RAISING RAISINS

**Investigation:** Observing raisins moving up and down in cold, clear, bubbly soda

**Process Skills:** Observing and comparing

**Materials:** Raisins, clear plastic cups with straight sides (although plastic cups do not work as well as glass, they are much safer than glass), and cold, clear, bubbly, recently uncapped soda

## Procedure:

*Getting started:*
Slowly pour some cold, clear, bubbly soda into a cup until the glass is about three-quarters full. Observe the bubbles rising in the soda. Have children drop three to five raisins into the soda and watch for some surprises. When the raisins are dropped into the soda, they will sink to the bottom of the cup and after a few moments jiggle around. Soon, a few raisins will start back up. The raisins will move up and down in the soda while the soda is bubbling.

*Questions and comments to guide children:*
- What are those things going up in the soda?
- What is happening to the raisins?
- What do you see on the raisins?
- I wonder what's making the raisins go up and down.

*What children and adults will do:*
The children will find the "bobbing" raisins fun and interesting. If the raisins do not move up and down in the soda, tear a couple of raisins into pieces and drop the pieces into the bubbling soda. Although the intent is for the children to relate the bubbles on the raisins with the rising and sinking of the raisins, a number of children will not make the connection.

*Closure:*
Help children observe that bubbles eventually stop forming in the soda and when this happens the raisins stop dancing.

## Follow-up Activity:

Try different objects in the soda to see if those objects will go up and down like the raisins. Try popcorn, dry macaroni, beans, small pieces of flattened clay, and any other objects the children want to test.

## Center Connection:
The children may want to see the dancing raisins again. Have some cold soda and raisins ready.

## Literature Connection:

*Wallop and Whizz and the Bottle of Fizz*
by Philip Hawthorn, Educational Development Corporation, 1996.

*Floating and Sinking*
by Jack Challoner, Raintree Steck-Vaughn, 1998.

*What Is Density?*
by Joanne Barkan, Children's Press, 2006.

*Floating and Sinking (Science All Around Us)*
by Karen Mole, Heinemann, 2002.

*Floating and Sinking (First Facts: Our Physical World)*
by Ellen Sturn Niz, Capstone, 2006.

# BUBBLES RAISING RAISINS

- **Science A-1** Begins to use senses and a variety of tools and simple measuring devices to gather information, investigate materials and observe processes and relationships.

- **Science A-5** Begins to describe and discuss predictions, explanations and generalizations based on past experiences.

- **Language Development B-1** Develops increasing abilities to understand and use language to communicate information, experiences, ideas, opinions, needs, questions and for other varied purposes.

- **Mathematics B-5** Builds an increasing understanding of directionality, order and positions of objects, and words such as up, down, over, under, top, bottom, inside, outside, in front and behind.

*Source: "Head Start Child Outcomes Framework." See Appendix A in this book for the framework.

## What To Look For

| Not Yet | Child does not watch what happens with the raisins. |
|---|---|
| Emerging | Child watches the raisins, but does not discuss or ask questions. |
| Almost Mastered | Child asks to drop in some of the raisins, talks about what is happening; shows surprise and interest as the activity progresses. |
| Fully Mastered | Child eagerly asks questions about the activity and asks to participate; asks questions and suggests trying out other objects in the soda water. |

## BUBBLES RAISING RAISINS

### Family Science Connection:

Place before your child some clear, cold, recently uncapped soda, some raisins, and a clear plastic cup. Ask your child if he or she can use these things to show you something interesting. If your child has seen raisins rising and falling in bubbly soda, he or she may be able to demonstrate that experience. If not, pour some cold, clear, bubbly soda into a clear plastic cup, add a few raisins, and watch what happens (the raisins move up and down in the soda). Invite your child to tell you about what is happening (bubbles collect on the raisins and cause the raisins to rise; bubbles pop at the surface of the soda and the raisins start back down).

**Comments or questions** that may add a *sense of wonder* to this activity:

- What makes the raisins go up in the soda?

- What makes the raisins go back down once they get to the top of the soda?

- Can raisins go up and down without bubbles?

## BURBUJAS Y PASAS

### La ciencia en familia:

Coloque frente a su hijo(a) un refresco transparente, frío y recién abierto, unas pasas y un vaso transparente. Pregúntele a su hijo(a) si él(ella) puede usar estas cosas para mostrarle a Ud. algo interesante. Si su hijo(a) ha visto pasas subiendo y bajando en un refresco gaseoso, tal vez le pueda demostrar lo que ha experimentado. Si no, vierta un refresco transparente y frío en un vaso transparente, agregue unas pasas y vea lo que sucede (las pasas suben y bajan en el refresco). Invite a su hijo(a) a que le diga lo que está sucediendo (las burbujas se forman debajo de las pasas causando que éstas suban a la superficie, luego las burbujas estallan y se caen las pasas).

**Comentarios o preguntas** que pueden *despertar curiosidad* en esta actividad:

- ¿Qué hace que las pasas suban en el refresco?

- ¿Qué hace que las pasas regresen hacia abajo una vez que han subido a la superficie?

- ¿Podrían subir y bajar las pasas sin burbujas?

# Section 4:
# CRITTERS

Children love to investigate living things, and many "critters" can be brought into the classroom or observed outside in their natural habitats. (Please read "Teaching Respect for Living Things," page xxiii, before working with critters.)

If you do keep a critter in your classroom children will become quite attached to it. We know of a teacher who brought a walking stick into her classroom. She allowed the children to hold it, and they were very careful with it. Nevertheless, one of the children accidentally held it too tight, and one leg broke off. The children were devastated. Imagine their surprise when the leg grew back! The walking stick became the class pet, and all the children learned something about respecting living things.

When investigating critters with children, the tendency of some adults is to ask a lot of closed questions: "How many eyes are there?" "What color is it?" Your challenge will be to ask open-ended questions that encourage children to think and figure out how to find the answer to their own questions: "What does the critter eat?" "Where can this critter hide?" You will find you don't need to ask very many questions because the children will have so many of their own!

## Critters:
## Selected Internet Resources

**Insects**
- Pictures and Facts About Hundreds of Insects—*www.ivyhall.district96.k12.il.us/4th/kkhp/1insects/bugmenu.html*
- Information on Keeping Insects in the Classroom—*www.uky.edu/Ag/Entomology/ythfacts/mascots.htm*
- Insect Activities and Ideas for the Classroom—*http://teachingheart.net/teachinsects.html*

**Fish**
- Online Story and Resources About Fish—*www.storyplace.org/preschool/activities/newfish.asp?themeid=22*

**Birds**
- Backyard Birding, Nesting Information, and Bird Food Recipes—*www.bcpl.net/~tross/by/backyard.html*
- Share the Wonder of Birds With Kids (Birding Activities to Do With Young Children)—*http://birding.about.com/library/weekly/aa041000a.htm?once=true&*
- Bird Sounds and Songs (Click and Listen)—*www.math.sunysb.edu/~tony/birds*

# CRITTERS: ROLY-POLYS

**Investigation:** Observing the behavior of roly-polys

**Process Skills:** Observing, comparing, classifying, communicating

**Materials:** Roly-polys, hand lenses, clear plastic sandwich boxes, plastic cups, moist soil, plastic spoons, plastic wire

## Procedure:

*Getting started:*
Place a container of roly-polys in the center of the table. Give the children some clues about the roly-polys in the box. Ask children what they think they are. Distribute one hand lens and one roly-poly to each child; place it in a clear sandwich box or cup for easy viewing. Listen to what they say and watch what they do before asking questions.

*Questions and comments to guide children:*
- What do they look like?
- What do the roly-polys eat?
- Tell me about your roly-poly.
- How do they move?
- Which end is the head? How can you tell?
- Is it as big as your fingernail?

*What children and adults will do:*
The children will observe the roly-polys in a plastic box or cup and try to learn as many things as possible about the way they look and move. Children will have many questions. When their question can be answered by an observation, encourage them to try to find out the answer. (CAUTION: Do not have children handle the roly-polys.)

*Closure:*
Ask the children to tell you what they have discovered about the roly-polys.

## Follow-up Activity:
Give children modeling clay and pipe cleaners to make their own roly-poly models.

## Center Connection:

Place some of the roly-polys in the science center so children can continue to observe them. Make a bug box from a plastic soft drink bottle to put them in. (Small "bug box" with magnifier lids can also be purchased from science supply companies.)

## Literature Connection:

*Backyard Insects*
by Millicent E. Selsam, Scholastic, 1988.

*The Best Bug to Be*
by Delores Johnson, Macmillan, 1992.

*A Pill Bug's Life*
by John Himmelman, Children's Press, 2000.

*Bugs Are Insects*
by Anne Rockwell, Harper Trophy, 2001.

# CRITTERS: ROLY-POLYS

## Assessment Outcomes & Possible Indicators*

- **Science B-1** Expands knowledge of and abilities to observe, describe and discuss the natural world, materials, living things and natural processes.

- **Creative Arts B-1** Gains ability in using different art media and materials in a variety of ways for creative expression and representation.

- **Creative Arts B-2** Progresses in abilities to create drawings, paintings, models, and other art creations that are more detailed, creative or realistic.

  *Source: "Head Start Child Outcomes Framework." See Appendix A in this book for the framework.

## What To Look For

| Not Yet | Child does not show interest in examining the roly-polys. |
|---|---|
| Emerging | Child is willing to observe roly-polys with adult guidance, imitates others who use hand lenses; asks some questions, listens to discussion. |
| Almost Mastered | Child observes and compares the roly-polys, discusses findings, asks questions. |
| Fully Mastered | Child observes the roly-polys; describes the observations; asks several questions and shares findings with others. |

## CRITTERS: ROLY-POLYS

### Family Science Connection:

**Go on a critter hunt** around the **neighborhood** or on the **school grounds** or at a **park.** Take time to **find** all kinds of critters. Look for them in weeds, dirt, trees, cracks in the sidewalk, and near trash cans. (CAUTION: A critter hunt requires direct adult supervision. "Weeds" could be poisonous plants; trash cans may contain bacteria or mold; lawns may have been sprayed with toxic chemicals.) **Talk about how the critters look, smell, move, and might feel. Compare** the **differences** in what you observe about these many critters. Repeat this activity many times throughout the year to **identify** if different critters are found and can be **observed** seasonally.

**CAUTION:** Parents, use your best judgment when it comes to touching critters! Don't eat any!

**Comments or questions** that may add a *sense of wonder* to this activity:

- Tell me about this bug. Where is its head? Does it have long or short legs? Eyes?

- Are there many other critters that move like this one?

## INSECTOS

### Ciencia en familia:

**Vayan en búsqueda de insectos** por el **vecindario**, en el **patio de la escuela, o en el parque. Busquen** toda clase de insectos. Busquen insectos en la hierba, tierra, arboles, ranuras en las banquetas o caminos, y junto a los botes de basura. (PRECAUCIÓN: Una búsqueda de insectos requiere la supervisión directa de un adulto. "La hierba" puede ser plantas tóxicas; cubos de la basura pueden contener bacterias o moho; el césped puede haber sido rociado con productos químicos tóxicos.) **Hablen acerca de cómo son los insectos, como huelen, como se mueven, y como se pueden sentir. Compare** las **diferencias** de lo que observan de estos diferentes insectos. Repitan esta actividad varias veces durante el año para **identificar** si encuentran diferentes insectos y si pueden **observarlos** en diferentes estaciones.

**ADVERTENCIA:** ¡Padres, use su criterio para tocar insectos! ¡No coman ningún insecto!

**Comentarios o preguntas** que pueden *despertar curiosidad* en esta actividad:

- Dime algo acerca de este insecto. ¿Dónde está su cabeza? ¿Tiene patas largas o cortas? ¿Ojos?

- ¿Hay muchos otros insectos que se mueven como éste?

# CRITTERS: MEALWORMS

**Investigation:** Observing and learning about the behavior of mealworms

**Process Skills:** Observing, comparing, communicating

**Materials:** *Per child*: Mealworms, hand lenses, clear plastic sandwich box or cup, plastic spoon
*Per group*: One small bowl of water, small potato or apple slices

## Procedure:

*Getting started:*
Place a box on the table and invite the children to guess what's in the box from a few "clues" about mealworms. After guessing, place a mealworm inside a clear plastic box or cup. Allow time for the children to observe their mealworms. Listen to their comments and observations before asking questions.

*Questions and comments to guide children:*
· Tell me about the mealworms.
· What are their bodies shaped like?
· Which way is your mealworm moving?
· Can you tell me how it moves?
· Does the mealworm feel softer than the roly-poly?

*What children and adults will do:*
Children will watch the mealworms and touch them. Notice what children are interested in. Follow their leads when choosing questions to ask. Ask only two or three questions during one group time?

*Closure:*
Ask them if several of them could go together to show how a mealworm walks. Ask how many legs a mealworm has. How many children do we need to make a mealworm? Since there are two legs per segment, have several children go together to form a mealworm.

## Follow-up Activity:

On another day, ask the children what would happen if they were to blow gently across the body of the meal worm. WAIT FOR THEIR PREDICTIONS: Model a gentle blow and have the children gently blow and observe the response. Ask what they think mealworms would do if two drops of water were placed near their heads? WAIT FOR PREDICTIONS then model—two drops near head. Children can just dip a finger into a bowl of water and drop the water near their mealworm's head.

## Center Connection:

Under direct adult supervision, children place the mealworms in an uncovered plastic container (watch for sharp edges) and cover them gently with oatmeal or bran flakes and add several pieces of raw potato and apple for moisture. (CAUTION: Remind students not to eat any part of this setup—not oatmeal, bran flakes, potato, apple, OR mealworms!)

## Literature Connection:

*A Mealworm's Life*
by John Himmelman, Children's Press, 2001.

*Mealworms (Life Cycles)*
by Donna Schaffer, Bridgestone Books, 1999.

# CRITTERS: MEALWORMS

- **Science B-1** Expands knowledge of and abilities to observe, describe and discuss the natural world, materials, living things and natural processes.

- **Approaches to Learning A-1** Chooses to participate in an increasing variety of tasks and activities.

  *Source: "Head Start Child Outcomes Framework." See Appendix A in this book for the framework.

## What To Look For

| Not Yet | Child does not show interest in examining the mealworms. |
|---|---|
| Emerging | Child is willing to observe mealworms with adult guidance, imitates others who use hand lenses; asks some questions, listens to discussion. |
| Almost Mastered | Child observes and compares the mealworms, discusses findings, asks questions. |
| Fully Mastered | Child observes the mealworms; describes the observations; asks several questions and shares findings with others. |

# CRITTERS: OBSERVING EARTHWORMS

**Investigation:** Observing and learning about the behavior of earthworms

**Process Skills:** Observing, comparing, communicating

## Materials:

*Per child*: One earthworm (or red wiggler) (CAUTION: Earthworms can be carriers of Toxocara larvae, causing health problems if swallowed. Have children work only under direct adult supervision and be certain that they wash their hands with soap and water after handling the worms), hand lens, clear plastic box or cup, moist paper towel, plastic spoon;

*Per group*: Moist soil and a small amount of food for worms: cornmeal, used coffee grounds, brown sugar, chopped leaves, one small bowl of water

## Procedure:

*Getting started:*
After a rainy day during which children have noticed worms, go on a Worm Hunt. Give each child a paper cup and spoon. Search in the grassy and dirt areas for worms. Bring the worms back inside.

*Questions and comments to guide children:*
- Tell me about the earthworms.
- Do they have any eyes? Legs? Mouth?
- Which way is your earthworm moving?
- What does the worm feel like?
- What do you think they like to eat?

*What children and adults will do:*
Children will watch the earthworms and touch them. Notice what children are interested in. Encourage them to use hand lenses. Follow their lead when choosing questions to ask. Ask only two or three questions during one group time.

*Closure:*
Ask the children to share what they like about earthworms. Chart their responses. Take the worms back outside and place them back in their "homes."

## Follow-up Activity:

On another day, ask the children what would happen if they were to blow gently across the body of the earthworm. WAIT FOR THEIR PREDICTIONS. Model a gentle blow and have the children gently blow and observe the response. Ask what they think earthworms would do if two drops of water were placed near the worm's heads. WAIT FOR THEIR PREDICTIONS then model—two drops near head. Children can just dip a finger into a bowl of water and drop the water near the earthworm's head.

## Center Connection:

Place some of the earthworms in an uncovered plastic container and cover them gently with moist soil/planter mix. (CAUTION: Choose mixes that do not contain asbestos fibers or toxic lawn chemicals.) Lightly mix some food, coffee grounds, brown sugar, and chopped leaves into the moist soil. Be sure to keep the soil moist.

## Literature Connection:

*Inch by Inch*
by Leo Lionni, Astor-Honor, 1962 (available in Spanish).

*The Big Fat Worm*
by Nancy Van Laan, Knopf, 1987.

*An Earthworm's Life*
by John Himmelman, Children's Press, 2001.

*Life Cycle of an Earthworm*
by Bobbie Kalman, Crabtree Publishing, 2004.

## Assessment Outcomes & Possible Indicators*

- **Science B-1** Expands knowledge of and abilities to observe, describe and discuss the natural world, materials, living things and natural processes.
- **Science B-2** Expands knowledge of and respect for their body and the environment.
- **Language Development B-1** Develops increasing abilities to understand and use language to communicate information, experiences, ideas, opinions, needs, questions and for other varied purposes.

*Source: "Head Start Child Outcomes Framework." See Appendix A in this book for the framework.

## What To Look For

| Not Yet | Child does not show interest in examining the earthworms. |
|---|---|
| Emerging | Child is willing to observe earthworms with adult guidance, imitates others who use hand lenses; asks some questions, listens to discussion. |
| Almost Mastered | Child observes and compares the earthworms, discusses findings, asks questions. |
| Fully Mastered | Child observes the earthworms; describes the observations; asks several questions and shares findings with others. |

# FAMILY PAGE / PÁGINA PARA LA FAMILIA

## CRITTERS: OBSERVING EARTHWORMS

### Family Science Connection:

**On or right after a rainy day,** go on a **worm hunt**. Spend time **observing** water puddles and muddy places in the yard. See if you can find those long worms that come out right after a continuous rain. **Talk** about how these **critters move, slide, and dive** quite easily in the mud. Think about what they might eat and where they go when everything dries. If you have a hard time finding worms, dig around a bit with a spoon or shovel and you should find some moving critters. Checking out a children's book about worms from the library could also be a way to see worms if the hunt fails.

**Comments or questions** that may add a *sense of wonder* to this activity:

- Let's watch the earthworm to see how it moves its body in the mud.

- How does the earthworm like to move?

## INSECTOS: OBSERVANDO LOMBRICES DE TIERRA

### Ciencia en familia:

**Durante un día lluvioso o el día después,** salgan a **buscar lombrices**. Pasen tiempo **observando** charcos de agua y lugares lodosos en el patio. Vean si pueden encontrar esas lombrices largas que salen después de que ha llovido mucho. **Hablen** acerca de cómo se **mueven, deslizan, y se clavan** muy fácilmente en el lodo. Piensen acerca de cómo se alimentan y adónde van cuando todo se seca. Si les es difícil encontrar lombrices, escarben un poco con una cuchara o una pala y podrán encontrar algunos insectos en acción. Si no pueden encontrar lombrices, pueden sacar prestados de la biblioteca libros infantiles relacionados con las lombrices.

**Comentarios o preguntas** que pueden *despertar curiosidad* en esta actividad:

- Observemos a la lombriz de tierra para ver cómo se mueve su cuerpo en el lodo.

- ¿Cómo le gusta moverse a la lombriz de tierra?

# CRITTERS: SNAILS

**Investigation:** Observing large land snails (*Helix aspersa*) (*see Safety Note on p. 182) (a two-day activity)

**Process skills:** Observing, comparing, classifying

**Materials:** Snails (*Helix aspersa*), leaves, hand lenses, eyedroppers, water, cups, string, sandpaper, acetate, cornmeal, granola, plastic knives, transparent meat or sandwich trays, index cards, popsicle sticks

## Procedure:

*Getting started:*
On Day One, put out snails (one for each child) on a tray or paper and let children explore. If available, place snails into a transparent meat tray for easier observation. Watch what they do and listen to what they say before commenting or asking questions. Have hand lenses, leaves, cornmeal, and granola available for children to use. Index cards and/or popsicle sticks will enable the more squeamish children to control the snails in the tray.

*Questions and comments to guide children:*
- How does your snail move? Try looking from the underside of the tray.
- What does it like to eat? How can we find out?
- Does your snail have eyes? Teeth?
- Does your snail like water? (Remember, however that *Helix* are land snails and will drown in too much water!)
- How do you think your snail "makes a living"?

*What children and adults will do:*
Children will begin observing the snails right away. (CAUTION: Remind children not to put their fingers into their mouths or noses while handling these critters [and, of course, have them wash their hands with soap and water after completing the activity.] This activity re-quires direct supervision [perhaps one adult for every three or four children] so that high standards of hygiene are maintained. Any children in your classroom with immune-system challenges should not handle a snail, but can observe while an adult holds the snail.)

Follow children's leads as you comment on what is interesting to them. Encourage those children who do handle the snails to use the materials you have out with the snails. Give them plenty of time to explore.

*Closure:*
Ask children to tell you what they found out about their snails. When the activity is completed, *Helix* should be returned to the environment from which they were collected. If obtained from a supplier, provide the snails with a classroom home in a terrarium. For details, see the following website: *www.weichtiere. at/Mollusks/Schnecken/land/weinberg/pet_snails.html*

## Follow-up Activities:

On Day Two, put out the snails again. **(Recall the cautionary notes above.)** This time add tap water in small cups, eyedroppers, string, sandpaper, acetate, and plastic knives to the materials you had available on Day One. Children will still need time to explore before you begin asking questions. Then encourage them to find out whether snails like to walk on something rough like sandpaper or something smooth like acetate. Ask if they think their snail could walk on the edge of a knife. Hold a piece of string taut and challenge children to see if a snail can "walk a tightrope." Later ask children to draw "something about your snail." Write down what they say about their snails.

## Center Connection:

Have playdough or clay available in the art area in case children would like to make a representation of their snail.

## Literature Connection:

*Are You a Snail?*
by Judy Allen, Kingfisher, 2000.

*Snail*
by Karen Hartley and Chris Macro, Heinemann Library, 1998.

*Snailology*
by Michael Elsohn Ross, Carolrhoda Books, 1996.

*Snail, Where Are You?*
by Tomi Ungerer, Blue Apple Press, 2005.

*The Snail's Spell*
by Joanne Ryder, Viking Penguin, 1982.

*Under One Rock: Bugs, Slugs, & Other Ughs*
by Anthony D. Fredericks and Jennifer Dirubbio, 2001.

**\*Safety Note:** Use only *Helix* (large brown garden snails) for this activity, as aquatic snails (those living in ponds and the like) may carry microorgansms that can be harmful. *Helix aspersa,* the most common garden snail found in California and other states, are not known to carry or convey any organisms harmful to children, although this snail is currently on the U.S. Department of Agriculture (USDA) list of plant pests. Due to agricultural and environmental concerns, transporting this snail across state lines (e.g., by buying through a biological supply house) is controlled by the USDA. States to which *Helix* may be shipped include Arizona, California, New Mexico, Texas, and Washington. In these states, *Helix* can only be shipped to addressees holding a permit to do so. For information, visit the USDA website at *www.aphis.usda.gov/ppq/permits/plantpest/snails_slugs.htm*. For more general information on land snails in the classroom, go to *http://lhsfoss.org/fossweb/teachers/materials/plantanimal/landsnails.htm*

# CRITTERS: SNAILS

## Assessment Outcomes & Possible Indicators*

- **Science B-1** Expands knowledge of and abilities to observe, describe and discuss the natural world, materials, living things and natural processes.

- **Science A-1** Begins to use senses and a variety of tools and simple measuring devices to gather information, investigate materials and observe processes and relationships.

- **Science A-3** Begins to participate in simple investigations to test observations, discuss and draw conclusions and form generalizations.

- **Creative Arts B-2** Progresses in abilities to create drawings, paintings, models, and other art creations that are more detailed, creative or realistic.

  *Source: "Head Start Child Outcomes Framework." See Appendix A in this book for the framework.

## What To Look For

| | |
|---|---|
| **Not Yet** | Child does not show interest in examining the snails. |
| **Emerging** | Child is willing to observe snails with adult guidance, imitates others who use hand lenses; asks some questions, listens to discussion. |
| **Almost Mastered** | Child observes and compares the snails, discusses findings, asks questions. |
| **Fully Mastered** | Child observes the snails; describes the observations; asks several questions and shares findings with others. |

# CRITTERS: JUMPING CRICKETS

**Investigation:** Observing crickets

**Process Skills:** Observing, comparing, classifying, communicating

**Materials:** *Per child:* One cricket in clear, plastic cup or box, one hand lens, small piece of moist bread for food, one sheet of white paper, pencil or crayon

## Procedure:

*Getting started:*
Place a cricket in a cup and cover it with plastic wrap. Give one cup and a hand lens to each child and ask them to take a very close look at the cricket. Tell the children that the crickets do not have any teeth and they do not bite or sting. However, children should not handle crickets because the projections on the crickets' skin surfaces can cause cuts.

*Questions and comments to guide children:*
- What do you see?
- How do the crickets move?
- Wow, look at that!
- Can the cricket move up the side of the plastic cup?
- Are all the crickets the same?
- Listen carefully. Can you hear any chirping?
- What do you think crickets might eat?
- Where do you think they live?

*What children and adults will do:*
The children will observe the crickets. Follow children's interests as you decide which two or three questions you want to ask.

## Follow-up Activity:

Give each child a sheet of paper and a pencil or crayon and ask the student to draw a cricket. Collect their pictures and display them somewhere in the room.

## Center Connection:

Place a few crickets in a clear box with plastic wrap with air holes on top in the center. Always have hand lenses available for children's use.

## Literature Connection:

*Nicholas Cricket*
by Joyce Maxner, HarperCollins, 1991.

*The Very Quiet Cricket*
by Eric Carle, Philomel, 1990.

*Chirping Crickets*
by Melvin Berger, HarperTrophy, 1998.

*Leaping Grasshoppers*
by Christine Zuchora-Walske, Lerner Publishing Group, 2000.

*A Pocketful of Cricket*
by Rebecca Caudill, Henry Holt, 2004.

# CRITTERS: JUMPING CRICKETS

## Assessment Outcomes & Possible Indicators*

- **Science B-1** Expands knowledge of and abilities to observe, describe and discuss the natural world, materials, living things and natural processes.

- **Science B-4** Shows increased awareness and beginning understanding of changes in materials and cause-effect relationships.

- **Language Development B-2** Progresses in abilities to initiate and respond appropriately in conversation and discussions with peers and adults.

- **Creative Arts B-2** Progresses in abilities to create drawing, paintings, models, and other art creations that are more detailed, creative or realistic.

  *Source: "Head Start Child Outcomes Framework." See Appendix A in this book for the framework

## What To Look For

| Not Yet | Child does not show interest in examining the jumping crickets. |
|---|---|
| Emerging | Child is willing to observe jumping crickets with adult guidance, imitates others who use hand lenses; asks some questions, listens to discussion. |
| Almost Mastered | Child observes and compares the jumping crickets, discusses findings, asks questions. |
| Fully Mastered | Child observes the jumping crickets; describes the observations asks several questions and shares findings with others. |

## CRITTERS: JUMPING CRICKETS

### Family Science Connection:

**In the neighborhood, at the park, or around the yard,** lightly shake the bushes to see if any jumping or flying bugs appear. (CAUTION: Be aware there can be hornet, bee, or wasp nests in bushes.) You might find a butterfly, grasshopper, or cricket. These critters can move very fast so be prepared to **pay close attention** to where they go so you can follow. **Talk** about what they look like—their **color, shape, and size**. Continue to **observe** them as they sit still and see if they look like part of their environment (camouflaged). If you get lucky enough to catch one of the critters you find, put it in a glass jar (with holes in the top for air) with some leaves and take it to school so everyone can **observe and learn more about your bug! If you cannot find any crickets, then go to the library and find a book about crickets.**

**Comments or questions** that may add a *sense of wonder* to this activity:

- Can you help me find the cricket's eyes, ears, legs, nose, or mouth?

- Let's listen to hear if the cricket makes any sounds. Can you make the sound of the cricket?

## INSECTOS: GRILLOS SALTARINES

### Ciencia en familia:

**En el vecindario, en el parque, o en el patio**, muevan con cuidado los arbustos para ver si sale algún insecto saltarín o volador. (PRECAUCIÓN: Tome en cuenta que puede haber un avispero en los arbustos.) Tal vez encuentren una mariposa, un saltamontes, o un grillo. Estos insectos se mueven muy rápidamente, así que estén listos y **presten mucha atención** para ver adónde van para que puedan seguirlos. **Hablen** acerca de cómo se ven—su **color, forma, y tamaño**. Continúen **observándolos** cuando se queden quietos y vean si se confunden con el ambiente (camuflaje). ¡Si tienen suerte y pueden atrapar a uno de esos insectos, pónganlo en un frasco de vidrio (hagan agujeros en la tapa para que entre aire), pongan algunas hojas dentro del frasco y llévenlo a la escuela para que todos puedan **observar y aprender acerca de su insecto! Si no pueden encontrar grillos, vayan a la biblioteca y saquen libros acerca de grillos.**

**Comentarios o preguntas** que pueden *despertar curiosidad* en esta actividad:

- ¿Puedes ayudarme a encontrar los ojos, orejas, patas, nariz, o boca del grillo?

- Escuchemos para ver si el grillo hace algún ruido. ¿Puedes imitar el sonido del grillo?

# CRITTERS: SWIMMING FISH

**Investigation:** Observing fish in a bowl

**Process Skills:** Observing, comparing, communicating

**Materials:** *Per child*: paper and pencil or crayon, hand lens
*Per group of two or three children*: One goldfish in a large plastic container, fish food (CAUTION: Make sure there is no electrical equipment near the water that houses the fish. Also, some fish may be ill with bacteria or fungus infestations and will display unusual behavior; do not use these fish. As always, wash hands with soap and water after each activity.)

## Procedure:

*Getting started:*
Ask children to describe a fish to you. You may want to draw a fish from their descriptions. Make a list of all of the things they are not sure of about a fish. Then ask the children to look for all of those things when they are observing the fish.

*Questions and comments to guide children:*
- What do you think those things might be?
- What do you think fish like to eat?
- I wonder what they use their fins for.
- How does the tail move? Back and forth, up and down, or in circles?

*What children and adults will do:*
The children will observe their fish and try to notice its body parts and how it moves, and the answers to some of the above questions. Follow children's interest when deciding which two or three questions to ask.

*Closure:*
Ask the children to describe the fish. Give each child a piece of paper and a crayon or pencil. Ask them to draw a picture of the fish as they are observing it.

## Follow-up Activity:

Ask the children to make up a story about their little goldfish and put all of their pictures on display or in a Big Book called, "Our Goldfish."

## Center Connection:

Place a few goldfish in a plastic bowl on the table in the center. Place a few hand lenses nearby so the children can observe the fish closely. Have the children observe the fish during feeding time at a regular time each day. Let children take turns feeding the fish. (CAUTION: Monitor feeding. Overfeeding can bring about bacterial and fungal infestations.)

## Literature Connection:

*Swimmy*
by Leo Leonni, Pantheon, 1963 (available in Spanish as *Nadarín*).

*Un Cuento de Un Pez Grande*
by Joanne Wylie, Children's Press, 1984.

*My Camera: At the Aquarium*
by Janet Perry Marshall, Little, Brown, 1989.

*Hello, Fish! Visiting the Coral Reef*
by Sylvia A. Earle, National Geographic Childrens Books, 2001.

*What Do You Do With a Tail Like This?*
by Steve Jenkins, Houghton Mifflin, 2003.

# CRITTERS: SWIMMING FISH

## Assessment Outcomes & Possible Indicators*

- **Literacy D-2** Begins to represent stories and experiences through pictures, dictation, and in play.

- **Creative Arts B-2** Progresses in abilities to create drawings, paintings, models, and other art creations that are more detailed, creative or realistic.

  *Source: "Head Start Child Outcomes Framework." See Appendix A in this book for the framework.

## What To Look For

| Not Yet | Child does not show interest in examining the swimming fish. |
|---|---|
| Emerging | Child is willing to observe swimming fish with adult guidance, imitates others who use hand lenses; asks some questions, listens to discussion. |
| Almost Mastered | Child observes and compares the swimming fish, discusses findings, asks questions. |
| Fully Mastered | Child observes the swimming fish; describes the observations, asks several questions, and shares findings with others. |

## CRITTERS: SWIMMING FISH

### Family Science Connection:

As a **family**, take a walk along your nearest pier, lake, river, or pond and ask people who are fishing what fish they might have caught. Politely ask if you can see the fish they have in their net, bucket, or bag. As you **discuss** what you see, **count** the number of fish each person caught, **looking** to see if the fish are still **breathing, swimming, or moving** or are **still. Talk** about how fish get around in water using their fins and tail. A storybook about fish might be fun to check out at the library.

**Comments or questions** that may add a *sense of wonder* to this activity:

- Can we find the fins, eyes, tail, and color of the fish we see along the pier lake, river, or pond?

- Can you notice if the fish are breathing? How can we tell if they are breathing?

## INSECTOS: PECES

### Ciencia en familia:

Como **familia**, tomen un paseo al muelle, lago, o rió más cercano y pregúntenle a los pescadores qué peces han pescado. Pregunten con amabilidad si pueden ver los peces que tienen en sus redes, baldes, o bolsas. A medida que **platican** de lo que ven, **cuenten** el número de peces que cada persona ha atrapado y **vean** si los peces todavía están **respirando, nadando, o moviéndose** o si están **quietos. Hablen** acerca de la manera en que los peces nadan en el agua usando sus aletas y cola. Sería divertido sacar prestado de la biblioteca un libro acerca de peces.

**Comentarios o preguntas** que pueden *despertar curiosidad* en esta actividad:

- ¿Podemos encontrar las aletas, ojos, cola, y color en los peces que vemos por el muelle, lago, o rió?

- ¿Puedes darte cuenta si los peces están respirando? ¿Cómo sabemos si están respirando?

# CRITTER CAMOUFLAGE

**Investigation:** Observing how various critters can be camouflaged on different surfaces

**Process Skills:** Observing, comparing, communicating

**Materials:** Various critters and different kinds of surfaces where they are found (e.g., leaves, twigs, weeds, ground covers, flowers)

## Procedure:

*Getting started:*
Provide children with different types of surfaces. Discuss with the children what *protective coloring* means and how critters need to hide to protect themselves.

*Questions and comments to guide children:*
- Which surface is best to hide your animal? Why?
- Let's put your critter on something else and see if we can still see it. Is it easier to see now? Harder?

*What children and adults will do:*
Have the children carefully place whatever animal they are working with on the different surfaces to observe and judge for themselves, the best surface on which animals could hide.

*Closure:*
Introduce the word *camouflage*. Ask the children which surface provided the best camouflaging conditions and why.

## Follow-up Activity:

Children can make their own "critters" out of clay or play dough, paint them, and place them on the best camouflaged surface.

## Center Connection:

Set out a few different surfaces in the center and let the children try them out with real, plastic, or student-made "critters."

## Literature Connection:

*How to Hide a Butterfly and Other Insects*
by Ruth Heller, Grosset & Dunlap, 1992.

*Who's Hiding Here?*
by Yoshi, Picture Book Studio, 1987.

*Can You See Me?*
by Shirley Greenway, Ideals Publications, 1992.

*I See Animals Hiding*
by Jim Arnosky, Scholastic, 2000.

*Where Once There Was a Wood*
by Denise Fleming, Owlet Books, 2000.

*What Color Is Camouflage?*
by Carolyn B. Otto and Megan Lloyd, Harper Trophy, 1996.

*Find the Fish*
by Cate Foley, Children's Press, 2000.

*Find the Insect*
by Cate Foley, Children's Press, 2000.

## Assessment Outcomes & Possible Indicators*

- **Science A-3** Begins to participate in simple investigations to test observations, discuss and draw conclusions and form generalizations.

- **Science B-1** Expands knowledge of and abilities to observe, describe and discuss the natural world, materials, living things and natural processes.

- **Language Development A-3** Understands an increasingly complex and varied vocabulary.

- **Creative Arts B-2** Progresses in abilities to create drawings, paintings, models, and other art creations that are more detailed, creative or realistic.

  *Source: "Head Start Child Outcomes Framework." See Appendix A in this book for the framework.

## What To Look For

| Not Yet | Child does not participate in placing critters on different surfaces. |
|---|---|
| Emerging | Child shows interest; places animal on various items; asks one or two questions; participates in adult-led discussion. |
| Almost Mastered | Places animal on various surfaces, asks questions, and discusses observations. |
| Fully Mastered | Places animal on various surfaces, is interested in other children's findings, makes comparisons, initiates discussions, and asks several questions. |

# FAMILY PAGE / PÁGINA PARA LA FAMILIA

## CRITTER CAMOUFLAGE

### Family Science Connection:

Look for places **in the yard, at the park, or along the shoreline** where the family might find hidden critters. **Look very closely at trees, bushes, branches, leaves, flowers, sand, shells, and rocks.** Many insects and water bugs blend in with their environment so it might take some patience and time to find and observe these critters. Notice if the critters you find have the same **surface, texture, shape, colors, and smell as what they are resting or moving on.** Enjoy watching these critters move in their camouflage coats. (CAUTION: Watch for bees, wasps, and other potentially dangerous insects. Always wash hands with soap and water after handling anything out-of-doors.)

**Comments or questions** that may add a *sense of wonder* to this activity:

- What is it that helped you find the critter as it was hiding? Did the critter move, make a special sound, or have a smell that made you find it?

- Tell me some more about the critter you found.

## INSECTOS CAMUFLAJEADOS

### Ciencia en familia:

Busquen lugares en el patio, **en el parque, o la orilla de la playa,** donde la familia puede encontrar insectos escondidos. **Miren con mucho cuidado los árboles, arbustos, ramas, hojas, flores, arena, conchas, y rocas.** Muchos insectos y animales pequeños marinos se ven como parte del ambiente y tal vez sea necesario tener un poco de paciencia y tiempo para encontrar y observar a estos insectos. **Fíjense si el insecto que han encontrado tiene la misma superficie, textura, forma, colores, y olor que el lugar donde está parado o moviéndose.** Disfruten viendo estos insectos moverse en sus cubiertas camuflajeadas. (PRECAUCIÓN: Esté atento a abejas, avispas, y otros insectos que pueden ser peligrosos. Siempre lavese las manos con jabón y agua después de tocar cualquier cosa afuera.)

**Comentarios o preguntas** que pueden *despertar curiosidad* en esta actividad:

- ¿Qué te ayudó a encontrar al insecto cuando éste se estaba escondiendo? ¿Se movió el insecto, hizo un sonido especial, o tenía un olor que te ayudó a encontrarlo?

- Dime más cosas divertidas acerca del insecto que te encontraste.

# SPIDERWEB COLLECTING

**Investigation:** Observing a teacher collect an old or abandoned spiderweb

**Process Skills:** Observing, comparing, communicating

**Materials:** Hand lenses, spray paint, paper in a contrasting paper to the paint, sticks (skewers) or rulers, spray misters (adjusted to produce a fine mist) (CAUTION: Use spray paint (latex) that contains low or no VOCs.)

## Procedure:

*Getting started:*
Go on a walk to look for spiderwebs. Caution children not to touch the spiders. When you find one, check to see if the spider is nearby. If so, just observe the movement of the spider for a while. If not, spray the web with the spray mister to make it easier to observe. Then allow the children to look at a strand of the web with a hand lens.

*Questions and comments to guide children:*
- What is the shape of the spiderweb?
- It looks like there are bugs caught in the spider's web.
- Is a spider in the web? What is it doing? How do you think the spider made its web? What makes you think so?
- What is holding up the web?
- If you can, touch the web. How does it feel?
- Where does the spider hide if it is not in the web?

*How to preserve and collect the spiderweb:*
- Make sure the spider has left the web and is not around.
- Spray the front and back of the web with spray paint that contains low or no VOCs.
- Before the paint dries, place a piece of construction paper behind the web and carefully move the paper forward making the web stick to the paper.
- You may want to spray the web and construction paper with a clear acrylic paint after it has dried to preserve it.
- Try to collect several different types of webs; hang them on the wall and compare them.

## Follow-up Activities:

(1) Read a book about spiders to the children (one that shows pictures of spiders making a web). (2) Give each group of two children a small ball of yarn and allow them to make a spiderweb between the legs of a small chair turned upside down.

## Center Connection:

Place several books about spiders in the center with yarn and a few branches that could be used to make spiderwebs in them.

## Literature Connection:

*The Very Busy Spider*
by Eric Carle, Putnam, 1984.

*I Love Spiders*
by John Parker, Scholastic, 1988.

*Zoe's Webs*
by Thomas West, Scholastic, 1989.

*Spiders and Their Webs*
by Darlyne A. Murawski, National Geographic Children's Books, 2004.

# SPIDERWEB COLLECTING

- **Science A-1** Begins to use senses and a variety of tools and simple measuring devices to gather information, investigate materials and observe processes and relationships.

- **Science B-1** Expands knowledge of and abilities to observe, describe and discuss the natural world, materials, living things and natural processes.

- **Literacy B-1** Demonstrates progress in abilities to retell and dictate stories from books and experiences; to act out stories in dramatic play; and to predict what will happen next in a story.

- **Creative Arts B-2** Progresses in abilities to create drawings, paintings, models, and other art creations that are more detailed, creative or realistic.

- **Physical Health & Development A-2** Grows in hand-eye coordination in building with blocks, putting together puzzles, reproducing shapes and patterns, stringing beads and using scissors.

- **Physical Health & Development C-4** Builds awareness and ability to follow basic health and safety rules such as fire safety, traffic and pedestrian safety, and responding appropriately to potentially harmful objects, substances and activities.

*Source: "Head Start Child Outcomes Framework." See Appendix A in this book for the framework.

## What To Look For

| | |
|---|---|
| **Not Yet** | Child is not interested in observing a spiderweb. |
| **Emerging** | Child shows some interest; observes, asks one or two questions, and listens while others discuss observations. |
| **Almost Mastered** | Child observes spiderwebs, asks questions, and discusses observations. |
| **Fully Mastered** | Child makes observations, independently points out similarities and differences of spiderwebs, and asks several questions. |

## SPIDERWEB COLLECTING

### Family Science Connection:

Looking for spiders and their webs can be fun and fascinating but please **do not touch the spiders** you happen to observe. Go on a spiderweb hunt and see if you can find the **different sizes and shapes** that make up webs. As you and an older member of the family find webs, **notice** what they are connected to, if bugs are trapped in the web, and if the spider is weaving more web. **Compare** the spider's size to the web size. (CAUTION: In your hunt, avoid going into old buildings or heavy foliage sites—for example, old sheds or big, deep bushes—where poisonous insects and poisonous plants might be found. Instead, check a simple garden with flowering plants, or even fence posts.)

**Comments or questions** that may add a *sense of wonder* to this activity:

· Do bigger spiders make bigger webs?

· What is the spider doing?

## COLECCIONANDO TELARAÑAS

### Ciencia en familia:

Buscar arañas y sus telarañas puede resultar divertido y fascinante, pero por favor **no toquen las arañas** que observen. Vayan en busca de telarañas y vean si pueden encontrar las **diferentes medidas y formas** en que están hechas las telarañas. Cuando ustedes y un miembro mayor de la familia encuentren telarañas, **fíjense** a qué está conectada la telaraña, y si la araña tiene insectos atrapados en la telaraña, o si la araña está tejiendo más en la telaraña. **Comparen** la medida de la araña con el tamaño de la telaraña. (PRECAUCIÓN: En su búsqueda, evite ir a edificios viejos o sitios con plantas tupidas—por ejemplo, depósitos viejos o arbustos grandes y profundos donde insectos y plantas venenosas pueden ser encontrados. En vez, busque en un jardín simple con plantas en flor o aún en verjas.)

**Comentarios o preguntas** que pueden *despertar curiosidad* en esta actividad:

· ¿Tienen las arañas más grandes telarañas más grandes?

· ¿Qué está haciendo la araña?

# MAKING A GIANT SPIDERWEB

**Investigation:** Making a giant spiderweb out of yarn

**Process Skills:** Observing, comparing

**Materials:** A picture of a spiderweb, two colors of yarn, a wad of masking tape (CAUTION: Remind children to keep masking tape out of their hair and yarn out of their mouths!)

## Procedure:

*Getting started:*
Do this activity after doing the "Spiderweb Collecting" activity.

*Questions to guide children:*
  • What do spiderwebs look like?
  • What is holding up the web?
  • How does the spider know it has caught something?

*What children and adults will do:*
Children and adults work together to build a giant spiderweb out of yarn that is attached to a corner of the room. Discuss what to do next with the children as you build the web. When finished, attach a separate color of yarn to the center of the web to represent the spider "alarm" line. Pull the alarm line across the surface of the web to the outer edge of the web. Have a child hold the end of the yarn and close his or her eyes. Have another child throw a wad of sticky tape into the center of the web. When the tape hits the web, the child holding the alarm line feels a slight tug, and knows that something hit the web. If the child were a spider, it would run into the web to attack its prey. Allow the children to take turns trying to throw the tape onto the web and feeling the pull of the alarm line.

## Follow-up Activity:

Build a giant spiderweb outside.

## Center Connection:

Place books about spiders at the center with small twigs suitable for making small spiderwebs with yarn.

## Literature Connection:

*The Very Busy Spider*
by Eric Carle, Putnam, 1984.

*About Arachnids: A Guide for Children*
by Cathryn Sill, Peachtree, 2006.

*Spinning Spiders*
by Melvin Berger, HarperTrophy, 2003.

# MAKING A GIANT SPIDERWEB

- **Science B-4** Shows increased awareness and beginning understanding of changes in materials and cause-effect relationships.

- **Language Development A-2** Shows progress in understanding and following simple and multiple-step directions.

- **Creative Arts B-1** Gains ability in using different art media and materials in a variety of ways for creative expression and representation.

- **Physical Health & Development B-2** Demonstrates increasing abilities to coordinate movements in throwing, catching, kicking, bouncing balls, and using the slide and swing.

*Source: "Head Start Child Outcomes Framework." See Appendix A in this book for the framework.

## What To Look For

| Not Yet | Child does not participate. |
|---|---|
| Emerging | Child participates by imitating others, with the guidance of an adult. |
| Almost Mastered | Child is able to discuss findings with the group. |
| Fully Mastered | Child is attentive and makes observations about the web even when it is not his or her turn, asks questions for clarification; adds own observations to the discussion. |

# LOOKING FOR BIRDS

**Investigation:** Observing birds in the environment

**Process Skills:** Observing, comparing

**Materials:** None (Optional: digital camera)

## Procedure:

*Getting started:*
Begin a discussion about birds by asking children where they have seen birds. Some may even have a bird as a pet. Go for a walk around the school, looking for birds.

*Questions and comments to guide children:*
- What is the bird doing?
- How is it moving?
- What helps it fly?
- Do all the birds look the same?
- How is that bird different than the last one you saw?
- I wonder if the tree is its home.

*What children and adults will do:*
Depending on the area and the day, there may be many birds, few, or none. Have children close their eyes and listen for birds. When one of the children spots a bird, stop everyone so they can observe the bird and listen to it. Pictures of the birds observed can greatly enhance the activity.

*Closure:*
After the walk, let children talk about and perhaps draw pictures of their birds. Ask children if they would like more birds to visit their school grounds. Ask what they think they could do so that more birds would want to visit. Listen to their responses, then tell children that birds use a lot of energy when they fly so they need to eat quite often. Ask them what they think birds might like to eat. Put out a few samples of food and watch for which foods the birds seem to like.

## Center Connection:

Put bird books in the science and book areas. Put feathers in the art area. Put recordings of bird songs in the music area.

## Literature Connection:

*Feathers for Lunch*
by Lois Ehlert, Harcourt Brace Jovanovich, 1990.

*Forest Woodpecker*
by Keizaburo Tejima, Philomel, 1989.

*Bald Eagle*
by Gordon Morrison, Houghton Mifflin, reprinted 2003.

*Birds, Nests, and Eggs*
by Mel Boring, Northwood Press, 1998.

*Take a Backyard Bird Walk*
by Jane Kirkland, Stillwater Publishing, 2001.

*Watching Water Birds*
by Jim Arnosky, National Geographic Children's Books, 2002.

## Finger Play:

*4 brown owls sitting in a tree*
*One flew away and then there were 3*
*3 brown owls sitting there too*
*One flew away and then there were 2*
*2 brown owls sitting in the sun*
*One flew away and then there was 1*
*It flew away and then there were none.*

(Substitute the name of any bird the children have seen.)

## Assessment Outcomes & Possible Indicators*

- **Science A-3** Begins to participate in simple investigations to test observations, discuss and draw conclusions and form generalizations.

- **Science B-1** Expands knowledge of and abilities to observe, describe and discuss the natural world, materials, living things and natural processes.

- **Language Development B-2** Progresses in abilities to initiate and respond appropriately in conversation and discussions with peers and adults.

  *Source: "Head Start Child Outcomes Framework." See Appendix A in this book for the framework.

## What To Look For

| Not Yet | Child does not show interest in examining the birds. |
|---|---|
| Emerging | Child is willing to observe birds with adult guidance, imitates others; asks some questions, listens to discussion. |
| Almost Mastered | Child observes and compares the birds, discusses findings, asks questions. |
| Fully Mastered | Child observes the birds; describes the observations, asks several questions, and shares findings with others. |

# FAMILY PAGE / PÁGINA PARA LA FAMILIA

## LOOKING FOR BIRDS

### Family Science Connection:

**At the park or when camping in the forest or on the beach,** take a **quiet walk** and **look** and **listen** for birds. Once you find a few, **observe** what they are doing. It's also fun to find a nest of babies, but you might have to look high in the trees or deep into a bush because the mother likes to keep her babies safe. (If you find a nest at eye level, don't go too close. Mother birds have been known to attack intruders!) Try to **count softly** all the birds you see and remember their different colors. When you leave their home area, share all the things you saw and can remember about the birds you spotted. Take pictures to share with friends and family members.

**Comments or questions** that may add a *sense of wonder* to this activity:

- Where did we see most of the birds? In the trees? In the air? In the brush? Near or on the water?

- Wow, we saw so many birds that had different colors! Can you remember all the colors of the birds?

## EN BUSCA DE AVES

### Ciencia en familia:

**En el parque o acampando en el bosque o la playa, paseen en silencio** y **observen** y **escuchen** a las aves. Una vez que hayan encontrado algunas, **observen** lo que están haciendo. También es divertido encontrar nidos de aves, pero tal vez tengan que buscar en las copas de los arboles o dentro de unos densos matorrales porque a la mamá le gusta poner a sus bebés en lugares seguros. (PRECAUCIÓN: Si encuentra un nido a nivel de los ojos, no se acerque mucho. Pajaros suelen atacar intrusos.) **Traten de contar** callados las aves que ven y recuerden todos sus diferentes colores. Cuando dejen el lugar donde habitan, compartan todas las cosas que vieron y lo que puedan recordar acerca de las aves que encontraron.

**Comentarios o preguntas** que pueden *despertar curiosidad* en esta actividad:

- ¿Dónde vimos más aves? ¿En los árboles? ¿En el aire? ¿En los matorrales? ¿Cerca o sobre el agua?

- ¡Caramba, vimos muchas aves que tenían diferentes colores! ¿Pueden recordar todos los colores de las aves?

# FEEDING THE BIRDS

**Investigation:** Attracting birds to the school yard by putting out food

**Process Skills:** Observing, comparing, communicating

**Materials:** Clean half-gallon or quart size milk cartons, heavy string, 12-inch-long stick or dowel, jar lids, assortment of bird food such as bird seed, popped popcorn, stale bread, or leftover fruit

## Procedure:

*Getting started:*
Ask children to collect empty milk cartons or save them from lunches at school. Cartons should be thoroughly cleaned and dried. Ahead of time, cut away several cartons as shown in the diagram. To make a perch, place a pencil or wood dowel through small holes you have cut into the sides of the carton. Birds will be able to perch on the dowel and reach inside to get to the food. Carefully punch another hole 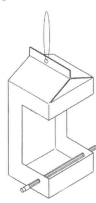 in the top. Tie heavy string through hole and make loop for hanging. Show children the bird feeders. Ask children what they think the birds will like to eat. "How can we find out?" Have an assortment of food ready. Let each child select one kind of food to put in a feeder. (CAUTION: Remind children not to eat any bird food. Commercial bird food may contain pesticides or fungicides.)

*Questions and comments to guide children:*
- Which food do you think the birds will like best?
- How can we find out?
- I see the bird eating _____.
- How is the bird eating?
- Are all the birds eating the same food?

*What children and adults will do:*
Children will choose foods. After children make the selections, designate one feeder for each type of food. Let children fill the feeders. (For example, all the children who chose popcorn would put popcorn in one of the feeders.) Peanut butter should be put in a jar lid for easier clean. Hang the feeders from the eaves or tree limbs. If possible hang them so they are visible from the classroom windows.

*Closure:*
Explain to the children that it may take several days for birds to find the feeders. They should keep looking every day!

## Follow-up Activity:

Make a graph by putting up a chart with a picture of each kind of food across the top (see "Simple Graphing for Young Children" on p. xxxiii). Encourage the children to watch for birds visiting the feeders and notice which food the birds choose to eat. Every time children see a bird eating they should tell you so that you can add to the chart. One way to do this would be to glue a piece of popcorn onto the chart each time a bird eats from the popcorn-filled feeder, add a seed when the bird eats seeds, and so forth.

## Center Connection:

Make bird watching a regular part of your outdoor time.

## Literature Connection:

*Feeding the Gulls*
by Deanna Calvert, Children's Press, 2004.

*A Mother's Journey*
by Sandra Markle, Charlesbridge, 2005.

# FEEDING THE BIRDS

- **Science B-2** Expands knowledge of and respect for their body and the environment.

- **Science A-3** Begins to participate in simple investigations to test observations, discuss and draw conclusions and form generalizations.

- **Science A-4** Develops growing abilities to collect, describe and record information through a variety of means, including discussions, drawings, maps and charts.

- **Approaches to Learning A-1** Chooses to participate in an increasing variety of tasks and activities.

  *Source: "Head Start Child Outcomes Framework." See Appendix A in this book for the framework.

## What To Look For

| | |
|---|---|
| **Not Yet** | Child does not participate in choosing foods for the birds. |
| **Emerging** | Child chooses a food with encouragement from an adult, asks one or two questions, and listens attentively while others engage in discussion. |
| **Almost Mastered** | Child chooses a food, predicts what birds will use the feeder, makes observations, asks questions, and discusses the prediction and observations. |
| **Fully Mastered** | Child enthusiastically chooses food, makes predictions based on previous observations, asks several questions, makes comparisons of several feeders, and initiates discussion. |

# BUILDING BIRD NESTS

**Investigation:** Using different materials to build a bird nest

**Process Skills:** Observing, comparing, classifying

**Materials:** A real bird nest, Styrofoam trays, take-out containers or plastic bowls, grapevine, thin twigs, a variety of different-size sticks, lint from the dryer, a mixture of mud and papier-mâché (1 cup papier-mâché to 6 cups wet sand).

## Procedure:

*Getting started:*
For several days before this activity, read—and discuss the many issues that are introduced in—the book *The Magpies' Nest.* Let the children know that they will have the opportunity to build their own nests. On the day of the activity lay out all the materials so children can see they are distinctly different. Talk about the materials and ask questions about them. Look carefully at the real bird nest.

*Questions and comments to guide children:*
  · How do you think a bird could use this to build its nest?
  · If you were building a nest, which material would you choose?
  · How would a bird carry that twig?
  · What material would you start with?
  · Joanne has decided to start with the mud.

*What children and adults will do:*
Children will choose materials and begin building their nests in one of the Styrofoam trays provided. It is important to remember that the goal is not the product. The products will look like piles of mud and sticks. What is important is that children have an opportunity to see and work with different nest-building materials and that they think about how a bird might go about making a nest. Talk about the different materials and how they might protect a bird's egg and a baby bird.

*Closure:*
Together look at all the nests. Compare the different materials and sizes and shapes. You might ask what size bird they think could fit in each of the different nests.

## Center Connection:

Leave the various materials in the art area so that children can experiment with making different kinds of bird nests.

## Literature Connection:

*The Magpies' Nest*
by Joanne Foster, Clarion Books, 1995.

*Mute Swans*
by Wendy Pfeffer, Silver Press, 1996.

*Birds Build Nests*
by Yvonne Winer, Charlesbridge, 2002.

# BUILDING BIRD NESTS

- **Science B-2** Expands knowledge of and respect for their body and the environment.

- **Language Development A-1** Demonstrates increasing ability to attend to and understand conversations, stories, songs, and poems.

- **Literacy B-1** Demonstrates progress in abilities to retell and dictate stories from books and experiences; to act out stories in dramatic play; and to predict what will happen next in a story.

- **Mathematics B-1** Begins to recognize, describe, compare and name common shapes, their parts and attributes.

  *Source: "Head Start Child Outcomes Framework." See Appendix A in this book for the framework.

## What To Look For

| Not Yet | Child does not participate. |
|---|---|
| Emerging | Child watches attentively as others build nest, participates with the help of an adult, asks few questions. |
| Almost Mastered | Child makes nest independently, participates with the help of an adult, asks questions, and discusses observations. |
| Fully Mastered | Child enthusiastically makes nests using prior knowledge and observations, is self-motivated, compares various nests, and initiates discussion. |

# WATER AND WATER MIXTURES

Water is a naturally interesting material for younger children to explore. Water can be investigated by itself or as it mixes with other substances. There is almost no end to the different water-related activities you can make available.

Water is also somewhat mysterious as it evaporates from the sidewalk or "disappears" into the sand. We can help children realize there is no magic involved by asking simple questions: "I wonder where the water is now. What will happen if we add more water? More sand?"

Children enjoy working with water because they need no adult help, and they can control the activity themselves. It also feels good to have one's hands in a bowl of water and cornstarch or a bucket full of wet sand.

Children can also learn about colors as they mix paint with water and primary colors with each other. We know one boy who made 17 different shades of green just by mixing blue and yellow together!

## Water and Water Mixtures: Selected Internet Resources

### Water Play
- Cognitive, Social, Physical Aspects of Water Play—*www.communityplaythings.com/c/ Resources/Articles/SandandWaterPlay/ MMostWaterPlay.htm*
- Water and Lake Art—*http:// kindernature.storycounty.com/display. aspx?DocID=20054191037*

### Water Information
- Drinking and Ground Water Resources for Kids—*www.epa.gov/OGWDW/kids*
- Water Instructional Resources for Teachers—*www.eelink.net/pages/ EE+Activities+-+Water*

### Bubbles
- Bubble Background Information—*www. bubbles.org*
- SoapBubbler.com—*http://homepage.mac. com/keithmjohnson/soapbubbler.com*

# LOOKING THROUGH WATER

**Investigation:** Looking through empty clear cups and water-filled cups to see how things look

**Process Skills:** Observing, communicating

**Materials:** Clear plastic cups, water, straws, plastic spoons and forks

## Procedure:

*Getting started:*
Give each child two cups, one empty and one half filled with water. Ask children to look through their cups at each other and at objects around the room. Encourage them to look through both the empty and filled cups. Watch and listen to what they say before asking any questions. (CAUTION: Make sure all electrical receptacles in the classroom are GFCI [ground fault circuit interrupter]–protected to protect children from shock when using water.)

*Questions to guide children:*
- What do you see when you look through the water?
- How does your friend look?
- Does she or he look the same as when you look through the empty cup?

*What children and adults will do:*
Children will want to walk around the room looking at things. Encourage them to look at objects from different distances to see if the image changes. Give each child two straws, one to put in each cup. Ask them to describe what their straws look like in the cups. Give children plastic spoons and forks. Ask them to predict how they will look in the empty and water-filled cups.

*Closure:*
Have children draw pictures of something "strange" they saw. Display their pictures. Encourage children to talk about what they saw and record their words on their pictures.

## Follow-up Activity:

After a rainy day has left puddles on the playground, let children go outside and look in the puddles. This works best on a sunny day when children can see reflections of themselves, other people and buildings in the puddles. During outside time, have clear plastic cups and water available so that children can continue their investigations.

## Literature Connection:

*The Rain Puddle*
by Adelaide Holl, Lothrop, 1965.

*Crawdad Creek*
by Scott Russell Sanders, National Geographic Children's Books, 2002.

*Water*
by Susan Canizares and Pamela Chanko, Scholastic, 1998.

## Assessment Outcomes & Possible Indicators*

- **Science A-3** Begins to participate in simple investigations to test observations, discuss and draw conclusions and form generalizations.

- **Language Development A-4** For non-English-speaking children, progresses in listening to and understanding English.

- **Literacy D-2** Begins to represent stories and experiences through pictures, dictation, and in play.

  *Source: "Head Start Child Outcomes Framework." See Appendix A in this book for the framework.

## What To Look For

| | |
|---|---|
| **Not Yet** | Child does not pick up cups or shows no interest. |
| **Emerging** | Child plays with or picks up cup, but is not using it correctly; loses interest in activity and is not very talkative. |
| **Almost Mastered** | Child looks through cup with adult's instruction; sees objects through cup and begins to answer a few questions. |
| **Fully Mastered** | Child looks through cup and sees objects through cup; sees a difference by looking through the cup with water compared to the empty cup, and talks about the differences. |

## LOOKING THROUGH WATER

### Family Science Connection:

**At a pool,** point out how clear the water looks and how the sun shines right through the water. If possible, find an object that can be placed at the bottom of the pool. **Describe** the object **before** you put it in the water and then **describe it as seen at the bottom of the pool.** Has it changed or does it look the same?

**At home** use a small wading pool and try the same activity. **Talk about the two experiences.**

**Comments or questions** that may add a *sense of wonder* to this activity:

- I wonder what will happen when we put ____ in the water. Has it changed or does it look the same?

- I wonder if the object in the water will look smaller near the top of the water or look smaller at the bottom of the water.

## VIENDO A TRAVÉS DEL AGUA

### Ciencia en familia:

**En una piscina,** señale lo clara que se ve el agua y cómo brilla el sol a través del agua. Si es posible, encuentre objetos que puedan ser colocados en el fondo de la piscina. **Describa** el objeto **antes** de ponerlo en el agua y luego **describa cómo se ve en el fondo de la piscina.** ¿Ha cambiado o se ve igual?

**En casa** use una alberca pequeña y trate de realizar la misma actividad. **Hablen acerca de las dos experiencias.**

**Comentarios o preguntas** que pueden *despertar curiosidad* en esta actividad:

- Me pregunto qué pasará si ponemos ____ en el agua. ¿Ha cambiado o se ve igual?

- Me pregunto si el objeto en el agua se verá más pequeño cerca la superficie del agua o más pequeño en el fondo del agua.

# WATER PAINTING

**Investigation:** Discovering that water evaporates into the air

**Process Skills:** Observing, comparing

**Materials:** Wide paint brushes, water in containers

## Procedure:

*Getting started:*
On a sunny day give children buckets of water and wide paintbrushes. Let children experiment with painting the tables and benches, steps, sidewalk, shed, or anything else outside. Watch what they do and listen to what they say before asking questions.

*Questions to guide children:*
- How does the (bench) look when it's wet?
- Is it still wet?
- Where do you think the water is going?

*What children and adults will do:*
Children love to water paint. Encourage them to notice the changes as the water dries. Ask them to paint something that is in the shade. Ask them to notice if it dries as fast as something in the sun.

*Closure:*
Have each of the children paint a big water spot on the ground and then outline the spot with chalk. Have them all sit back and watch what happens. If some spots are in the shade, ask children to predict which will dry faster. After a few minutes have children draw around the spot that is still wet. (Some spots will have disappeared altogether.) Ask children where they think the water went. Tell them it is in the air even though they can't see it.

## Follow-up Activity:

Try painting with ice cubes! Tape butcher paper onto tables (outside if possible); put out cups or plates of tempera paint. Children can dip their ice cubes in the paint and apply to the butcher paper. As they paint the ice cube will dilute the paint, creating more of a watercolor effect. Ask children to talk about how the paint is changing as they work with it.

## Center Connection:

Let children repeat this activity many times during outdoor times for further exploration.

## Literature Connection:

*Water Play*
by Cally Chambers, Hodder & Stoughton Children's Division, 1992.

*I Get Wet*
by Vicki Cobb, HarperCollins, 2002.

# WATER PAINTING

- **Science A-1** Begins to use senses and a variety of tools and simple measuring devices to gather information, investigate materials and observe processes and relationships.

- **Science B-1** Expands knowledge of and abilities to observe, describe and discuss the natural world, materials, living things and natural processes.

- **Language Development B-4** Progresses in clarity of pronunciation and towards speaking in sentences of increasing length and grammatical complexity.

  *Source: "Head Start Child Outcomes Framework." See Appendix A in this book for the framework.

## What To Look For

| Not Yet | Child does not participate or shows no interest in water painting. |
|---|---|
| Emerging | Child participates but imitates others and is not very talkative or observant. |
| Almost Mastered | Child paints with water and talks to others about what is happening; does not notice changes as the water dries, or the differences in the sun and shade. |
| Fully Mastered | Child paints with water and notices changes as the painting dries; eagerly responds to discoveries and leads some of the discussion; shares discoveries with adults and peers. |

# ABSORBING WATER

**Investigation:** Finding out which items absorb water and which do not

**Process Skills:** Observing, classifying, comparing, communicating

**Materials:** Plastic egg cartons or sorting trays; a variety of small items, some of which absorb water (cotton, paper towel, cloth, sponge) and some which do not (bottle cap [not metal], coin, plastic toys, foil); water; eyedroppers

## Procedure:

*Getting started:*
Give each child an egg carton, an eyedropper, a container of water, and a variety of items. Tell the children they are going to experiment to see what happens when they put some water on each of their items. Have children choose which items they want for their experiment and put each in one section of their carton or sorter. Show children how to use the eyedropper. Ask them to put some water on each of their items. Watch what they do and listen to what they say before asking questions.

*Questions and comments to guide children:*
• What's happening to the water?
• Which things are soaking up the water?
• Which are not?
• How does the (cotton) look now?
• Allison says the cotton feels mushy.

*What children and adults will do:*
Children will notice some of the items changing appearance and will use their own words to describe the new look and feel. They will notice the water staying on top and around some items. As children make discoveries and talk about what they are seeing, repeat aloud some of their ideas.

*Closure:*
Let children squeeze the items to see if they leave absorbed water. Use the words "absorbing water" when discussing with the children what they found out. Clarify the term by asking, "Which ones 'drink' the water?" Ask children to tell you which of their items absorbed water and which did not. Use a sorting mat to group items into the two groups.

## Follow-up Activity:

Whenever there are puddles on the ground and the Sun is out, have children outline the puddles with chalk. After a while look together at the puddles to see what is happening. Have them take a different-colored chalk to outline the puddles that remain. Repeat this several times as the puddle shrinks. Ask, "What do you think happened to the water?"

## Center Connection:

Leave an assortment of items and an eyedropper in the science center for further exploration. Fill a water table or tub with sudsy water. Let children wash doll clothes, dolls, dishes, and plastic toys. Encourage them to notice which absorb water and which do not.

## Literature Connection:

*Peter Cottontail Sponge Art*
by Golden Books, 2001.

*Wanda's Washing Machine Fun*
by Anna Mcquinn, Tiger Tales, 2005.

# ABSORBING WATER

- **Science A-1** Begins to use senses and a variety of tools and simple measuring devices to gather information, investigate materials and observe processes and relationships.

- **Language Development A-3** Understands an increasingly complex and varied vocabulary.

- **Language Development B-1** Develops increasing abilities to understand and use language to communicate information, experiences, ideas, opinions, needs, questions and for other varied purposes.

- **Approaches to Learning C-2** Grows in recognizing and solving problems through active explorations, including trial and error, and interactions and discussions with peers and adults.

*Source: "Head Start Child Outcomes Framework." See Appendix A in this book for the framework.

## What To Look For

| | |
|---|---|
| **Not Yet** | Child does not show interest in adding water to various objects. |
| **Emerging** | Child chooses one or two items and adds water, but is not very talkative or observant. |
| **Almost Mastered** | Child chooses a few items, adds water, notices when water stays on top or goes around the items. |
| **Fully Mastered** | Child chooses most of the items, adds water, notices when the water is and is not absorbed by the item, eagerly responds to discoveries, and leads some of the discussion. |

## ABSORBING WATER

### Family Science Connection:

**At home** when something spills, see if younger children in the house can figure out the best rag, towel, paper towel, napkin, or tissue to use to clean up the spill. **Experiment** each time to see if one towel or rag is better than another. **Talk** about why one towel or rag might work better than another to clean up the spill.

**Comments or questions** that may add a *sense of wonder* to this activity:

- Let's see if the rag, towel, paper towel, napkin, or tissue picks up the most.

- Can you think about why the rag picked up more of the spill than the tissue?

## ABSORBIENDO AGUA

### Ciencia en familia:

**En casa**, cuando algo se derrame, vea si los niños pequeños de la casa pueden escoger el mejor trapo, toalla, toalla de papel, servilleta, o pañuelo papel para limpiar lo derramado. **Experimente** cada vez para ver si una toalla o trapo es mejor que el otro. **Hablen** acerca del por qué una toalla o trapo podría servir mejor que otro para limpiar lo derramado.

**Comentarios o preguntas** que pueden *despertar curiosidad* en esta actividad:

- Veamos si el trapo, toalla, toalla de papel, servilletas, o pañuelo de papel recoge más líquido.

- ¿Puedes explicar por qué piensas que el trapo recogió más líquido que el pañuelo de papel?

# Water and Water Mixtures

# ABSORBING COLORS

**Investigation:** Finding out what happens when various foods are placed in water; what happens when foods or flowers are placed in colored water

**Process Skills:** Observing

**Materials:** Containers with water, onions, radishes, carrots, bread, celery, flowers, colored water (CAUTION: Remind students not to eat food used in experiments.)

## Procedure:

*Getting started:*
Have each child select a container; then pour about an inch of water in it. Then let each select a vegetable. Have a variety available. Tell the children they are going to put the vegetables in water.

*Questions to guide children:*
- Which vegetable are you going to choose?
- What will happen if we leave it in the water?

*What children and adults will do:*
Children will talk about what is going to happen. Some may think the vegetable is going to grow or "get cooked." Put out some bread or crackers and ask them what will happen if they put this in water (in a separate container). Let them try it out to see if they are right.

*Closure:*
Tell the children they will be observing these foods every day to see if the foods change.

## Follow-up Activity:

The next day, change the activity by letting children add food coloring to new containers of water. Have them place celery and white flowers in the containers. They could also try adding onions, radishes, and carrots from the day before to make comparisons.

## Center Connection:

Put all the containers together in an accessible area so children can see the changes. You might want to take "before" and "after" pictures to reinforce the changes that have taken place.

## Literature Connection:

*Experiments With Foods*
by Salvatore Tocci, Children's Press, 2004.

## Assessment Outcomes & Possible Indicators*

- **Science A-2** Develops increased ability to observe and discuss common properties, differences and comparisons among objects and materials.

- **Language Development B-1** Develops increasing abilities to understand and use language to communicate information, experiences, ideas, opinions, needs, questions and for other varied purposes.

- **Approaches to Learning C-3** Progresses in abilities to classify, compare and contrast objects, events and experiments.

*Source: "Head Start Child Outcomes Framework." See Appendix A in this book for the framework.

## What To Look For

| Not Yet | Child does not pick out any objects or shows no interest. |
|---|---|
| Emerging | Child watches others and copies them; picks a small amount of objects; is not very talkative or observant. |
| Almost Mastered | Child picks out objects and notices some of the changes in water; notices changes the next day with adult's help; says one or two things about object. |
| Fully Mastered | Child picks out objects, notices the change in water, and independently notices the changes the next day; eagerly responds to what is seen and leads the discussion; has a strong curiosity about all of the objects and sees a difference using colored water. |

# WATER MIXTURES

**Investigation:** Discovering what happens when different materials are mixed with water

**Process Skills:** Observing, exploring, classifying, communicating

**Materials:** Clear plastic cups (five for each child) or muffin tins, sand, salt, sugar, flour, pepper, five-flavor Life Savers, water, stirring sticks, sorting mat (CAUTION: Remind students not to eat food used in experiments.)

## Procedure:

*Getting started:*
Fill each cup halfway with water. Show the children the six materials you have (sand, salt, sugar, flour, pepper, five-flavor Life Savers) and explain that they are going to see what happens when each one is mixed with water. Let someone in the group decide which to start with. Before each material is mixed into the water, ask children to predict what will happen.

*Questions and comments to guide children:*
- What happened when we put the _____ in water?
- Can you still see it?
- Where do you think it went?
- How can we tell?
- What happens to the _____ when it is stirred into the water?
- I wonder what will happen if you stop stirring.

*What children and adults will do:*
With each material let each child put a spoonful of the mixture in water and stir. Ask children to describe what is happening, then let the children decide whether it has dissolved ("disappeared") or whether it has not dissolved (can still be seen). Using a large sorting mat or divider of some sort, put the cups of solution along with some of the dry material on the "dissolved" or "not dissolved" side. Repeat with each material.

*Closure:*
After all materials have been tried and the water mixtures sorted, ask children to describe what they found out.

## Follow-up Activity:

This time ask the children **not** to stir as they drop a five-flavor Life Saver into water in a clear plastic cup. Ask them what they think will happen to the Life Saver if it is left in the water for a while. The dissolving takes a little while so have children do something else, then check back periodically. The children should see bubbles rising from the Life Saver (air that has been trapped inside the candy). As the Life Saver "disappears," it goes into the water at the bottom of the cup. A layer of color will form at the bottom of the cup if the water is not stirred. Leave the liquids in the cups for several days and watch the color gradually spread throughout all the liquid.

## Center Connection:

Children may want to experiment with other materials in water during outdoor time. Provide cups, water, and stirrers. Add water, salt, and pepper to the house area so children can pretend to cook. The aroma of the pepper adds to the realism.

## Literature Connection:

*Mr. Putter and Tabby Stir the Soup*
by Cynthia Rylant, Harcourt Paperbacks, 2004.

# WATER MIXTURES

## Assessment Outcomes & Possible Indicators*

- **Science A-2** Develops increased ability to observe and discuss common properties, differences and comparisons among objects and materials.

- **Language Development A-3** Understands an increasingly complex and varied vocabulary.

- **Language Development B-1** Develops increasing abilities to understand and use language to communicate information, experiences, ideas, opinions, needs, questions and for other varied purposes.

- **Mathematics B-4** Shows growth in matching, sorting, putting in series and regrouping objects according to one or two attributes such as color, shape or size.

*Source: "Head Start Child Outcomes Framework." See Appendix A in this book for the framework.

## What To Look For

| Not Yet | Child does not participate or shows no interest in the activity. |
|---|---|
| Emerging | Child participates but imitates others and is not very talkative or observant; loses interest quickly. |
| Almost Mastered | Child sees that some items dissolved and some did not; predicts what will happen next but doesn't sort items. |
| Fully Mastered | Child sees that some items dissolved and some did not; predicts what will happen next; sorts items that dissolved and did not dissolve; eagerly responds to observations and leads some of the discussion; has a strong curiosity and eagerly repeats the process. |

# FAMILY PAGE / PÁGINA PARA LA FAMILIA

## WATER MIXTURES

### Family Science Connection:

**At home,** any time Mom, Dad, or brothers and sisters **mix** water with drinkable ingredients like frozen juice, Kool Aid, or tea, ask the younger children to help mix them. **Describe** how the ingredients are **dissolving** in the water to make a delicious drink. Enjoy your **experiment** by drinking it all up! Then **talk** about how water gets mixed with a lot of foods to make the foods taste good.

Examples of foods that are mixed with water to make the food taste good:

| | |
|---|---|
| pancakes | soups |
| mashed potatoes | steamed vegetables |
| cake mix | legumes |
| tortillas | rice |

**Comments or questions** that may add a *sense of wonder* to this activity:

- As we stir, let's watch the water get mixed up with the food.

- Can you still see the water in the mixture? If not, what might have happened?

## MEZCLAS DE AGUA

### Ciencia en familia:

**En casa** cuando mamá, papá o los hermanos y hermanas **mezclen** agua con ingredientes para beber como jugo congelado, Kool Aid, o té, pida a los niños más pequeños que ayuden a mezclarlos. **Describan** cómo se **disuelven** los ingredientes en el agua para hacer una deliciosa bebida.¡Disfruten su **experimento** tomándoselo todo! Luego **hablen** acerca de cómo se puede mezclar el agua con diferentes ingredientes para hacer que los alimentos sepan bien.

Ejemplos de comidas que se mezclan con agua para tener mejor sabor:

| | |
|---|---|
| crepas | arroz |
| puré de papas | caldo |
| pastel | legumbres al vapor |
| tortillas | frijoles |

**Comentarios o preguntas** que pueden *despertar curiosidad* en esta actividad:

- Al batirla, veamos cómo se mezcla el agua con el ingrediente.

- ¿Todavía puedes ver el agua en la mezcla o ha desaparecido?

# WATER DROPS

**Investigation:** Finding out how different liquids affect how liquid drops behave (a two-day activity)

**Process Skills:** Observing, classifying, comparing

**Materials:** Liquids, colored water, water with soap, vegetable oil, plastic eyedroppers for each child, popsicle sticks, straws, large containers for the water, water with soap, small individual cups, a square of waxed paper for each child (CAUTION: Make sure all electrical receptacles in the classroom are GFCI [ground fault circuit interrupter]–protected to protect children from shock when using water.)

## Procedure:

*Getting started:*
DAY 1: Give each child a small cup. Let the children pour colored water from a pitcher into the cups so that they are half full. Give children eyedroppers and let them practice using the eyedroppers until they are able to draw water into them and squirt it back into the cup. Once they are all reasonably proficient, give them each a piece of waxed paper. Ask them to try dropping a small amount of water onto their paper in order to make drops. Give them popsicle sticks to move the water drops around.

*Questions and comments to guide children:*

- What's the smallest drop you can make?
- Jana put her baby drops together to make a bigger drop.
- How did you do that, Jana?
- Can you move a drop around on your paper?

*What children and adults will do:*
Children will notice the water separates into individual drops and that it is hard to get it to "stay together." Adults will have extra pieces of waxed paper available so that a soggy piece can be replaced. As a variation, give children straws so they can try blowing the drops around.

*Closure:*
Ask children to describe what they found out about their drops of water. Tell them that tomorrow they will be finding out about drops of soapy water and vegetable oil.

DAY 2: Repeat the above activity with colored soapy water and then with small amounts of vegetable oil. Ask children to compare the experiences by asking questions such as:

- Which liquid made the smallest drops? Largest?
- Was it easier to make a water drop or an oil drop?
- What happens when you put a drop of water inside a drop of oil?

## Center Connection:

Provide tubs of colored water and eyedroppers outside along with a plastic cloth. Encourage children to drop water onto the plastic cloth and move the water around with sticks or straws. Try putting out one tub of red-colored water and one tub of another color. Add a little oil to the water. Ask, "What happens when two drops 'bump into' each other?"

## Literature Connection:

*A Drop of Water*
by Walter Wick, Scholastic, 1997.

*A Drop of Water*
by Gordon Morrison, Houghton Mifflin/ Lorraine, 2006.

# WATER DROPS

- **Science A-1** Begins to use senses and a variety of tools and simple measuring devices to gather information, investigate materials and observe processes and relationships.

- **Science A-3** Begins to participate in simple investigations to test observations, discuss and draw conclusions and form generalizations.

- **Language Development B-1** Develops increasing abilities to understand and use language to communicate information, experiences, ideas, opinions, needs, questions and for other varied purposes.

*Source: "Head Start Child Outcomes Framework." See Appendix A in this book for the framework.

## What To Look For

| Not Yet | Child is unengaged or shows no interest in the water experiment. |
|---|---|
| Emerging | Child sits still and watches or has difficulty using the dropper correctly, is not very talkative or observant. |
| Almost Mastered | Child uses dropper correctly; imitates and copies what others are doing with their water drops; is curious and makes one or two comments. |
| Fully Mastered | Child uses dropper correctly and is very involved; eagerly responds to what is happening and leads some of the activity; is very curious. |

# WATER MAGIC

**Investigation:** Finding out what happens when some materials stay in water for a long time

**Process Skills:** Exploring, observing, comparing, communicating

**Materials:** Plastic egg cartons or sorting trays; a variety of items that change when soaked in water (beans, noodles, rice, crackers, cardboard, raisins, jelly beans) and some that do not (shells, rocks, coins, plastic toys); water (CAUTION: Make sure all electrical receptacles in the classroom are GFCI [ground fault circuit interrupter]– protected to protect children from shock when using water.)

## Procedure:

*Getting started:*
This activity should follow the "Absorbing Water" activity. Ask children to predict which items will change when they are put in water. Give children a plastic egg carton or sorting tray. Let them put some water in each compartment, then choose one different item to put in each. Listen to what they say before asking any questions.

*Questions to guide children:*
- What do you see?
- What is happening to the (noodle)?
- Do you see something different happening to the jelly bean?
- What will happen if we leave all these things in the water?

*What children and adults will do:*
Children will notice some of the items changing appearance and will use their own words to describe the new look. Encourage children to touch the items to see if the texture is changing as well. As children make discoveries and talk about them, repeat aloud some of their findings.

*Closure:*
Tell the children the items are going to stay in the water overnight. Ask them to predict whether or not they will change and how. On the following day let children compare the dry items with those that have been soaking in water.

## Center Connection:

Leave the dry and wet items in the science area for a while. Encourage children to look at both with a hand lens to see the effects the water had.

## Literature Connection:

*Our Big Home: An Earth Poem*
by Linda Glaser, Scholastic, 2000.

*Rainy Day Slug*
by Mary Palenick Colborn, Sasquatch Books, 2000.

*The Mole Sisters and the Rainy Day*
by Roslyn Schwartz, Annick Press, 2000.

# Assessment Outcomes & Possible Indicators*

- **Science A-1** Begins to use senses and a variety of tools and simple measuring devices to gather information, investigate materials and observe processes and relationships.

- **Language Development A-3** Understands an increasingly complex and varied vocabulary.

- **Language Development B-1** Develops increasing abilities to understand and use language to communicate information, experiences, ideas, opinions, needs, questions and for other varied purposes.

- **Approaches to Learning C-2** Grows in recognizing and solving problems through active explorations, including trial and error, and interactions and discussions with peers and adults.

*Source: "Head Start Child Outcomes Framework." See Appendix A in this book for the framework.

# What To Look For

| Not Yet | Child does not show interest in adding water to various objects. |
|---|---|
| Emerging | Child chooses one or two items and adds water, but is not very talkative or observant. |
| Almost Mastered | Child chooses a few items, adds water, and notices when the water is and is not absorbed by the item; does not notice change in texture or compare differences the next day. |
| Fully Mastered | Child chooses most of the items, adds water, notices when the water is and is not absorbed by the item; notices changes in texture and compares the differences of the items the next day; eagerly responds to discoveries and leads some of the discussion. |

# BUBBLE MAKERS

**Investigation:** Making bubbles and bubble makers

**Process Skills:** Observing, comparing, communicating

**Materials:** Straws, liquid soap (e.g., Dawn), glycerin or corn syrup, buckets, water, toilet rolls, tubing, cups, and various bubble makers (plastic rings from soda can holders, small hoops, pipe cleaners, strawberry baskets) (CAUTIONS: 1. Be aware that soaps and other liquids can cause eyes to burn. 2. Water spilled on the floor, including from popped bubbles, can be a slip/fall hazard. Wipe up any spilled water immediately. 3. Make sure all electrical receptacles in the classroom are GFCI [ground fault circuit interrupter]–protected to protect children from shock when using water.)

## Procedure:

*Getting started:*
Prepare the soap solution using 1 cup liquid soap and 1 gallon of water and 50 drops of glycerin, or use a solution of 1 cup Dawn dish soap, ¼ cup of corn syrup, and 5–10 cups of water. Use individual tubs or a water table. Demonstrate how bubbles can be created by using your hand as a bubble maker. Put out bubble-making materials listed above. Ask children how they can use the materials in front of them to create a bubble maker. Allow them to manipulate the materials to come up with a bubble maker.

*Questions and comments to guide children:*
- How did you make your bubble?
- Which of the bubble makers makes the biggest bubbles?
- What is happening to your bubble?
- What do you see inside your bubble?

- Mai's bubbles bumped into each other.
- Where does your bubble go after it pops?

*What children and adults will do:*
Children love making bubbles! They will experiment with all the materials you make available. Encourage them to try different materials to change the size of their bubbles.

*Closure:*
Children won't want to stop, so tell them they will have a chance to make bubbles again on another day. If it is a sunny day, encourage them to talk about the colors they saw in their bubbles. Let them tell you their "bubble stories." Write them down and post by the water table.

## Follow-up Activity:

On another day, add food coloring to the solution. Put down butcher paper so that when bubbles pop on the paper they will leave colored splotches.

## Center Connection:

Put bubbles in the water table or in a tub outdoors on any sunny day.

## Literature Connection:

*Pop! A Book About Bubbles*
by Kimberly Brubaker Bradley, HarperTrophy, 2001.

*Bubble Trouble*
by Stephen Krensky, Aladdin, 2004.

*Benny's Big Bubble: A Picture Reader*
by Jane O'Connor, Penguin, 1997.

*Bubble Bubble*
by Mercer Mayer, School Specialty, 2003.

*How to Make Monstrous, Huge, Unbelievably Big Bubbles*
by David Stein, Klutz, 2005.

## Assessment Outcomes & Possible Indicators*

- **Science A-1** Begins to use senses and a variety of tools and simple measuring devices to gather information, investigate materials and observe processes and relationships.

- **Language Development B-1** Develops increasing abilities to understand and use language to communicate information, experiences, ideas, opinions, needs, questions and for other varied purposes.

- **Approaches to Learning A-1** Chooses to participate in an increasing variety of tasks and activities.

*Source: "Head Start Child Outcomes Framework." See Appendix A in this book for the framework.

## What To Look For

| | |
|---|---|
| **Not Yet** | Child does not participate or shows no interest in trying to make bubbles. |
| **Emerging** | Child participates but imitates others and is not very talkative or observant. |
| **Almost Mastered** | Child plays in mixture and responds to what he or she sees; does not see how children were able to make or change their bubbles; is curious and makes one or two comments. |
| **Fully Mastered** | Child plays in mixture and makes many discoveries; is very involved and sees how to make or change bubbles; eagerly responds to what everyone is doing and leads some of the activity; has a strong curiosity. |

# SAND SCULPTURES

**Investigation:** Making things with sand and water

**Process Skills:** Observing, comparing, communicating

**Materials:** Sand, water, pie pans, molds, sieves, funnels, dump trucks, cars, pails, shovels, balance sale, magnifying lens

## Procedure:

*Getting started:*
Either inside at a sand table or outside in the sandbox, let the children begin by exploring dry sand with shovels, sieves, and funnels. Very soon add water to the sand. Have other materials such as cars, dump trucks, pie pans, and molds readily available.

*Questions and comments to guide children:*
- That cake looks delicious. How did you make it?
- What will happen if we add more water?
- Do you need dry sand or wet sand to make a pie?
- Does all the sand go through the sieve?

*What children and adults will do:*
Children will make models of things in their experience (birthday cakes, hamburgers, ditches, freeways). Wet sand allows children to try out many more ideas than dry sand does. Listen to what children say and observe what they do, then join in their play (pretend to take a bite of cake, help with the tunnel). Encourage them to use their sand in many different ways.

*Closure:*
Bring out a bucket of water for children to dip materials in to remove wet sand (from hands and arms, too!).

## Follow-up Activities:

On another day bring out the balance and magnifying lens so children can further explore wet and dry sand. Take a trip to the beach or lake so children can build with a different kind of sand. Bring a sample of the sand back with you so the children can compare the kinds of sand.

## Center Connection:

Change the props you make available for sand play to keep the sand area interesting.

## Literature Connection:

*Mary Ann's Mud Day*
by J. M. Udry, Harper and Row, 1967.

*Sand Cake*
by Frank Asch, Parents Magazine Press, 1978.

*Sand Castle*
by Brenda S. Yee, Greenwillow, 1999.

# SAND SCULPTURES

## Assessment Outcomes & Possible Indicators*

- **Science A-1** Begins to use senses and a variety of tools and simple measuring devices to gather information, investigate materials and observe processes and relationships.

- **Science A-2** Develops increased ability to observe and discuss common properties, differences and comparisons among objects and materials.

- **Language Development B-1** Develops increasing abilities to understand and use language to communicate information, experiences, ideas, opinions, needs, questions and for other varied purposes.

- **Creative Arts B-2** Progresses in abilities to create drawings, paintings, models, and other art creations that are more detailed, creative or realistic.

*Source: "Head Start Child Outcomes Framework." See Appendix A in this book for the framework.

## What To Look For

| Not Yet | Child does not participate or shows no interest in sculpting with sand. |
|---|---|
| Emerging | Child plays in sand and identifies the differences between wet and dry sand; does not try out many ideas in wet sand; is not very talkative. |
| Almost Mastered | Child plays in sand and identifies the differences between wet and dry sand; tries out different ideas in wet sand; is talkative but not very curious. |
| Fully Mastered | Child plays in wet and dry sand and identifies the differences; is very talkative; eagerly tries different models and has many ideas of different objects to make. |

# FAMILY PAGE / PÁGINA PARA LA FAMILIA

## SAND SCULPTURES

### Family Science Connection:

**Go to the beach** and bring items from the kitchen that can be used to play with in the sand. **Cookie cutters, big spoons, molds, sieves, pie pans, bowls—and of course sand toys are great, too!** Using the **imagination of the whole family**, make something creative in the wet sand. Use lots of **water** to make the sculpture stick together. **Talk** about how dry sand will not stick together like the wet sand does. **Explore and compare** how the wet sand does what you want it to do while the dry sand cannot be molded into a shape.

**Comments or questions** that may add a *sense of wonder* to this activity:

- What happens when we add just a little water to the sand?

- If we put lots of water in the sand, what happens to the sand?

## ESCULTURAS DE ARENA

### Ciencia en familia:

**Vayan a la playa** y lleven objetos de la cocina que puedan usar para jugar en la arena. **Cortadores de galletas, cucharas grandes, moldes, moldes para hornear, coladores—¡y por supuesto juguetes para la arena son excelentes también!** Usando la imaginación de toda la familia, hagan algo creativo con la arena mojada. Usen mucha agua para hacer que las esculturas se mantengan. **Hablen** acerca de que la arena seca no se mantiene junta como lo hace cuando está mojada. **Exploren y comparen** cómo la arena mojada hace lo que uno quiere mientras que la arena seca no se puede moldear.

**Comentarios o preguntas** que pueden *despertar curiosidad* en esta actividad:

- ¿Qué pasa cuando agregamos sólo un poco de agua a la arena?

- ¿Si ponemos mucha agua a la arena que le sucederá a la arena?

# Water and Water Mixtures

# MIXING COLORS

**Investigation:** Mixing two primary colors to create a secondary color

**Process Skills:** Observing

**Materials:** Red, yellow, and blue nontoxic children's paint; paintbrushes; paint cups or plates; paper

## Procedure:

*Getting started:*
When introducing mixing of colors, always start with the primary colors. Choose only two of the primary colors. Put both colors on plates or in cups for children to use. Let them spend time painting before you begin talking about the colors. (CAUTIONS: 1. Water spilled on the floor can be a slip/fall hazard. Wipe up any spilled water immediately. 2. Make sure all electrical receptacles in the classroom are GFCI [ground fault circuit interrupter]–protected to protect children from shock when using water.)

*Questions to guide children:*
- What happened when you painted (red) on top of the (yellow)?
- What will happen if you add more (yellow)?

*What children and adults will do:*
Children may want to paint several pictures. Some will be interested in the effects of mixing colors but not all will. Point out the different shades that children are producing as they use proportionately more of one color or the other. Encourage them to experiment by adding more of one color or the other.

*Closure:*
Have children share their pictures and talk about the colors they made.

## Follow-up Activities:

On another day repeat the activity with a different combination of two primary colors. For a different experience provide red, yellow, and blue crepe paper and clear cups of water. Let children dip paper into water to see what happens. Keep colors separate at first. Then let the children try dipping two different colors in the same cup to see a new color being formed.

On another day give the children each a small amount of vanilla pudding. (Remember: No eating.) Provide food coloring in two primary colors. Let children choose to add two drops of one color. Then let them add two drops of the other color if they want to make a new color.

Put red paint on one hand and yellow on the other. Have children rub their hands together to see what happens.

## Center Connection:

Put two primary colors in the easel cups so children can continue their explorations.

## Literature Connection:

*Little Blue and Little Yellow*
by Leo Lionni, I. M. Oblensky, 1959.

*Cherries and Cherry Pits*
by Vera B. Williams, Greenwillow, 1986.

*Pinta Ratones*
by Ellen Walsh, Harcourt Brace Jovanovich, 1989.

*Mouse Paint*
by Ellen Walsh, Harcourt Brace Jovanovich, 1989.

*The Color Kittens*
by Margaret Wise Brown, Golden Books, 2000.

## Assessment Outcomes & Possible Indicators*

- **Science A-1** Begins to use senses and a variety of tools and simple measuring devices to gather information, investigate materials and observe processes and relationships.

- **Language Development A-4** For non-English-speaking children, progresses in listening to and understanding English.

- **Language Development B-1** Develops increasing abilities to understand and use language to communicate information, experiences, ideas, opinions, needs, questions and for other varied purposes.

- **Creative Arts B-1** Gains ability in using different art media and materials in a variety of ways for creative expression and representation.

    *Source: "Head Start Child Outcomes Framework." See Appendix A in this book for the framework.

## What To Look For

| Not Yet | Child does not participate or shows no interest in painting. |
|---|---|
| Emerging | Child paints but does not mix colors or see that colors are mixed. |
| Almost Mastered | Child paints and sees that there is a new color, but doesn't realize that it was formed by mixing the two colors. |
| Fully Mastered | Child paints and sees that there is a new color and notices it is a mixture of the two colors; mixes different variations of new color (e.g., darker, lighter); is very talkative and eagerly mixes more colors on other days. |

## MIXING COLORS

### Family Science Connection:

**At home get a paint set, brushes, and paper.** Spend some time painting with any colors that each of you chooses to use. As you paint, **identify** the colors that each picture has in it. Begin to **play** with colors by **mixing** two colors together and seeing which third color you can create. **Describe** these new or existing colors. When you are all finished creating various colors from mixtures of colors, **count** how many different colors you have created.

**Comments or questions** that may add a *sense of wonder* to this activity:

· What happens when we mix two colors together?

· Let's count how many new colors we have made.

## MEZCLANDO COLORES

### Ciencia en familia:

**En casa tome un juego de pinturas, pinceles, y papel.** Pasen tiempo pintando con los colores que cada uno escoja. Mientras pintan, **identifiquen** los colores que tiene cada uno de los dibujos. Empiecen a **experimentar** con colores **mezclando** dos colores juntos y viendo qué otro color pueden crear. **Describa** estos colores nuevos o existentes. Cuando hayan terminado de crear varios colores mediante la mezcla de colores, **cuenten** cuántos colores diferentes han creado.

**Comentarios o preguntas** que pueden *despertar curiosidad* en esta actividad:

· ¿Qué sucede cuando mezclamos dos colores?

· Contemos cuántos colores nuevos hemos creado.

# COLOR DESIGNS

**Investigation:** Dipping paper towels and other materials in colored water to make designs and test absorption properties

**Process Skills:** Observing, comparing, communicating

**Materials:** Small bowls or muffin tins with food coloring mixed with a little water, paper towels, coffee filters, waxed paper, newsprint, tissue paper (CAUTIONS: 1. Water spilled on the floor can be a slip/fall hazard. Wipe up any spilled water immediately. 2. Make sure all electrical receptacles in the classroom are GFCI [ground fault circuit interrupter]– protected to protect children from shock when using water.)

## Procedure:

*Getting started:*
Put out small bowls of red, yellow, and blue food coloring mixed with a little water. Encourage children to fold their towels any way they want, then to dip a corner into a color, and then dip each of the other corners in different colors. Have them unfold their towels to see the design.

*Questions and comments to guide children:*

- What is happening to the colored water?
- How did the color get onto all those places?
- What would happen if you dipped the same corner in two colors?
- Look at that!

*What children and adults will do:*
Children will want to make several of the towel designs. Encourage them to try different combinations of color and different amounts of colored water. Provide a clothesline and clothespins to hang them up.

On the next day repeat this activity but provide newsprint, tissue paper, waxed paper, and coffee filters. Ask children to predict which will make the best designs. As they try out using different materials, encourage them to talk about what is happening.

*Closure:*
On both days have children show or point to their designs and talk about how they were made. After children use all the different kinds of paper have them decide which made the best designs.

## Follow-up Activity:

On another day let children experiment with felt-tip pen inks, food coloring, and other dyes in another way. Put a drop of dye or ink in the center of a white napkin or paper towel. Let children use eyedroppers to drop some water onto the ink or dye spot. Ask, "What is happening to the ink (dye) spot?" Let children make designs by dropping dye in several spots and adding water to each spot.

## Center Connection:

Put the same materials in the art center or outside for children to continue their investigations.

## Literature Connection:

*What Is Pink?*
by Christina Rossetti, Macmillan, 1971.

*Is It Red? Is It Yellow? Is It Blue?*
by Tana Hoban, Greenwillow, 1978.

## Assessment Outcomes & Possible Indicators*

- **Science A-2** Develops increased ability to observe and discuss common properties, differences and comparisons among objects and materials.

- **Science A-3** Begins to participate in simple investigations to test observations, discuss and draw conclusions and form generalizations.

- **Language Development B-1** Develops increasing abilities to understand and use language to communicate information, experiences, ideas, opinions, needs, questions and for other varied purposes.

- **Creative Arts A-1** Participates with increasing interest and enjoyment in a variety of music activities, including listening, singing, finger plays, games and performances.

*Source: "Head Start Child Outcomes Framework." See Appendix A in this book for the framework.

## What To Look For

| Not Yet | Child does not participate or shows no interest in making designs. |
|---|---|
| Emerging | Child dips paper towel and imitates others, but is not talkative or observant. |
| Almost Mastered | Child dips paper towel in the three colors and is curious about the new colors, but doesn't realize that it was mixed by the three colors; makes no predictions about different materials the next day. |
| Fully Mastered | Child dips paper towel and sees all of the new colors made; eagerly responds to changes and leads most of the discussion; has a strong curiosity about the colors and wants to explore more; makes predictions the next day for different materials. |

# WATER DROPS AS ART

**Investigation:** Dropping water on a semi-absorbent surface to see what happens

**Process Skills:** Observing, comparing, communicating

**Materials:** Shoe boxes or cardboard boxes cut so they are shallow, white paper (notebook or copier paper, not construction paper), eyedroppers, cups or bowls of colored water (CAUTIONS: 1. Water spilled on the floor can be a slip/fall hazard. Wipe up any spilled water immediately. 2. Make sure all electrical receptacles in the classroom are GFCI [ground fault circuit interrupter]–protected to protect children from shock when using water.)

## Procedure:

*Getting started:*
Cut paper to fit inside each box. Have colored water ready for children to use. Give each child an eyedropper. Children can work in pairs. Ask one child to drop colored water from the eyedropper into the box while the other tilts the box to see what happens to the water.

*Questions and comments to guide children:*

· What happens when you add more water?
· Does the water go in a different place or the same place?
· Bernie says his looks like a river.
· Maxine made lots of rivers.

*What children and adults will do:*
Children will drop water of different colors onto the paper. Some will notice that the water sticks to itself and then begins making new paths. Sometimes it collects in a heavy drop just before it bursts to start a new "river."

*Closure:*
Put all the boxes together on the rug. Ask the children to look at the various boxes and compare the results. Some may look like beautiful paintings! They can be dried and hung on the wall to decorate the classroom.

## Follow-up Activity:

On another day cover a large area of the floor with butcher paper. Have children stand around the edges of the butcher paper. Have tables nearby with cups of water, colored with red, yellow, and blue food coloring. Encourage children to take a dropper and fill it with one color of water at a time. Hold their hands out over the paper and let the water drop onto the paper. There will be some puddles. Some children will use the droppers to suck the water back up and re-drop it. Others will get down and use the dropper to push and pull the water into lines and circles.

## Center Connection:

Put the same materials into the art area so children can continue their investigations.

## Literature Connection:

*Experiments With Colors*
by Salvatore Tocci, Children's Press, 2004.

*Song of the Water Boatman and Other Pond Poems*
by Joyce Sidman, Houghton Mifflin, 2005.

## Assessment Outcomes & Possible Indicators*

- **Science A-1** Begins to use senses and a variety of tools and simple measuring devices to gather information, investigate materials and observe processes and relationships.

- **Science A-3** Begins to participate in simple investigations to test observations, discuss and draw conclusions and form generalizations.

- **Language Development B-1** Develops increasing abilities to understand and use language to communicate information, experiences, ideas, opinions, needs, questions and for other varied purposes.

- **Creative Arts A-1** Participates with increasing interest and enjoyment in a variety of music activities, including listening, singing, finger plays, games and performances.

- **Social & Emotional Development C-1** Increases abilities to sustain interactions with peers by helping, sharing and discussion.

*Source: "Head Start Child Outcomes Framework." See Appendix A in this book for the framework.

## What To Look For

| Not Yet | Child is unengaged or shows no interest in dropping colored water on paper. |
|---|---|
| Emerging | Child watches others but is not involved or doesn't use dropper correctly; is not very talkative or observant. |
| Almost Mastered | Child uses dropper correctly and is involved; imitates and copies what others are doing; is curious and makes one or two comments about what the water is doing. |
| Fully Mastered | Child uses dropper correctly and is very involved; notices how the drops of water interact with each other (makes rivers, bigger drops, sticks together); eagerly responds to changes and leads most of the activity; has a strong curiosity. |

# MAKING OOBLECK

**Investigation:** Mixing water with cornstarch to see what happens

**Process Skills:** Exploring, comparing, communicating

**Materials:** Cornstarch, water, large bowls or pans or plastic cups, large spoons

## Procedure:

*Getting started:*
Give each child a bowl, or two children could share a large bowl or pan, or each child can make individual portions in a plastic cup. Have children measure equal amounts of cornstarch and water into their bowls. Give them spoons to stir the mixture. Give them time to explore their oobleck before you ask any questions. (CAUTIONS: 1. Water spilled on the floor can be a slip/fall hazard. Wipe up any spilled water immediately. 2. Make sure all electrical receptacles in the classroom are GFCI [ground fault circuit interrupter]–protected to protect children from shock when using water.)

*Questions and comments to guide children:*

- How does it feel?
- How long can you hold some in your hand?
- What happens when you stir it?
- Dominique made hers into a ball.

*What children and adults will do:*
Experimenting with the oobleck yourself along with the children will help you make appropriate comments and ask questions that will help children make discoveries. As children do different things with their oobleck, point out their discoveries to others in the group—"Look at how Nathan is pouring his!" Encourage children to describe what is happening. Use words yourself like *solid, liquid, thin, thick,* and *changing.*

*Closure:*
Save the oobleck in one or two bowls to use during another time. Cleanup is easy. When dry, the mixture will come right up. Have children assist with cleanup.

## Follow-up Activities:

On another day add food coloring to the oobleck for a different experience. On yet another day add plastic dinosaurs!

## Center Connection:

Some children will want to continue exploring the oobleck during their free choice or outdoor time.

## Literature Connection:

*Bartholomew and the Oobleck*
by Dr. Seuss, Random House, 1949.

*What Is the World Made Of? All About Solids, Liquids, and Gases*
by Kathleen Zoehfeld, HarperTrophy, 1998.

# MAKING OOBLECK

- **Science A-1** Begins to use senses and a variety of tools and simple measuring devices to gather information, investigate materials and observe processes and relationships.

- **Science A-2** Develops increased ability to observe and discuss common properties, differences and comparisons among objects and materials.

- **Language Development A-3** Understands an increasingly complex and varied vocabulary.

- **Language Development B-1** Develops increasing abilities to initiate and respond appropriately in conversation and discussions with peers and adults.

  *Source: "Head Start Child Outcomes Framework." See Appendix A in this book for the framework.

## What To Look For

| | |
|---|---|
| **Not Yet** | Child does not participate or shows no interest in mixing the materials. |
| **Emerging** | Child plays with oobleck but is unengaged and not involved with discussion. |
| **Almost Mastered** | Child plays with oobleck and is talkative and answers some adults' questions. |
| **Fully Mastered** | Child plays with oobleck, makes many discoveries and shares with group; child is very talkative and describes what is happening. |

# FAMILY PAGE / PÁGINA PARA LA FAMILIA

## MAKING OOBLECK

### Family Science Connection:

**In the kitchen, give each family member** a large bowl or pan. **Together measure** equal parts of water and cornstarch in each of the bowls. Each person can stir the ingredients in his or her own bowl. As you stir, **watch** how the ingredients change. **Smell** and **touch** the oobleck. **Play** with the mixture and **describe** how it **looks** and **feels**.

**Comments or questions** that may add a *sense of wonder* to this activity:

- How does the oobleck feel? Soft? Hard? Cold? Wet?

- What happens when you squeeze it?

## HACIENDO "OOBLECK"

### Ciencia en familia:

**En la cocina**, dele a cada miembro de la familia un tazón grande o un recipiente. **Mezclen juntos** partes iguales de maizena (corn starch) y agua en cada uno de los recipientes. Cada persona puede revolver los ingredientes en su tazón o recipiente. A medida que mezclan **observen** cómo cambian los ingredientes. **Huelan y toquen** el oobleck. **Jueguen** con la mezcla y **describan** cómo se **ve** y se **siente**.

**Comentarios o preguntas** que pueden *despertar curiosidad* en esta actividad:

- ¿Cómo se siente el oobleck? ¿Suave? ¿Duro? ¿Frío? ¿Mojado?

- ¿Qué sucede cuando lo exprimes?

# Water and Water Mixtures

# SNAPPY

**Investigation:** Manipulating a new material to see what it feels like and what can be done with it

**Process Skills:** Observing, classifying

**Materials:** Glue, water, borax

## Procedure:

*Getting started:*
Make a batch of snappy by following this recipe:

> 2 cups glue
> 2½ cups water
> 1 teaspoon borax

Boil the water or use warm water. Pour most of it into a bowl. Add the glue and mix. Dissolve the borax into the rest of the boiling water. Add to glue mixture. Store in an airtight container. Put out on a table for children to use. (CAUTION: Keep students away from boiling water!)

*Questions and comments to guide children:*
- How does the snappy feel?
- What can you do with it?
- I wonder what will happen if I try to make a ball.
- I like the way it feels!

*What children and adults will do:*
Children will work with the snappy for a long time, pushing, pulling, rolling, and stretching. Don't put any tools (cookie cutters, scissors, sticks) out the first time you give children snappy to experience. Tools will distract them from experiencing the actual material. Use the snappy yourself. Talk about what you and the children are doing and discovering.

*Closure:*
As children put the snappy away, ask them what they liked best about the snappy.

## Follow-up Activities:

On another day you can add food coloring to water to make colored snappy. Add tools if you see children losing interest in using snappy by itself.

## Center Connection:

Make snappy available in the art area for children to use during free choice time.

## Literature Connection:

*What Is a Scientist?*
by Barbara Lehn, Millbrook Press, 1999.

# Assessment Outcomes & Possible Indicators*

- **Science A-1** Begins to use senses and a variety of tools and simple measuring devices to gather information, investigate materials and observe processes and relationships.

- **Science A-3** Begins to participate in simple investigations to test observations, discuss and draw conclusions and form generalizations.

- **Language Development B-1** Develops increasing abilities to understand and use language to communicate information, experiences, ideas, opinions, needs, questions and for other varied purposes.

  *Source: "Head Start Child Outcomes Framework." See Appendix A in this book for the framework.

# What To Look For

| Not Yet | Child does not participate or shows no interest in using the snappy. |
|---|---|
| Emerging | Child plays with snappy but is unengaged and not involved with discussion. |
| Almost Mastered | Child plays with snappy and is talkative and answers some adults' questions. |
| Fully Mastered | Child plays with snappy, makes many discoveries and shares with group; child is very talkative and describes what is happening. |

# Section 6:
# SEEDS

Many young children have not yet made the connection between seeds and the food that these seeds produce. Because food is so basic and relevant to children's lives, it is a simple matter to have children discover for themselves that there are seeds in many foods.

From there it is a simple matter to give children seeds to classify and compare. Certain seeds grow very quickly—radishes, grass, limas—so children can see the entire cycle of seed to plant to seed again. Children can plant seeds and harvest the results.

Taking care of seeds in a garden can become a social activity as well as one in which children share the responsibility for watering and caring for plants they grow. A productive garden teaches children a great deal about where food comes from and what plants need to grow and can be a source of pride for the gardeners.

## Seeds:
## Selected Internet Resources

### Gardens and Gardening
- Garden Ideas for Kids—*http://aggie-horticulture.tamu.edu/nutrition/ideas/forkids.html*
- Gardening for Visually Impaired or Multi-Impaired Children—*www.nfb.org/Images/nfb/Publications/fr/fr18/fr05sf12.htm*
- Kids' Valley Garden—Let's Plant Some Stuff!—*www.copper-tree.ca/garden/index.html*
- KinderGarden—*http://aggie-horticulture.tamu.edu/kindergarden/kinder.htm*

### Plants and Flowers
- Interactive Online Plants and Flowers Games—*www.primarygames.com/science/flowers/games.htm*
- Pumpkin Science Information—*http://scienceforfamilies.allinfo-about.com/features/pumpkinscience.html*

# SEEDS IN OUR FOOD

**Investigation:** Looking for seeds in fruit

**Process Skills:** Observing, comparing, classifying, communicating

**Materials:** Avocados, melons, oranges, lemons, grapefruit, tomatoes, apples, sturdy plastic knives, paper plates, bowls, hand lenses

## Procedure:

*Getting started:*
Put all the fruit on the table. Pass them around so children have a chance to touch and smell each one. Ask if they know the name of each one. Let each child choose one to work with. Listen to what they say about the fruit.

*Questions and comments to guide children:*
- What does this look like on the inside?
- How can we find out?
- What did you find?
- What are these things?
- All these fruits have seeds!
- How are they different?

*What children and adults will do:*
Children will try to open their fruit with their knives, their hands, and their mouths. (Fruits with thick or hard skin such as melons and lemons can be very difficult for children to cut. Adults should cut such fruits with knives.) When one of the children uses the word *seeds*, repeat the word and tell children there are seeds in all these fruits.

*Closure:*
Encourage children to talk about what they have found out. Ask if anyone knows what seeds do. Whatever children answer, ask, "What makes you think so?" "How do you know?" "How can we find out?"

## Follow-up Activities:

This activity could be spread out over several days with one or two fruits investigated each day. Have children look for less obvious seeds in bananas and strawberries. Look for seeds during lunchtime. In the fall let children investigate the inside of a pumpkin. Wash and dry the seeds, toast them in the oven, and eat!

## Center Connection:

Save the seeds and skin from each fruit and put with a picture of the fruit in the science center. Have hand lenses ready.

## Literature Connection:

*From Seed to Plant*
by Gail Gibbons, Holiday House, 1991.

*A Fruit Is a Suitcase for Seeds*
by Anca Hariton, First Avenue Editions, 2006.

*How a Seed Grows*
by Helene J. Jordan, HarperTrophy, rev. ed., 1992.

SEEDS IN OUR FOOD

## Assessment Outcomes & Possible Indicators*

- **Science A-1** Begins to use senses and a variety of tools and simple measuring devices to gather information, investigate materials and observe processes and relationships.

- **Language Development B-1** Develops increasing abilities to initiate and respond appropriately in conversation and discussions with peers and adults.

- **Language Development B-3** Uses an increasingly complex and varied spoken vocabulary.

- **Physical Health & Development A-1** Develops growing strength, dexterity and control needed to use tools such as scissors, paper punch, stapler and hammer.

*Source: "Head Start Child Outcomes Framework." See Appendix A in this book for the framework.

## What To Look For

| Not Yet | Child shows no interest in finding out what is inside the fruit. |
|---|---|
| Emerging | Child opens and explores one fruit but does not show interest in what other children are discovering in their fruit. |
| Almost Mastered | Child finds seeds in one fruit, then looks at others and compares the look and feel of seeds in other fruits; uses a hand lens to explore and comments on the differences. |
| Fully Mastered | Child describes the seeds found in one fruit; compares and discusses the differences in all the fruit; asks questions about seeds and how/why they are different; continues to explore seeds during free choice time. |

**256**   **National Science Teachers Association**

# FAMILY PAGE / PÁGINA PARA LA FAMILIA

## SEEDS IN OUR FOOD

### Family Science Connection:

**At home** as the family prepares meals together, look for seeds in the food (e.g., avocados, melons, apples, papaya, lemons, corn, or oranges). Ask the younger children to help **identify** the seeds. Maybe you can **collect** all the **seeds** that are found that day and see if the family can remember the food that the seeds came from. **Talk** about how most plants have seeds in them so we can grow more of them.

**Comments or questions** that may add a *sense of wonder* to this activity:

- Let's count the number of seeds we collected today.

- This seed came from which plant?

## SEMILLAS EN NUESTROS ALIMENTOS

### Ciencia en familia:

**En casa**, mientras la familia prepara los alimentos, busque las semillas en la comida (aguacates, manzanas, papaya, limones, maíz, o naranjas). Pida a los niños más pequeños que le ayuden a **identificar** las semillas. Tal vez pueda **juntar** todas las **semillas** ese día y ver si la familia recuerda los alimentos de donde provinieron. **Hablen** acerca de cómo la mayoría de las plantas tienen semillas dentro y es así como nosotros podemos hacer crecer más plantas de esas semillas.

**Comentarios o preguntas** que pueden *despertar curiosidad* en esta actividad:

- Contemos el número de semillas que recolectamos hoy.

- ¿De qué planta vino esta semilla?

# WHERE DO SEEDS COME FROM?

**Investigation:** Observing seeds in fruits and vegetables

**Process Skills:** Observing, classifying, comparing, communicating

**Materials:** Assorted fruits and vegetables (e.g., apple, watermelon, squash, beans, tomato, pumpkin, peas, ear of corn); one hand lens per child, small paper plates, plastic spoons (CAUTION: Check with parents for children's food allergies before doing this activity.)

## Procedure:

*Getting started:*
(Do this activity after "Seeds in Our Food.") Show the children a small assortment of seeds. Ask them what they are and where they come from. Discuss their ideas. Hopefully, they will mention different fruits and vegetables. Take out an assortment of fruits and vegetables from a bag or box and place them on the table. Have the children observe, smell, thump, and try to name each item.

*Questions and comments to guide children:*
- Where do we find seeds?
- Do you think all these fruits and vegetables have seeds in them?
- How can we find out?
- What does it look like inside the fruit or vegetable?

*What children and adults will do:*
Cut slices of seeds from each piece of fruit or vegetable. Give a small slice of each food and a spoon to each child. Have them remove and observe the seeds. Children will touch, smell, and taste the foods as they look for seeds. (CAUTION: Tasting and eating seeds must be done under sanitary conditions. Make sure surface used is clean. Have children wash their hands with soap and water before and after the activity.)

*Closure:*
While the children are observing each item, take one or two seeds from each fruit and vegetable. For closure ask children to tell you what they found out about seeds. Have the group dictate a "seed story." Write the story on a piece of poster board or easel paper. Include drawings when appropriate. Post it in the science center by the collection of seeds.

## Center Connection:

Place the leftover slices at the center for further observation.

## Literature Connection:

*The Very Hungry Caterpillar*
by Eric Carle, Philomel, new ed., 1994.

*Ten Seeds*
by Ruth Brown, Knopf, 2001.

*The Shaman's Apprentice: A Tale of the Amazon Rain Forest*
by Lynne Cherry and Mark J. Plotkin, Gulliver Books, 1998.

# WHERE DO SEEDS COME FROM?

- **Science A-2** Develops increased ability to observe and discuss common properties, differences and comparisons among objects and materials.

- **Language Development B-1** Develops increasing abilities to understand and use language to communicate information, experiences, ideas, opinions, needs, questions and for other varied purposes.

- **Language Development B-3** Uses an increasingly complex and varied spoken vocabulary.

- **Literacy D-2** Begins to represent stories and experiences through pictures, dictation, and in play.

*Source: "Head Start Child Outcomes Framework." See Appendix A in this book for the framework.

## What To Look For

| Not Yet | Child shows no interest in the seeds found in fruits and vegetables; may smell and taste the food. |
|---|---|
| Emerging | Child finds the seeds in several of the fruits and vegetables; talks about having found seeds but does not try to compare them. |
| Almost Mastered | Child explores each seed with and without magnifier; describes each seed and places most or all of the seeds into groups based on different characteristics. |
| Fully Mastered | Child explores each seed with and without a magnifier; describes each seed by various characteristics, then regroups, using other categories. |

# SORTING SEEDS

**Investigation:** Observing seeds

**Process Skills:** Observing, classifying, comparing

**Materials:** Several types, sizes, and colors of seeds/beans (a bag of 18-bean soup mix may be purchased at any grocery store and is useful for this activity), hand lens

## Procedure:

*Getting started:*
(Do this activity after "Where Do Seeds Come From?") Distribute an assortment of the same types of seeds to each child. Ask them to put together all the seeds that seem to be the same. Encourage them to use magnifiers. Listen to what children say and observe what they do before asking questions. (CAUTIONS: 1. Make sure the seeds are chemical free—that is, not prepared with fungicides or herbicides. 2. Remind children not to eat the seeds. 3. Have children wash their hands with soap and water after doing this activity.)

*Questions to guide children:*
- Which seeds seem to look alike?
- Which seeds feel alike?
- Do any have a black dot on them?
- Are any wrinkled?
- How did you sort or group your seeds?
- Which seed is your favorite? Why?

*What children and adults will do:*
The children will sort (group) their seeds according to different properties or characteristics such as: color, size, shape, texture, and smell. Encourage children to describe the similarities and differences among the seeds. As children begin grouping by an attribute, describe to children what other children are doing—for example, "Julie is putting all the red beans together."

*Closure:*
Have each child share something about his or her seeds. If time, ask the children to hold up their largest seed, smallest, most wrinkled, and so forth.

## Follow-up Activity:

Ask children to regroup their seeds/beans in a different way. Work with a friend and find a new way together.

## Center Connection:

Place the leftover seeds at the center for further observation.

## Outside Connection:

Give each child a large sock to put on over his or her shoe. Go for a walk in a field. When you return, have children remove their socks and look for seeds that may be sticking to them. This will probably be most effective in summer or early fall. (CAUTION: Many fields today have been sprayed with pesticides and herbicides. Try to select fields that are known to be chemically free. Have children wash their hands with soap and water after doing this activity.)

## Literature Connection:

*The Button Box*
by Margarette S. Reid, Puffin, reprint, 1995.

*Make a Match: A Preschool Sorting Game*
by Tish Rabe, Innovative Kids, 2006.

# SORTING SEEDS

- **Science A-2** Develops increased ability to observe and discuss common properties, differences and comparisons among objects and materials.

- **Language Development A-3** Understands an increasingly complex and varied vocabulary.

- **Mathematics C-2** Shows increasing abilities to match, sort, put in series, and regroup objects according to one or two attributes such as shape or size.

- **Social & Emotional Development C-1** Increases abilities to sustain interactions with peers by helping, sharing and discussion.

  *Source: "Head Start Child Outcomes Framework." See Appendix A in this book for the framework.

## What To Look For

| | |
|---|---|
| **Not Yet** | Child picks up the seeds but does not attempt to describe or sort them. |
| **Emerging** | Child looks at each seed; watches as others notice and describe the characteristics of the seeds. |
| **Almost Mastered** | Child explores each seed with and without a magnifier; describes each seed and places most or all of the seeds into groups based on different characteristics. |
| **Fully Mastered** | Child explores each seed with and without a magnifier; describes each seed and asks questions; groups seeds by various characteristics, then regroups, using other categories. |

# FAMILY PAGE / PÁGINA PARA LA FAMILIA

## SORTING SEEDS

### Family Science Connection:

Have the **family** collect seeds from foods eaten over the week. Put the seeds on a plate where they can dry out. Each day as the seeds dry out, **observe** how the seeds are changing. If you have a magnifying glass, use it to get a closer look at each seed. When all the various seeds are dried, get a muffin pan or old egg carton and begin to **sort the seeds into groups.** You might decide to group the seeds by size or shape. Or allow the **younger members of the family** to choose how they want to **categorize the seeds.** As the seeds are being grouped into a sorter, have the children **talk** about the **differences and similarities** among the groups.

**Comments or questions** that may add a *sense of wonder* to this activity.

- Which group of seeds are your favorite? What do you like about them? Their shape? Their wrinkled texture? Their size?

- I wonder—if we planted the seeds, do you think they would grow?

## AGRUPANDO SEMILLAS

### Ciencia en familia:

En **familia**, guarden las semillas de comidas que prepararon durante la semana. Ponga las semillas en un plato dónde se puedan secar. Cada día, a medida que las semillas se secan, **observe** cómo están cambiando las semillas. Si usted tiene una lupa, úsela para ver de cerca cada semilla. Cuando las diferentes semillas estén secas, consigan un molde para panecillos o una cartera de huevos vieja y **ordenen las semillas por grupos.** Pueden agrupar las semillas por tamaño o forma. O permítale a **los miembros más jóvenes de la familia** escoger cómo quieren **categorizar las semillas.** A medida que están agrupando las semillas, pídale a los niños que **hablen** acerca de las **diferencias y parecidos** entre los grupos.

**Comentarios o preguntas** que pueden *despertar curiosidad* en esta actividad:

- ¿Cuál es tu grupo de semillas favorito? ¿Qué te gusta de estas semillas? ¿Su forma? ¿Su textura arrugada? ¿Su tamaño?

- Si plantamos las semillas, ¿piensas que crecerán?

# HOW ARE SEEDS ALIKE?

**Investigation:** Sorting seeds by one attribute

**Process Skills:** Observing, classifying, comparing

**Materials:** Several types, sizes, and colors of seeds/beans in individual, plastic sealable bags (a bag of 18-bean soup mix may be purchased at any grocery store and is useful for this activity); one "happy face" sorting mat per child; hand lenses

## Procedure:

*Getting started:*
(Do this activity after "Sorting Seeds.") Have sorting mats ready for each child (see "Simple Graphing for Young Children," p. xxxiii). Distribute one bag of seeds to each child. Let children explore their seeds. Encourage them to use hand lenses.

*Questions and comments to guide children:*
- What can you tell me about the seeds you put together?
- Why did you choose those seeds?
- Are all the seeds you chose exactly the same?
- How are they different?
- These seeds all seem to be black.

*What children and adults will do:*
After an exploration time, have the children put all the seeds on the left side of the "happy face" sorting mat, or in a pile on the table. Call out a characteristic for a seed—for example, *white, wrinkled,* or *bumpy.* Any seed(s) that have that characteristic should be moved over to the "happy face" side of the mat. Leave all the rest of the seeds on the left-hand side of the mat. Have children share their choices with the group and put them all back on the left-hand side to sort again with a new property.

*Closure:*
As soon as you think children have the idea, let them take turns calling out a property to sort the seeds.

## Follow-up Activity:

Give the children other objects to sort using their sorting mats (e.g., buttons, crayons, or small assorted objects).

## Center Connection:

Children will initiate their own game of sorting the seeds if you leave some of the sorting mats and a collection of the seeds in the center.

## Literature Connection:

*Seeds: Pop! Stick! Glide!*
by Patricia Lauber, Crown, 1988.

*The Empty Pot*
by Demi, Henry Holt and Company, 1990.

## Assessment Outcomes & Possible Indicators*

- **Science A-4** Develops growing abilities to collect, describe and record information through a variety of means, including discussions, drawings, maps and charts.

- **Language Development A-2** Shows progress in understanding and following simple and multiple-step directions.

- **Mathematics C-2** Shows increasing abilities to match, sort, put in series, and regroup objects according to one or two attributes such as shape or size.

  *Source: "Head Start Child Outcomes Framework." See Appendix A in this book for the framework.

## What To Look For

| Not Yet | Child explores the seeds but does not attempt to compare or group seeds by a property. |
|---|---|
| Emerging | Child watches others use the sorting mat before participating; does not independently choose which seeds move to the "happy face" side of the mat; instead, follows what others do. |
| Almost Mastered | Child participates in the sorting mat activity by following the adult's directions and then regroups seeds as other children name different properties by which to sort. |
| Fully Mastered | Child participates in the sorting mat activity and sometimes leads the group by calling out a new property by which to sort; asks questions about the seeds. |

# SOAKING SEEDS

**Investigation:** Observing seeds absorb water, change size, and become soft

**Process Skills:** Observing, comparing

**Materials:** *Per child:* One lima bean seed, hand lens, small cup, water, a few pieces of spaghetti or rice

## Procedure:

*Getting started:*
(Do this activity after "Water Magic.") Give a lima bean seed and hand lens to each child. Ask children to observe the seed and tell you what they see. (CAUTIONS: 1. Water spilled on the floor can be a slip/fall hazard. Wipe up any spilled water immediately. 2. Make sure all electrical receptacles in the classroom are GFCI [ground fault circuit interrupter]–protected to protect children from shock when using water.)

*Questions to guide children:*
- What does the outside of the seed look like?
- How does it feel?
- What do you think it looks like inside? How can we find out?
- What can we do to soften the seed up so we can open it up and look inside?
- What will happen if the seed is put in water?
- Do you think it will change?
- How can we find out?

*What children and adults will do:*
Ask children to try to open their seed. Give them a minute or so to try, then ask if the children have any suggestions on how to soften the seed so they can look inside. Have children examine a piece of uncooked spaghetti or rice and ask if they know how uncooked spaghetti and rice get soft and chewy. They may remember what happened to the objects soaked in water in the activity "Water Magic." Hopefully they will suggest putting the seed into water. If not, remind them of what happened in the "Water Magic" activity. Ask what they think will happen if the seed is soaked in water overnight. Listen to children's predictions. Ask if they think the bean will change in some way. Will it become smaller, stay the same, or become larger?

*Closure:*
Invite the children to look at their seeds several times during the day to see what is happening.

## Follow-up Activity:

Use the activity "Seeds to Plants" the following day.

## Center Connection:

Leave the soaking beans where children can check on them.

## Literature Connection:

*Carrot Seed*
by Ruth Krauss, HarperTrophy, 1991.

*The Big Seed*
by Ellen Howard, Simon & Schuster, 1993.

# SOAKING SEEDS

- **Science A-3** Begins to participate in simple investigations to test observations, discuss and draw conclusions and form generalizations.

- **Science B-4** Shows increased awareness and beginning understanding of changes in materials and cause-effect relationships.

- **Approaches to Learning B-2** Demonstrates increasing ability to set goals and develop and follow through on plans.

- **Approaches to Learning C-2** Grows in recognizing and solving problems through active explorations, including trial and error, and interactions and discussions with peers and adults.

   *Source: "Head Start Child Outcomes Framework." See Appendix A in this book for the framework.

## What To Look For

| Not Yet | Child shows no interest in opening the lima bean seed or trying to explore the inside of the seed. |
| --- | --- |
| Emerging | Child attempts to open the seed but has no suggestions as to how to open it. |
| Almost Mastered | Child attempts to open the seed; when reminded, child eagerly puts the seed in water and predicts what will happen to it. |
| Fully Mastered | Child attempts to open the seed, then suggests putting it in the water to soften it; predicts the seed will change in some other way as well and checks on it often throughout the day. |

# SEEDS TO PLANTS

**Investigation:** Observing the inside of the lima bean seed

**Process Skills:** Observing, comparing

**Materials:** *Per child:* Three pre-soaked lima bean seeds from the previous day's activity ("Soaking Seeds"), hand lens, large, moist paper towel, small plastic plate

## Procedure:

*Getting started:*
Give children their own cup containing their soaking seed from the previous day's activity. Ask children to describe any changes they notice.

*Questions to guide children:*
- How have the seeds changed?
- What does the inside of the seed look like?
- Can you see light through the seed coat?
- Can you see the two small leaves inside the seed?

*What children and adults will do:*
After comparing the sizes, texture, shape, and firmness of their lima beans, ask children what they think the seed will look like inside. Listen to their ideas. Have the children follow you as you open your seed as follows:
- Carefully remove the outer "seed coat" of the seed (some children may need help). Tell them the seed coat protects the seed before it is planted.
- Open the seed at the seam between the two halves and observe the little plant that is represented by the two small leaves inside.
- Ask the children what they think will happen if they put a pre-soaked lima bean seed in between wet paper towels for a few days? Discuss their ideas.

*Closure:*
Give children two pre-soaked lima beans each. Have them loosely wrap the seeds in between a moist paper towel and place them on a plastic plate. Keep the towel moist at all times. Have the children place their seed plates in a special place in the classroom so they can check on them daily. (CAUTION: Seeds kept in wet paper towels for several <u>weeks</u> can develop mold spores and active mold bodies. Some children are highly allergic to these molds.)

## Follow-up Activity:

Have the children carefully unwrap their seeds daily to make their observations. Make sure their paper towels stay moist. Plant some of the seeds in the garden or in individual cups.

## Center Connection:

Leave some of the planted seeds in a window for children to measure as they grow (see "Simple Graphing for Young Children," p. xxxiii).

## Literature Connections:

*This Year's Garden*
by Cynthia Rylant, Aladdin Books, 1984.

*Pumpkin, Pumpkin*
by Jeanne Titherington, Greenwillow, 1986.

*The Carrot Seed*
by Ruth Krauss, Harper Junior, 1945, 1989.

*How Seeds Travel: Popguns and Parachutes*
by Jane Moncure, Child's World, 1990.

## Fingerplay:

*I dig, dig, dig and plant some seeds*
*I rake, rake, rake and pull some weeds*
*I wait and watch and soon I know*
*My garden sprouts and starts to grow*

(author unknown)

# SEEDS TO PLANTS

- **Science B-1** Expands knowledge of and abilities to observe, describe and discuss the natural world, materials, living things and natural processes.

- **Science B-4** Shows increased awareness and beginning understanding of changes in materials and cause-effect relationships.

- **Language Development A-1** Demonstrates increasing ability to attend to and understand conversations, stories, songs, and poems.

- **Language Development B-3** Uses an increasingly complex and varied spoken vocabulary.

*Source: "Head Start Child Outcomes Framework." See Appendix A in this book for the framework.

## What To Look For

| Not Yet | Child shows no interest in finding out how the seeds have changed. |
|---|---|
| Emerging | Child watches others explore the lima bean seed and follows the adult's directions in opening the seed and placing it in a towel. |
| Almost Mastered | Child discusses the changes in the seed, follows the adult's directions in opening the seed and placing it in the towel. |
| Fully Mastered | Child recognizes and discusses changes in the seed; asks questions and follows adult's directions in completing the activity; eagerly checks on the seeds each day and makes comparisons between different seeds and the size of the plants. |

## SEEDS TO PLANTS

### Family Science Connection:

**At home collect** three or four different kinds of seeds. Keep them in a dish with a damp paper towel for a week or two. On a daily basis, **observe** what changes take place. One seed may sprout while another seed does nothing. At the end of the experiment, **explore** each seed by breaking it open and seeing what is inside. **Talk** about how the inside of the seed looks.

**Comments or questions** that may add a *sense of wonder* to this activity:

· What looks different today about each of the seeds? Is each seed growing or shrinking? Has the color changed? Does it smell? Does the seed feel harder or softer?

· Today let's open each seed and see what's inside. Tell me what you see.

## DE SEMILLAS A PLANTAS

### Ciencia en familia:

**En casa coleccionen** tres o cuatro clases diferentes de semillas. Guárdenlas en un recipiente con una toalla de papel mojada por una o dos semanas. **Observen** diariamente los cambios que ocurren. Una semilla podría brotar mientras que otra semilla no sufre ningún cambio. Al finalizar el experimento, **exploren** cada semilla abriéndola y viendo lo que tiene dentro. **Hablen** de cómo se ven las semillas por dentro.

**Comentarios o preguntas** que pueden *despertar curiosidad* en esta actividad:

· ¿Qué se ve diferente hoy acerca de una de las semillas? ¿Está creciendo o encogiéndose cada semilla? ¿Ha cambiado el color? ¿Huele? ¿Se siente la semilla más dura o más blanda?

· Abramos hoy cada semilla y veamos qué hay dentro. Dime qué ves.

# TERRARIUMS

**Investigation:** Planting a terrarium

**Process Skills:** Observing, comparing

**Materials:** *Per child:* One container (clear 2-liter soda bottle with top cut off, gallon jar, OR fish bowl with hole large enough for hand OR large clear sandwich box); aquarium gravel, crushed charcoal (charcoal briquettes), potting soil, spoon, small plants, spray bottle of water

## Procedure:

*Getting started:*
Have each child choose a container and one plant. Working together follow the planting procedure:

Planting: Put a thin layer of gravel in a clean container. Add a thin layer of charcoal. Add in 2–3 inches of potting soil. Use spoon handle to make planting holes in the soil. Carefully remove plants from their pots and loosen the soil around their roots. Place them in the planting holes and gently press soil around them. Spray with water until soil is moist but not soggy. Add decorations like plastic animals if desired. Cover with a lid. (CAUTION: Make sure children wash their hands with soap and water after doing this activity.)

*Questions and comments to guide children:*
- Tell me about the plant you chose.
- How does it feel?
- How does it feel when you touch the roots?
- What do you think will happen to the plants?
- Our plant seems to be watering itself!

*What children and adults will do:*
Put the garden where it will get plenty of light but not direct sunlight, which would make it too hot. Watch it for a day or two. If the container fogs up, take off the top for a few hours to let the garden "breathe." Then put the top back on. Once the garden has the right amount of water, it won't need much care. If the soil looks dry, or if water doesn't drip down the sides anymore, open it and give it a little water. Ask children to check on their plants each day. If the plants get too big, prune carefully with scissors. Pick off dried or yellow leaves. A garden jar can last as long as two years.

## Center Connection:

Keep at least one terrarium in the classroom to observe.

## Literature Connection:

*A Garden Alphabet*
by Isabel Wilner, Dutton, 1991.

*Garden*
by Robert Maass, Henry Holt, 1998.

*Sandbox Scientist: Real Science Activities for Little Kids*
by Michael Elsohn Ross, Chicago Review Press, 1995.

# TERRARIUMS

## Assessment Outcomes & Possible Indicators*

- **Science B-1** Expands knowledge of and abilities to observe, describe and discuss the natural world, materials, living things and natural processes.

- **Science B-3** Develops growing awareness of ideas and language related to attributes of time and temperature.

- **Language Development B-1** Develops increasing abilities to understand and use language to communicate information, experiences, ideas, opinions, needs, questions and for other varied purposes.

- **Language Development B-3** Demonstrates increasing ability to set goals and develop and follow through on plans.

  *Source: "Head Start Child Outcomes Framework." See Appendix A in this book for the framework.

## What To Look For

| | |
|---|---|
| **Not Yet** | Child shows no interest in making a terrarium although he or she may want to play with the materials. |
| **Emerging** | With a great deal of help from an adult, child completes some of the steps to make a terrarium; explores some of the materials but does not discuss the materials or the process. |
| **Almost Mastered** | With some assistance from an adult, child makes a terrarium, completing all the steps; explores each material and describes each one; asks questions about the use of at least one of the materials. |
| **Fully Mastered** | Child eagerly makes a terrarium, may ask to make more than one; questions the use of each of the materials, learns the name of each and describes each; visits the classroom terrarium often and shares observations with others. |

# AN EAR OF CORN

**Investigation:**  Exploring an ear of corn

**Process Skills:**  Observing, communicating

**Materials:**  Ears of corn in their husks, newspaper

## Procedure:

*Getting started:*
Working in pairs, let the children explore the cornhusks. Watch what they do. Listen to what they say. After a few minutes encourage children to find out what is inside their cornhusks.

*Questions to guide children:*
- What does the husk feel like?
- How can we find out what's inside?
- What does the silk feel like?
- Why do you think the corn is covered with silk?
- How does your Mom (or other adult) cook corn at home?

*What children and adults will do:*
After an exploration period, children will begin pulling off the husks and silk. Encourage them to put the silk in one pile and the husks in another. They will talk about eating corn once they discover it. Have children look at the kernels. Ask them what they look like. If they don't make the connection to seeds, show them some other seeds and ask them if the corn kernels look like seeds.

*Closure:*
Tell children you are going to cook the corn so they can taste it. Find out how many have eaten corn on the cob. Cook and enjoy (see Follow-up Activity).

## Follow-up Activity:

Brush the ears of corn with melted margarine. Replace husks (without the silk) around the ear of corn. Fasten with rubber bands. Cook on full power in a microwave oven, allowing one minute for each ear and leave at least one inch of space between ears. (CAUTION: Make sure the ear of corn is cooled off after coming out of the microwave before allowing children to handle it.)

## Center Connection:

Put husks, silk, and one ear of corn in the science center with hand lenses.

## Literature Connection:

*Corn Is Maize, the Gift of the Indian*
by Aliki, Harper Trophy, 1986.

*Three Stalks of Corn*
by Leo Politi, Aladdin Books, 1994.

*The Ears of Corn: An Ike and Mem Story*
by Patrick Jennings, Holiday House, 2003.

# AN EAR OF CORN

## Assessment Outcomes & Possible Indicators*

- **Science B-1** Expands knowledge of and abilities to observe, describe and discuss the natural world, materials, living things and natural processes.

- **Language Development B-1** Develops increasing abilities to initiate and respond appropriately in conversation and discussions with peers and adults.

- **Language Development B-2** Progresses in abilities to understand and use language to communicate information, experiences, ideas, opinions, needs, questions and for other varied purposes.

- **Social & Emotional Development C-1** Increases abilities to sustain interactions with peers by helping, sharing and discussion.

  *Source: "Head Start Child Outcomes Framework." See Appendix A in this book for the framework

## What To Look For

| Not Yet | Child shows no interest in exploring an ear of corn. |
|---|---|
| Emerging | Child watches as partner explores the ear of corn and pulls off some of the husk and silk. |
| Almost Mastered | Child works with a partner to explore the corn, pulling off the husk and silk; listens to and discusses with partner discoveries about the corn; participates in eating the corn. |
| Fully Mastered | Child eagerly explores the corn with a partner, discussing and asking questions about corn of both adults and peers; describes personal connections to corn such as eating or growing corn at home. |

## AN EAR OF CORN

### Family Science Connection:

**At the market** look at all the **different kinds of corn** sold and **talk** together about their **similarities and differences**. Mom, dad, brothers, and sisters can also **point out** that corn is often mixed with other foods for better flavor, texture, or looks.

**At home** during dinner see if the family can **point out** all the ways we eat and use corn. **Discuss the feel, smell, look, and sound of corn** in all its forms.

**Grow** corn and other vegetables and **compare** homegrown to store bought.

**Comments or questions** that may add a *sense of wonder* to this activity:

· Let's name all the different ways we cook and eat corn!

· I wonder if corn tastes sweeter if it is cooked or eaten raw.

## UNA ESPIGA DE MAIZ

### Ciencia en familia:

**En el mercado**, busquen las **diferentes clases de maíz** que se venden y **hablen** juntos acerca de sus **parecidos** y **diferencias**. Mamá, papa, o los hermanos también pueden **señalar** que el maíz se mezcla con otras comidas para que tengan un mejor sabor, textura y apariencia.

**En casa** durante la cena, vea si su familia puede **señalar** todas las maneras en que comemos y usamos el maíz. **Platiquen sobre cómo se siente, huele, ve, y suena el maíz** en todas sus formas.

**Siembre** maíz y otras verduras y **comparen** los que crecen en casa con los que compran en la tienda.

**Comentarios o preguntas** que pueden *despertar curiosidad* en esta actividad:

· ¡Nombremos todas las diferentes maneras de cocinar y comer maíz!

· Me pregunto si el maíz sabe más dulce si es cocinado o si se come crudo.

# POPPING UP SOME CHANGE

**Investigation:** Investigating how heat changes things

**Process Skills:** Observing and comparing

**Materials:** Unpopped popcorn, a popcorn popper, paper towels or cups

## Procedure:

*Getting started:*
Hand out some unpopped popcorn kernels to the children. Ask the children to tell you about the kernels. Show the children that your kernels are just like their kernels. Put your kernels in a popcorn popper and make some popcorn. Make sure the children know that the popcorn popper heats up the popcorn to make it pop. Pass out some popped popcorn to the children and ask them to tell you about the popped popcorn. Focus on the differences between the unpopped and the popped popcorn.

*Questions to guide children:*
- What can you tell us about the unpopped kernels?
- What is the color of the kernels? Are the kernels hard or soft, shiny or dull, big or little?
- What does the popper do to make the popcorn pop? (heats up the popcorn)
- What can you say about the popped popcorn?
- How is the popped popcorn different from the unpopped kernels?
- What changes did the heat make in the popcorn?

*What children and adults will do:*
This is a science investigation that the children can eventually eat. There will, however, be the temptation to eat the popped popcorn before it is carefully investigated. Tell the children they can eat their popped popcorn after they have carefully observed it.

*Closure:*
Ask children to draw pictures of popcorn *before* it is popped and *after* it is popped. Have the children look at each other's pictures to see if they can tell which is the "before" (popping) picture and which is the "after" (popping) picture. Also, have children glue 10 kernels of popped corn and 10 kernels of unpopped corn in two parallel lines on a sheet of paper and compare them.

## Follow-up Activity:

The hard cover on the kernel is still on the popped popcorn. Challenge the children to find the kernel cover on the popped popcorn. From one small cup of kernels, find out how many small cups of popped popcorn you can get.

## Art Connection:

Have the children use popcorn kernels and popped popcorn in their art projects. The kernels and the popped popcorn can be pasted to drawings. Popped popcorn can be strung on string to make long strands.

## Literature Connection:

*The Popcorn Shop*
by Alice Low, Scholastic, 1994.

*Popcorn!*
by Elaine Landau, Charlesbridge, 2003.

## Assessment Outcomes & Possible Indicators*

- **Science B-4** Shows increased awareness and beginning understanding of changes in materials and cause-effect relationships.

- **Language Development B-3** Demonstrates increasing ability to set goals and develop and follow through on plans.

- **Literacy D-2** Begins to represent stories and experiences through pictures, dictation, and in play.

- **Creative Arts B-2** Progresses in abilities to create drawing, paintings, models, and other art creations that are more detailed, creative or realistic.

  *Source: "Head Start Child Outcomes Framework." See Appendix A in this book for the framework.

## What To Look For

| | |
|---|---|
| **Not Yet** | Child shows no interest in exploring the kernels or discussing their properties or in drawing a picture of the kernels. |
| **Emerging** | Child holds some kernels and listens as others describe their properties; eats the popcorn but does not draw a recognizable picture of the kernels. |
| **Almost Mastered** | Child explores the kernels, describing some of their properties; comments as the popcorn pops; eats the popcorn and draws "before and after" pictures of the kernels. |
| **Fully Mastered** | Child eagerly explores the kernels, describing their properties; comments and asks questions as the kernels pop; eats the popcorn; draws "before and after" pictures of the popcorn and dictates a story about how the popcorn kernels changed. |

# FAMILY PAGE / PÁGINA PARA LA FAMILIA

## POPPING UP SOME CHANGE

### Family Science Connection:

Next time you make popcorn, explore unpopped popcorn with your child. Notice that the kernels (seeds) are hard, small, and yellow/tan in color. After the popcorn has popped, explore the popcorn again, noticing that it is soft, large, and white in color. The corn changed from hard to soft, from small to large, and from yellow/tan to white. Heat from the popcorn popper made the changes. When you are cooking, explore and talk with your child about what the food is like before it is cooked and again what the food is like after it is cooked. Point out that heat sometimes changes things.

**Comments or questions** that may add a *sense of wonder* to this activity:

- What can we say about this uncooked food (popcorn, apples, potatoes)?

- How does this uncooked food feel, look, and taste?

- What can we say about this cooked food?

- How does this cooked food feel, look, and taste?

- How did cooking change the food?

## UN ESTALLIDO CAMBIO

### Ciencia en familia:

La próxima vez que prepare palomitas de maíz, explore con su hijo(a) el grano de maíz sin estallar. Vea que las semillas son duras, pequeñas y de color amarillo. Después de que ha estallado el grano, explore la palomita de maíz, advirtiendo que es suave, grande y de color blanco. El maíz cambió de duro a suave, de pequeño a grande, y de amarillo a blanco. El calor hizo los cambios. Cuando esté cocinando, explore y hable con su hijo(a) acerca de cómo es la comida antes de ser cocinada y cómo es la comida después de ser cocina. Señale que a veces el calor cambia las cosas.

**Comentarios o preguntas** que pueden *despertar curiosidad* en esta actividad:

- ¿Qué podemos decir acerca de esta comida sin cocinar (palomitas, manzanas, papas)?

- ¿Cómo se siente, cómo se ve y a qué sabe esta comida sin cocinar?

- ¿Qué podemos decir acerca de esta comida cocinada?

- ¿Cómo se siente, cómo se ve y a qué sabe esta comida cocinada?

- ¿Cómo cambió la comida al cocinarla?

# SEEDS AS FOOD

**Investigation:** Grinding corn (a two-day project)

**Process Skills:** Comparing, classifying, communicating

**Materials:** Corncobs with dried kernels of corn, fresh corncobs, metates (grinding stones), bowls

## Procedure:

*Getting started:*
Let children handle the corncobs and talk about what they see and feel. Give them time to explore the differences between the two kinds of corn before asking questions.

*Questions to guide children:*
- What do you notice about the corncobs?
- What do they feel like?
- How are they the same? Different?
- How could we get the corn kernels off the cob?
- Some of the kernels are different colors.

*What children and adults will do:*
Children will handle the corn, then begin picking off the kernels after you encourage them to use their fingers. They will notice the texture and colors.

*Closure:*
Have the children put all the dried kernels in one bowl and the fresh kernels in another. Tell them you are going to soak the dried kernels in water overnight. Ask them to predict what will happen.

## Follow-up Activities:

After letting the kernels soak overnight in water with a little lime juice, let the children take turns grinding the corn on a metate. On another day bring in pea pods and let children open them to discover the peas. Let them compare the number of peas in each pod. Tell them that peas are also seeds. Let children taste the peas (they are good raw, but could also be cooked).

Bring in Indian corn for children to observe. Encourage them to use their hand lenses. Try planting the entire cob. Dig a deep hole (as deep as the cob is long) and place the cob in the hole, vertically. Cover with soil, keep it watered, and see what happens! When the plant starts to sprout, let children measure the growth by marking on a plain stick.

Later, after thoroughly investigating seeds we eat, bring in seeds we do not eat such as those from an avocado, a plum, and an apple.

On another day, make popcorn, reminding children of the other ways the corn is used as food.

## Center Connection:

Save some of the dried kernels to put in the science center with a hand lens.

## Literature Connection:

*Corn Is Maize, The Gift of the Indian*
by Aliki, HarperTrophy, 1986.

*This Year's Garden*
by Cynthia Rylant, Bradbury Press, 1984.

*The Popcorn Shop*
by Alice Low, Scholastic, 1993.

*I Like Corn (Good Food)*
by Robin Pickering, Children's Press, 2000.

*My Cooking Spoon*
by Joanne Barkin, Warner Juvenile Books, 1989.

# SEEDS AS FOOD

- **Science A-1** Begins to use senses and a variety of tools and simple measuring devices to gather information, investigate materials and observe processes and relationships.

- **Science A-2** Develops increased ability to observe and discuss common properties, differences and comparisons among objects and materials.

- **Science A-3** Begins to participate in simple investigations to test observations, discuss and draw conclusions and form generalizations.

- **Science B-1** Expands knowledge of and abilities to observe, describe and discuss the natural world, materials, living things and natural processes.

- **Language Development B-1** Develops increasing abilities to understand and use language to communicate information, experiences, ideas, opinions, needs, questions and for other varied purposes.

- **Language Development B-2** Progresses in abilities to initiate and respond appropriately in conversation and discussions with peers and adults.

- **Physical Health & Development A-2** Grows in hand-eye coordination in building with blocks, putting together puzzles, reproducing shapes and patterns, stringing beads and using scissors.

    *Source: "Head Start Child Outcomes Framework." See Appendix A in this book for the framework.

## What To Look For

| Not Yet | Child shows no interest in exploring the fresh and dried kernels. |
|---|---|
| Emerging | Child watches others remove kernels from the cob before attempting to do the same; does not separate the two kinds of kernels. |
| Almost Mastered | Child participates in removing the kernels from the cobs, then separates the two kinds of kernels; discusses some of the differences; attempts to use the metate. |
| Fully Mastered | Child participates in removing the kernels from the cob, separates the two kinds of kernels, discusses in detail the differences; eagerly grinds the corn using the metate and asks many questions about the process. |

## SEEDS AS FOOD

### Family Science Connection:

**At home** during dinner **share** favorite corn recipes. Maybe these food ideas are old family favorites that can be cooked sometime during the week. **Talk** about all the ingredients that make these food ideas so tasty. As the cooking takes place, **count, measure, smell, and describe** the ingredients that make the corn recipes so special.

**At a family picnic** have family groups bring some unique corn potluck cooking. Then **compare** the different corn recipes.

**Comments or questions** that may add a *sense of wonder* to this activity:

· I wonder what ingredients are in your favorite corn dish.

· Let's talk about the different ways we cook corn.

## SEMILLAS COMO ALIMENTO

### Ciencia en familia:

**En casa** durante la cena **comparta sus** recetas favoritas en las que se use maíz. Quizás estas ideas de comida son recetas familiares de antaño, y puedan prepararlas alguna vez durante la semana. **Hablen** acerca de todos los ingredientes que hacen que estas comidas sean tan deliciosas. Cuando cocinen una de estas recetas, **cuenten, midan, huelan, y describan** los ingredientes que hacen tan especial a esta receta de maíz.

**En una comida familiar en el parque** pida a otras familias que traigan diferentes comidas de maíz para compartirlas. Después **comparen** las diferentes recetas de maíz.

**Comentarios o preguntas** que pueden *despertar curiosidad* en esta actividad:

· Me pregunto cuáles son los ingredientes en tu platillo favorito de maíz.

· Hablemos acerca de las diferentes maneras en que podemos cocinar maíz.

# SEED WREATH

**Investigation:** Using a variety of seeds to make a collage or wreath

**Process Skills:** Observing, collecting, comparing, communicating

**Materials:** A variety of seeds from fruits, vegetables, flowers, and grasses; nontoxic glue; paper plate or sturdy round pieces of cardboard

## Procedure:

*Getting started:*
Have the children help you begin saving seeds from the fruits and vegetables served at breakfast, lunch, and snack time (e.g., watermelon, orange, corn). You can also find seeds in grasses and flowers and sometimes in pods. Let the seeds dry. Plan this activity for when you have collected enough for a group of children to use. Ahead of time cut holes in the middle of the paper plates or round pieces of cardboard, producing a wreath shape. Let children look at and touch all the different seeds. (CAUTION: Remind children not to eat seeds used in this activity.)

*Questions and comments to guide children:*
• How are your seeds the same? Different?
• Do you remember where we got these seeds?
• I see Jana is making a pattern with her seeds.

*What children and adults will do:*
Observe which seeds children seem to be most interested in. Suggest they begin making a collage or picture with their seeds. Some children will make patterns, some will make pictures, and others will put down seeds randomly. Talk to children about the seeds they are using.

*Closure:*
Have each child say something about his or her collage. Display the collages for all to see.

## Center Connection:

Add a variety of seeds to the art area so children can continue to use them in collages. Continue to collect seeds from the fruits and vegetables served at school. Let children decide what they want to do with them.

## Literature Connection:

*More Than Moccasins: A Kid's Activity Guide to Traditional North American Indian Life*
by Laurie Carlson, Chicago Review Press, 1994.

*The Tiny Seed*
by Eric Carle, Picture Book Studio, 1987.

# SEED WREATH

- **Science A-2** Develops increased ability to observe and discuss common properties, differences and comparisons among objects and materials.

- **Mathematics C-1** Enhances abilities to recognize, duplicate and extend simple patterns using a variety of materials.

- **Creative Arts B-1** Gains ability in using different art media and materials in a variety of ways for creative expression and representation.

  *Source: "Head Start Child Outcomes Framework." See Appendix A in this book for the framework.

## What To Look For

| Not Yet | Child shows no interest in exploring all the different kinds of seeds or in making a seed wreath. |
|---|---|
| Emerging | Child watches others exploring the seeds; examines some of them but does not discuss the differences; glues seeds randomly on paper. |
| Almost Mastered | Child examines all the different seeds; discusses their properties then uses many seeds to make a wreath. |
| Fully Mastered | Child eagerly examines all the seeds; discusses their properties and begins to group them; makes a wreath using most or all of the different kinds of seeds, and making a pattern or picture on the paper; asks questions about the seeds while working. |

## SEED WREATH

**Teachers,** please have the children participate in this take-home activity before they make the classroom wreath. This take-home will help you prepare the materials for the lesson.

### Family Science Connection:

For the next week have the **family** save all the seeds from foods that have been eaten or found in the yard. **Talk** about what seeds are and why we know seeds are so important. To help keep the seeds in some kind of **order,** label an egg carton with the names of the different seeds you are **collecting.** As the seeds are collected, put them under the labeled name in the egg carton. All orange seeds go in one space, all chili seeds in another, and all apple seeds in another. Put the big seeds like the avocado in a bag and label it. At the end of the week, send the seeds to school so the children may continue their discussion about seeds and make a seed wreath.

**Comments or questions** that may add a *sense of wonder* to this activity:

- Let's put some of the seeds in order by size. Which seed is the biggest and which seed is the smallest?

- Do the bigger seeds have bigger fruit and the smaller seeds smaller fruit?

## GUIRNALDA DE SEMILLAS

**Maestros,** por favor piden que los niños participen en esta actividad en casa antes de hacer la guirnalda en clase. Esta actividad los ayudará en preparar los materiales para la lección.

### Ciencia en familia:

Pídale a la **familia** que durante la próxima semana guarden todas las semillas de todos los alimentos que han comido o encontrado en el patio. **Hablen** acerca de lo que son las semillas y por qué sabemos que las semillas son tan importantes. Para ayudar a mantener las semillas en **orden,** ponga etiquetas en una cartera de huevos con los nombres de las semillas que están **coleccionando.** Conforme vayan coleccionando las semillas pónganlas en la etiqueta correspondiente en la cartera de huevos. Todas las semillas de naranja en un espacio, todas las semillas de chile en otro, y todas las semillas de manzanas en otro. Pongan las semillas grandes como la de aguacate en una bolsa y pongan una etiqueta. Al finalizar la semana, manden las semillas a la escuela para que los niños sigan aprendiendo más acerca de las semillas y que hagan una guirnalda de semillas.

**Comentarios o preguntas** que pueden *despertar curiosidad* en esta actividad:

- Pongamos las semillas según su tamaño. ¿Cuál semilla es la más grande y cuál es la más pequeña?

- ¿Dan las semillas más grandes frutas más grandes y las semillas más pequeñas frutas más pequeñas?

# PONDERING PUMPKINS: THE OUTSIDES

**Investigation:** Investigating the outside properties of pumpkins

**Process Skills:** Observing and communicating

**Materials:** One or more pumpkins and one strip of paper for each pumpkin. Each strip should be about 2 inches wide and from 2 to 3 feet in length (or bigger around than the biggest pumpkin).

## Procedure:

*Getting started:*
Set out a few different-size pumpkins for small groups of children to explore. Ask the children to look at and touch the pumpkins to find out something about pumpkins. Invite the children to tell what they have learned from exploring their pumpkins.

*Questions and comments to guide children:*
- What can you say about pumpkins?
- Are pumpkins hard or soft? Are they rough or smooth? Are they heavy or light?
- What side of the pumpkin do you think rested on the ground?
- Each pumpkin was attached to a plant. What part of the pumpkin was attached to the plant?
- Are some pumpkins bigger around than some children?

*What children and adults will do:*
Challenge the children to figure out how to use the strip of paper to measure the "belt size" of the pumpkin. Show the children how to wrap the strip around the widest part of a pumpkin and tear off the excess. See if any pumpkin "belts" fit around any of the children. Hang up the labeled pumpkin belts to show the different belt sizes. Challenge the children to describe how the different pumpkins are alike and different. Record the pumpkin discoveries on chart paper. Ask which pumpkin belt belongs to the biggest pumpkin and which to the smallest pumpkin.

## Follow-up Activity:

Compare pumpkins to other fruit (e.g., squash, apples, melons). Discover where these fruits were attached to the plant.

## Center Connection:

Have different pumpkins for children to explore. Challenge the children to put these pumpkins in a row from the littlest to the biggest. Challenge children to show how these pumpkins rested in the field.

## Literature Connection:

*The Pumpkin Patch*
by Elizabeth King, Dutton, 1990.

*Pumpkins*
by Mary Lyn Ray, Harcourt Brace Jovanovich, 1993.

*Pumpkin Circle: The Story of a Garden*
by George Levenson, Tricycle Press, new ed., 1999.

## Assessment Outcomes & Possible Indicators*

- **Science A-1** Begins to use senses and a variety of tools and simple measuring devices to gather information, investigate materials and observe processes and relationships.

- **Science B-1** Expands knowledge of and abilities to observe, describe and discuss the natural world, materials, living things and natural processes.

- **Mathematics B-4** Shows growth in matching, sorting, putting in series and regrouping objects according to one or two attributes such as color, shape or size.

- **Mathematics C-4** Shows progress in using standard and non-standard measures for length and area of objects.

  *Source: "Head Start Child Outcomes Framework." See Appendix A in this book for the framework.

## What To Look For

| Not Yet | Child shows no interest in exploring or measuring the pumpkins. |
|---|---|
| Emerging | Child watches others, then begins to tentatively explore one pumpkin, touching and lifting it. |
| Almost Mastered | Child explores all the pumpkins, noticing differences in textures, colors, and weights; answers questions about the pumpkins; attempts to measure at least one of the pumpkins using a strip of paper. |
| Fully Mastered | Child eagerly explores each pumpkin using all senses; asks questions about the pumpkins; measures several pumpkins and compares the sizes. |

## PONDERING PUMPKINS: THE OUTSIDES

### Family Science Connection:

Before you carve a scary face into a pumpkin to make a jack-o'-lantern, explore the outside of the pumpkin. Look at the grooves. Try to tell how the pumpkin rested in the field. Notice other pumpkin characteristics (smoothness, hardness, orangeness, bumpiness). Compare the pumpkin with other fruits (squash, tomatoes, apples).

Tell the story of why we call a carved face in a pumpkin a jack-o'-lantern: Jack was a bad boy. As punishment, Jack was only allowed to walk around at night. Some people felt sorry for Jack. They carved a pumpkin and put a candle in the pumpkin. The pumpkin with its candle was known as Jack's lantern. Jack could use this lantern to see in the night.

**Comments or questions** that may add a *sense of wonder* to this activity:

- What is one thing you find special about a pumpkin?

- I'm going to say some things about these two things (a pumpkin and an apple or orange). You tell me whether I'm talking about the pumpkin or the other object.

## ¿QUÉ PASA CON LA CALABAZA? (EXTERIOR)

### Ciencia en familia:

Antes de que corte una cara en la calabaza para el Día de brujas, exploren el exterior de la calabaza. Mire las hendiduras. Imagínese cómo reposaba la calabaza en el campo. Vea las otras características de la calabaza (tersura, dureza, color, irregularidad). Compare la calabaza con otras frutas (calabacita, tomates, manzanas).

Cuente el relato de por qué en inglés se le llama *"jack-o'-lantern"* (Farol de Jack) a una calabaza con una cara cortada: Jack era un niño malo. Como castigo, Jack sólo podía salir a caminar de noche. Algunas personas se compadecieron de Jack. Cortaron una calabaza y pusieron una vela dentro. La calabaza con su vela se conocía como farol de Jack. Jack podía usar este farol para ver de noche.

**Comentarios o preguntas** que pueden *despertar curiosidad* en esta actividad:

- ¿Qué piensas que es especial acerca de la calabaza?

- Voy a decir unas características acerca de estas dos cosas (una calabaza y una manzana o naranja). Dime si estoy hablando de la calabaza o del otro objeto.

# PONDERING PUMPKINS: THE INSIDES

**Investigation:** Investigating the insides of pumpkins

**Process Skills:** Observing and communicating

**Materials:** One or more pumpkins; newspapers to cover table surfaces; small paper cups; a stiff, serrated table knife

## Procedure:

*Getting started:*
Give each group of children a pumpkin. Ask children to tell you what they think is inside the pumpkin.

*Questions and comments to guide children:*
- Is the inside of your pumpkin mostly full or mostly empty?
- What does the stringy stuff do?
- What does the inside feel like?
- It looks like the seeds are attached to something inside the pumpkin.
- How are the seeds alike? How are the seeds different?

*What children and adults will do:*
After finding out what children think the insides of pumpkins are like, have an adult carefully cut open the pumpkins in half horizontally around the middle. There is a great tendency to start pulling things apart without careful observation. Caution against initial, frenzied pulling and digging. Instead, as you ask questions, model careful looking with minimal digging and tearing. As you learn more, dig deeper and explore further in search of answers to questions. Ask the children to share what they have discovered about the insides of pumpkins. Return to some of the questions and find out how different children answer those questions.

## Follow-up Activity:

After washing and drying the seeds on a clean, sanitized surface, bake some of the seeds in an oven (add salt and steak sauce for flavoring) and then invite the children to taste some of the baked seeds. (CAUTION: Remember to check on possible food allergies before tasting.)

Have the children help you glue all the seeds from one pumpkin in a single line (end to end) on strips of paper. Tape the strips of paper together to see how long the single line of seeds from one pumpkin will stretch. You'll be amazed.

Make a pumpkin pie from scratch using the pumpkins from this lesson. Have the children notice the change in the pumpkin material from its raw state to its cooked state (heat changes the properties of materials).

## Center Connection:

Plant some of the dried pumpkin seeds and see if they grow.

## Literature Connection:

*Pumpkin, Pumpkin*
by Jeanne Titherington, Greenwillow, 1986.

*Pumpkin Circle: The Story of a Garden*
by George Levenson, Tricycle Press, new ed., 1999.

# PONDERING PUMPKINS: THE INSIDES

## Assessment Outcomes & Possible Indicators*

- **Science B-1** Expands knowledge of and abilities to observe, describe and discuss the natural world, materials, living things and natural processes.

- **Language Development B-1** Develops increasing abilities to understand and use language to communicate information, experiences, ideas, opinions, needs, questions and for other varied purposes.

- **Language Development B-3** Demonstrates increasing ability to set goals and develop and follow through on plans.

    *Source: "Head Start Child Outcomes Framework." See Appendix A in this book for the framework.

## What To Look For

| Not Yet | Child shows no interest in exploring the inside of a pumpkin. |
|---------|--------------------------------------------------------------|
| Emerging | Child watches others, then begins to tentatively explore the inside of a pumpkin; shows some interest in the seeds and other materials found in the pumpkin. |
| Almost Mastered | Child explores the pumpkin, pulling out seeds and other materials, commenting on what is discovered and answering some of the adult's questions. |
| Fully Mastered | Child eagerly explores the inside of a pumpkin, commenting and asking questions; independently compares and/or counts the seeds. |

## PONDERING PUMPKINS: THE INSIDES

### Family Science Connection:

When it comes to that family event of carving pumpkins into jack-o'-lanterns, take time to explore the outside and inside of the pumpkin as you create your jack-o'-lantern. Notice that the seeds are attached to the "stringy stuff" on the inside of the pumpkin. Marvel at how many seeds there are in one pumpkin. Explore other fruits in your home and see how many seeds are in those fruits and how the seeds are arranged and attached inside the fruits. Compare pumpkin seeds with other seeds.

**Comments or questions** that may add a *sense of wonder* to this activity:

- Are seeds grouped together inside a pumpkin? Are they grouped together in other fruit?

- I wonder if other fruits have as many seeds as a pumpkin.

- Will our seeds grow if we plant them?

- I wonder what part of the pumpkin is used to make pumpkin pie.

## ¿QUÉ PASA CON LA CALABAZA? (INTERIOR)

### Ciencia en familia:

Cuando llegue la faena familiar de cortar calabazas para formar jack-o'-lanterns, tómese el tiempo de explorar el interior y el exterior de la calabaza al crear su jack-o'-lantern. Vea que las semillas están unidas por esa "*cosa fibrosa*" dentro de la calabaza. Maravíllese de la cantidad de semillas que hay en una calabaza. Explore otras frutas en su hogar y vea cuántas semillas hay en esas frutas y cómo están acomodadas y unidas las semillas dentro de las frutas. Compare las semillas de calabaza con otras semillas.

**Comentarios o preguntas** que pueden *calidad de asombro* a esta actividad:

- ¿Están las semillas en grupos dentro de una calabaza? ¿Están agrupadas en otras frutas?

- Me pregunto si otras frutas tienen tantas semillas como una calabaza.

- ¿Crecerán nuestras semillas si las plantamos?

- Me pregunto qué parte de la calabaza se usa para hacer el pastel de calabaza.

## Section 7:

# NATURE WALKS

Every school is located within walking distance of interesting living things: pets, birds, plants, and colors and shapes in nature.

We want children to become good observers so that they will develop the basic observational skills we all need to have. Going on regular nature walks will alert children to the fact there are interesting things to look for no matter where they are. Collecting things in nature allows children to organize and compare objects and to make collections that can be discussed.

Going on a nature walk requires no materials. But we would suggest you get into the habit of giving your children hand lenses to take along. You will soon find that they reach for one whenever there is anything new to examine.

## Nature Walks:
## Selected Internet Resources

**Pets**
- Online Story and Resources About Pets—*www.storyplace.org/preschool/activities/petsonstory.asp*
- Classroom Activities Related to Pets—*www.avma.org/careforanimals/kidscorner/default.asp*

**Nature Walks**
- Learn to Lead Nature Walks for Kids—*www.childrensnatureinstitute.org*
- Growing Socks From Your Sock Walk—*http://scienceforfamilies.allinfo-about.com/features/growingsocks.html*

**Trees**
- Tree Resources for Teachers—*www.educationworld.com/a_lesson/lesson/lesson309.shtml*

# NATURE BRACELETS

**Investigation:** Finding interesting objects in nature to make into a bracelet

**Process Skills:** Observing, classifying

**Materials:** 2-inch-wide masking tape

## Procedure:

*Getting started:*
Make a masking tape bracelet for each child by placing a piece of masking tape around the wrist, sticky side out. Go outside; tell children they can make themselves bracelets by picking up interesting objects such as leaves, grass, flowers, and twigs and placing them on the tape. Have extra tape available so children have a bracelet for each wrist if desired. (CAUTION: Make sure the area is free of poisonous plants and dangerous litter or garbage before doing this activity.)

*Questions and comments to guide children:*

- What did you find?
- Can you find more (leaves) that look the same?
- Can you find something different?
- Can you find something longer? Shorter? A different color? Softer? Harder?
- This leaf smells like grass.

*What children and adults will do:*
Watch carefully to see what children choose to put on their bracelet. Some will make a pattern of just two or three materials; others will choose randomly. Some may discover that sand sticks to tape too! When you see what children are choosing, you may begin to ask questions. To expand their thinking, point out what different children are doing. Children will talk about the objects they chose for their bracelets. They will talk about what sticks and what doesn't.

*Closure:*
Gather children together and ask them to share their bracelets. Ask them to talk about what they chose to put on their bracelets.

**Center Connection:**
Have tape available outdoors so that children can choose to make another bracelet. Let children make a *class mural* out of the extra things they have collected. If children make bracelets at home, also, discuss the difference between the items found at home versus the items found at school.

**Literature Connection:**

*All New Native American Bracelets*
by Geri Dawn Weitzman, Troll Commmunications, 1997.

*I Took a Walk*
by Henry Cole, Greenwillow, 1998.

*Take a City Nature Walk*
by Jane Kirkland, Stillwater, 2005.

# NATURE BRACELETS

- **Science B-1** Expands knowledge of and abilities to observe, describe and discuss the natural world, materials, living things and natural processes.

- **Mathematics C-1** Enhances abilities to recognize, duplicate and extend simple patterns using a variety of materials.

- **Creative Arts B-1** Gains ability in using different art media and materials in a variety of ways for creative expression and representation.

   *Source: "Head Start Child Outcomes Framework." See Appendix A in this book for the framework.

## What To Look For

| Not Yet | Child does not participate in making a nature bracelet. |
|---|---|
| Emerging | Child participates with the help of an adult, asks one or two questions, does not join in group discussion. |
| Almost Mastered | Child collects items for bracelet, asks questions about the items, and discusses the items with peers and adults. |
| Fully Mastered | Child collects items for the bracelet, sorts and compares the items independently, shares discoveries with peers and adults. |

## NATURE BRACELETS

### Family Science Connection:

At home **have mom or dad put some masking tape (sticky side showing) around each child's wrist for the day.** At the end of the day, cut the tape off each child and **observe, identify, compare, and match** the various objects that stuck to the tape. Another way to try this activity is by attaching the tape to one's shirt. This way will allow for easier movement while playing or working.

**Comments or questions** that may add a *sense of wonder* to this activity:

- Wow, what did we collect on our sticky bracelets today?

- Tell me about the smallest thing that stuck to the bracelet. And about the biggest thing that stuck.

## PULSERAS DE LA NATURALEZA

### Ciencia en familia:

**En casa pide a mamá o papá que te ponga cinta adhesiva (con el pegamento por fuera) a cada una de las muñecas de tu mano** para traerla puesta todo el día. Al final del día, corten la cinta de cada niño y **observen, identifiquen, comparen, e igualen** los objetos varios que se hayan adherido a la cinta adhesiva. Otra manera de realizar esta actividad es poner la cinta con un seguro en su camisa. Así será más fácil que los niños se muevan mientras juegan o trabajan.

**Comentarios o preguntas** que pueden *despertar curiosidad* en esta actividad:

- ¡Veamos qué recogimos en nuestras pulseras adhesivas hoy!

- Dime acerca de lo más pequeño y lo más grande que se adhirió a la pulsera.

# OBSERVING WEEDS

**Investigation:** Looking for weeds in sidewalk cracks

**Process Skills:** Observing, comparing, classifying

**Materials:** Plastic sealable bags or paper bags, hand lenses

## Procedure:

*Getting started:*
Ask the children what they think a weed is. Where do they think they might find weeds? Give each child a plastic sealable bag or paper bag. Take them on a walk where they might find weeds in sidewalk cracks. (Research this ahead of time to make sure there are weeds for children to find, but also to make sure that there is no glass or other dangerous items on or near the sidewalk. If possible, make sure no herbicides or pesticides have been applied in the area.) Have children pull up weeds to put in their bags. Have children wash their hands with soap and water after doing the activity.

*Questions and comments to guide children:*
- How would you describe your weed?
- How do you think it got there?
- Does it have a smell?
- My weed is the same as Brenda's.
- How do the weeds look different?

*What children and adults will do:*
Children will find weeds and begin pulling them up. They may need help, especially if it hasn't rained in a while. Caution children to pull up weeds only (not the flowers and plants along the way). Discuss the difference between weeds and plants that have been put there purposely. (A weed is a plant growing where you don't want it to grow.)

*Closure:*
Back in the classroom, give each child a hand lens with which to examine the weeds. Ask children to describe what they see, feel and smell. Don't let them taste them! Have them put the weeds together and compare the different kinds. Have children tape their weeds all together on a big piece of stiff paper. Display it in the science center, with a heading such as "Our Weed Walk."

## Center Connection:

Put some of the weeds on a tray in the science center so children can further explore them. Children may want to add to the collection by bringing in weeds from home.

## Literature Connection:

*War of the Weeds (Fruit Troop)*
by Melody Carlson, Multnomah, 1998.

*Dandelions: Stars in the Grass*
by Mia Posada, Carolrhoda Books, 2000.

# OBSERVING WEEDS

## Assessment Outcomes & Possible Indicators*

- **Science A-1** Begins to use senses and a variety of tools and simple measuring devices to gather information, investigate materials and observe processes and relationships.

- **Science B-2** Expands knowledge of and respect for their body and the environment.

- **Approaches to Learning A-1** Chooses to participate in an increasing variety of tasks and activities.

    *Source: "Head Start Child Outcomes Framework." See Appendix A in this book for the framework.

## What To Look For

| | |
|---|---|
| **Not Yet** | Child shows no interest in looking for and collecting weeds. |
| **Emerging** | Child shows little interest; imitates others who collect weeds and use hand lenses; listens while others discuss discoveries. |
| **Almost Mastered** | Child observes weeds using hand lenses, asks questions, and discusses discoveries. |
| **Fully Mastered** | Child observes weeds independently with hand lens, makes comparisons of weeds, asks questions about differences and similarities of weeds, and initiates discussions of discoveries. |

# FAMILY PAGE / PÁGINA PARA LA FAMILIA

## OBSERVING WEEDS

### Family Science Connection:

**At home** in the **yard** or in the **neighborhood,** go on a weed hunt and find **three to five different kinds of weeds. Observe** the place they are growing and **compare** each one by look, smell, touch, and size. Are they all the same color? Are there any bugs crawling or living on these weeds? **Describe** together all the ideas about weeds you can.

**CAUTION:** Parents, always use your best judgment when children want to handle bugs and /or plants.

**Comments or questions** that may add a *sense of wonder* to this activity:

· Let's find the weeds that look most alike.

· Does each of the weeds have a different smell? What do the weeds smell like?

## OBSERVANDO LA MALEZA

### Ciencia en familia:

**En casa**, en el **patio** o en el **vecindario,** vayan en busca de maleza y encuentren de **tres a cinco clases diferentes de hierbas. Observen** el lugar en el que han crecido, **compárelas** según el tamaño observándolas, oliéndolas, y tocándolas. ¿Son todas del mismo color? ¿Hay algún insecto arrastrándose o viviendo en la hierba? **Describan** juntos todas las ideas que puedan acerca de la maleza.

**PRECAUCIÓN**: Padres, siempre usen su mejor criterio cuando sus niños quieran tocar los insectos y plantas.

**Comentarios o preguntas** que pueden *despertar curiosidad* en esta actividad:

· Encontremos las hierbas que se parecen más.

· ¿Tiene cada hierba un olor diferente? ¿A qué huelan las hierbas?

# ANIMAL WALK

**Investigation:** Going for a walk to look for animals in the neighborhood

**Process Skills:** Observing, classifying, comparing, communicating

**Materials:** Camera (optional), chart paper, markers

## Procedure:

*Getting started:*
Remind children of the rules to follow when going on a walk. Tell children they are going to go on a walk to look for animals. Follow children's leads when deciding on which questions to ask as you walk.

*Questions and comments to guide children:*
- What animals do you think we will see on our walk?
- I see an animal looking out of that window.
- I wonder if there are more animals inside that house.
- Does anyone hear a bird?
- Does that dog look the same as the dog we just saw?

*What children and adults will do:*
Children will talk about their own pets as they see similar animals. Adults can keep track of the number and kinds of animals seen on the walk. Children and adults look for clues that animals are nearby (tracks, food, bowls, sounds of animals). Encourage children to talk about how animals look, how they move, what they eat.

*Closure:*
Back in the classroom make a list on chart paper of all the animals children can remember seeing. Write each word with a simple drawing next to it. Or make a graph of children's favorite animals seen on the walk. Draw pictures or have pictures cut out ahead of time of the animals you are likely to see. If you take pictures, include them in the display.

## Follow-up Activity:

Visit a farm, zoo, or nature center where the children will see different animals they can compare to those seen on the walk.

## Center Connection:

Put books about animals in the book or science center. Add a pet to your classroom. Make a class "pet book" from children's drawings or photographs of their pets. Add pet food dishes to the house area.

## Literature Connection:

*Come With Me*
by Ashley Wolff, Dutton, 1990.

*The Third Story Cat*
by Leslie Baker, Little, Brown, 1987.

*Our Cat Flossie*
by Ruth Brown, Dutton, 1986.

*Cloudy*
by Deborah King, Putnam, 1989.

*Pets*
by Dave King, Aladdin, 1991.

*Why Does the Cat Do That?*
by Susan Bonners, Henry Holt, 1998.

# ANIMAL WALK

- **Science A-4** Develops growing abilities to collect, describe and record information through a variety of means, including discussions, drawings, maps and charts.

- **Language Development B-1** Develops increasing abilities to understand and use language to communicate information, experiences, ideas, opinions, needs, questions and for other varied purpose.

- **Literacy B-5** Progresses in learning how to handle and care for books; knowing to view one page at a time in sequence from front to back; and understanding that a book has a title, author and illustrator.

*Source: "Head Start Child Outcomes Framework." See Appendix A in this book for the framework.

## What To Look For

| Not Yet | Child shows no interest in looking for animals while on the walk. |
|---|---|
| Emerging | Child talks about his or her pet, observes other pets, asks one or two questions. |
| Almost Mastered | Child observes pets, asks questions, joins in discussion, is able to make comparisons. |
| Fully Mastered | Child makes comparisons of pets owned by others and him- or herself, initiates discussion about animals that are pets and animals that are not. |

# FAMILY PAGE / PÁGINA PARA LA FAMILIA

## ANIMAL WALK

### Family Science Connection:

**Go to the library** and find some **books about pet animals**. Together with a **family member** look at the pictures of the different pets and **talk** about which one would be a favorite to own. **Talk** about all the things you like about the pet and maybe visit a friend who owns that pet. Your family may even own the pet, so spend time **observing** everything you can about the animal.

**Comments or questions** that may add a *sense of wonder* to this activity:

- What are the many things you like about your favorite pet animal?

- Do animals understand what you tell them? How could you find out if they do understand what people say?

## HABLANDO DE ANIMALES

### Ciencia en familia:

**Vayan a la biblioteca** y busquen algunos **libros acerca de mascotas caseras**. Junto con un **miembro de la familia** vean las fotos de las diferentes mascotas y hablen acerca de cuál de todas sería la favorita. **Hablen** acerca de todas las cosas que les gustan del animal y si pueden vayan a visitar a un amigo que tenga esa mascota. Tal vez su familia ya tenga una en casa y entonces pueden **observar** todo lo que les gusta de ese animal.

**Comentarios o preguntas** que pueden *despertar curiosidad* en esta actividad:

- ¿Qué es lo que te gusta de tu mascota favorita?

- ¿Entienden los animales lo que les dices? ¿Cómo podrías averiguar si ellos entienden cuando la gente les habla?

# ADOPTING A TREE

**Investigation:** Making observations of a tree over time

**Process Skills:** Observing, comparing, communicating

**Materials:** Camera, paper, crayons, ball of string, scissors

## Procedure:

*Getting started:*
Choose a tree that is near the school and that changes through the year. A deciduous tree (one that loses its leaves) makes the best subject. If there are several trees near the classroom, ask children to choose one tree to be their special class tree. Visit for the first time as early in the school year as possible so that children will be able to observe many changes throughout the year. (CAUTION: Prior to the activity, inspect the area for poisonous plants or vines growing on or near the tree.)

*Questions and comments to guide children:*
  • What can you tell me about this tree?
  • I wonder if it is going to get any taller.
  • How does the bark feel?
  • How do the leaves look different from the last time we visited?

*What children and adults will do:*
Help children notice the many interesting attributes of the trunk, leaves, and branches. Follow their leads in deciding which questions to ask. Some children may be interested in the leaves on the ground, while others may notice the sap or some ants on the trunk of the tree. If this is not your first visit to the tree, help children notice the changes that have occurred. On different visits to the tree you can focus on different aspects of the tree. One time have the children make rubbings of the bark by placing a piece of plain paper against the bark and rubbing with a crayon. Have children work in pairs, with one holding the paper and the other doing the rubbing. On another visit children could measure the trunk with a piece of string. Then they can compare the size of their tree to others in the area.

*Closure:*
If leaves and twigs are on the ground, allow children to collect some to bring back to the classroom. Have children draw pictures of the class tree and dictate something about it.

## Follow-up Activity:

Visit the tree often to observe the many changes throughout the seasons. Record changes with a camera.

## Center Connection:

Put books about trees in the book or science center. Place photographs of the tree in the classroom at children's eye level. Sequence photographs in order of the time of the visit so children can begin to get a sense of time and changes that occur in nature.

## Literature Connection:

*The Giving Tree*
by Shel Silverstein, Harper & Row, 1964.

*The Seasons of Arnold's Apple Tree*
by Gail Gibbons, Harcourt Brace Jovanovich, 1984.

*The Great Kapok Tree*
by Lynne Cherry, Harcourt Brace Jovanovich, 1990.

# ADOPTING A TREE

## Assessment Outcomes & Possible Indicators*

- **Science B-3** Develops growing awareness of ideas and language related to attributes of time and temperature.

- **Literacy D-2** Begins to represent stories and experiences through pictures, dictation, and in play.

- **Mathematics C-4** Shows progress in using standard and non-standard measures for length and area of objects.

- **Creative Arts B-2** Progresses in abilities to create drawings, paintings, models, and other art creations that are more detailed, creative or realistic.

*Source: "Head Start Child Outcomes Framework." See Appendix A in this book for the framework.

## What To Look For

| Not Yet | Child goes on the nature walk but shows no interest in looking at or exploring a particular tree. |
|---|---|
| Emerging | Child watches others explore a tree by touching the bark and examining the parts of the tree, and listens to others' comments about their observations. |
| Almost Mastered | Child explores the tree, making comments about the parts of the tree; makes comments about changes on subsequent visits; participates in activities such as gathering leaves, making rubbings of the bark, and drawing pictures of the tree. |
| Fully Mastered | Child eagerly explores the tree during each visit and sometimes asks an adult if the class could make another visit; asks questions and discusses the changes that take place; shows interest in the photographs of the tree, draws pictures and dictates stories about the tree. |

## ADOPTING A TREE

### Family Science Connection:

**Mom or Dad,** take your child(ren) outside to **count** and **observe** the many trees that are growing in and around **your yard.** If you do not have trees, then take a walk in **the neighborhood** and check out one that you can **observe.** Look for fruit, leaves, seeds, bark, or twigs that may be hanging or have fallen from the tree. Pick one tree and spend time each day during one season and try to **identify** anything you can about the tree. **Together talk** about the size, shape, color, odor, and textures of the tree. See if you can **recognize** and **describe any changes** the tree goes through during the course of that season. Parents, point out any interesting changes about the tree that your child happened not to notice. **Collect** anything that has fallen from the tree and spend time **comparing** it with the same part that is still on the tree. Three books that are fun to read related to this activity are *The Giving Tree* by Shel Silverstein, *The Seasons of Arnold's Apple Tree* by Gail Gibbons, and *The Great Kapok Tree* by Lynne Cherry.

**Comments or questions** that may add a *sense of wonder* to this activity:

- Let's see how tall you are next to the tree. Show the child with your hand how short he or she is next to the tree.

- Tell me everything you like about this tree. Encourage the child to describe everything the child senses about the tree—colors, texture, shapes, size, odor.

## ADOPTE UN ÁRBOL

### La ciencia en familia:

**Mamá o papá,** lleven a su hijo o hijos afuera para que **cuenten** y **observen** los muchos árboles que están creciendo en **su patio** y en los alrededores. Si usted no tiene árboles, caminen **en el vecindario** y busquen un patio que puedan **observar.** Vea las frutas, hojas, semillas, corteza o ramitas que se puedan haber caído o estén todavía en el árbol. Seleccionen un árbol y pasen tiempo cada día durante una estación tratando de **identificar** lo que vean del árbol. **Hablen juntos** acerca del tamaño, figura, color, olor, y texturas del árbol. A ver si pueden **reconocer y describir cambios** en el árbol durante esa estación. Papás, señalen cambios interesantes acerca del árbol que su niño quizás no haya notado. **Recojan** algo que se haya caído del árbol y pasen tiempo **comparándolo** con la misma parte que todavía está en el árbol. Hay tres libros divertidos relacionados con esta actividad *The Giving Tree* por Shel Silverstein, *The Seasons of Arnold's Apple Tree* por Gail Gibbons, y *The Great Kapok Tree* por Lynne Cherry.

**Comentarios o preguntas** que pueden *despertar curiosidad* en esta actividad:

- Vamos a ver tu altura junto al árbol. Muestre a su hijo con la mano cuán alto es junto al árbol.

- Dime todo lo que te gusta de este árbol. Anime a su hijo(a) a describir todo lo que percibe de este árbol—colores, textura, figuras, tamaño, olor.

# VISIT TO A NURSERY

**Investigation:** Visiting a nursery to observe plants, flowers, and trees

**Process Skills:** Observing, comparing, classifying

**Materials:** Camera (optional)

## Procedure:

*Getting started:*
Visit the nursery first yourself to review what you will want children to see. Talk to the manager about any rules children will need to follow. Decide on the route you will follow as you walk through the nursery. In the classroom show children a few pictures of flowers, plants, and trees. Encourage them to look for many different colors, shapes, and smells while they are in the nursery. (CAUTION: Remember that some children are allergic to certain flowers, pollens, or grasses. Check with parents before making this trip.)

*Questions and comments to guide children:*
- I see two different yellow flowers.
- I wonder how tall that tree will grow?
- Which flower do you like the best?
- Has anyone ever seen a plant with leaves like that one?
- Can you find another flower that looks like this but is a different color?

*What children and adults will do:*
Children will notice and comment on the many different flowers, plants, and trees. Adults will need to remind them about the rules (e.g., do not touch the plants). Encourage them to observe in other ways—looking and smelling. Help children notice similarities and differences.

*Closure:*
If possible bring back some items from the nursery for children to plant and some to send home. Put photos of the trip on the wall at children's eye level. Later put them into a book.

## Follow-up Activities:

Have children make flowers, plants, or trees out of materials in your art area. Have available a wide variety of materials such as pipe cleaners, tissue paper, construction paper, buttons, nontoxic paint for children, nontoxic markers, and nontoxic glue. On another day, go for a neighborhood walk and look for flowers, plants, and trees similar to those children saw at the nursery.

## Center Connection:

Put books about flowers in the book or science center. Add flowers to your classroom. Use plants or flowers as table centerpieces. Add plants to the science center. Add seed and garden catalogs to the science or house area. Add gardening tools and clothes and put them next to the water/sand table. Fill the table with soil.

## Literature Connection:

*Red Leaf, Yellow Leaf*
by Lois Ehlert, Harcourt Children's Books, 1991.

*Planting a Rainbow*
by Lois Ehlert, Harcourt Brace Jovanovich, 1988.

*From Seed to Plant*
by Gail Gibbons, Holiday House Reprint, 1993.

*From Seed to Plant*
by Allan Fowler, Children's Press, 2001.

## Assessment Outcomes & Possible Indicators*

- **Science A-2** Develops increased ability to observe and discuss common properties, differences and comparisons among objects and materials.

- **Science B-1** Expands knowledge of and abilities to observe, describe and discuss the natural world, materials, living things and natural processes.

- **Language Development B-1** Develops increasing abilities to understand and use language to communicate information, experiences, ideas, opinions, needs, questions and for other varied purpose.

- **Creative Arts B-2** Progresses in abilities to create drawings, paintings, models, and other art creations that are more detailed, creative or realistic.

*Source: "Head Start Child Outcomes Framework." See Appendix A in this book for the framework.

## What To Look For

| Not Yet | Child goes on the visit but shows no interest in the plants, flowers, and trees. |
|---|---|
| Emerging | Child shows interest in the contents of the nursery by making comments about the plants, flowers, and trees. |
| Almost Mastered | Child comments and answers some of the adult's questions about the plants, flowers, and trees; may ask one or two questions. |
| Fully Mastered | Child eagerly explores the nursery, comments, and asks many questions; notices and comments on similarities and differences; attempts to represent what was seen on the visit by using various art materials. |

# BRANCH PUZZLES

**Investigation:** Putting pieces of a branch together to make a whole branch

**Process Skills:** Observing, comparing, and sequencing

**Materials:** Cut two 2-foot branches from the same kind of tree. The thicker end of each branch should be a little bigger around than your thumb. Cut one of the branches into three or more pieces. The more pieces there are, the harder the puzzle will be. Use some straight cuts across the branch and some angled cuts.

## Procedure:

*Getting started:*
Go for a walk with children and on your walk observe the trees. Focus on how the branches get thinner toward their ends. Feel the rough bark (older trees) on the trunk and the smoother bark on the small branches. After the walk, show the children the two branches and challenge them to put the branch puzzle together.

*Questions and comments to guide children:*
Some questions for the walk and tree study:
- Which part of the tree is biggest?
- Can you hug the tree and get your arms all the way around the trunk of the tree?

Some questions for the branch puzzle challenge:
- This is a whole branch. This branch was a whole branch, but was sawed into pieces. How could we put the pieces of this branch together to make a whole branch like this one?
- If we start with this widest piece, what piece should come next?

*What children and adults will do:*
Some children will have difficulty with the branch puzzle. In that case, you might put the branch puzzle together but make some mistakes. Ask the children to compare the whole branch to your branch to see if any mistakes have been made. Ask the children to help you correct the mistakes. Help the children observe color and texture for clues.

*Closure:*
Compare the ends of a branch. Which end is thicker? Which end is thinner? Which end was attached to the tree? How are the two ends different?

## Follow-up Activity:

If children find the branch puzzle too easy, cut the branch into more pieces. Make two branch puzzles from branches of two different kinds of trees. Mix the pieces from both branches and challenge the children to put together two different branches.

## Center Connection:

Have different sizes and kinds of branches for the children to explore.

## Art Connection:

Give the children strips of paper of different thickness. Ask the children to paste these strips to a piece of paper to make the branch of a tree.

## Literature Connection:

*Have You Seen Trees?*
by Joanne Oppenheim, Young Scott, 1967, 1995.

*This Is the Tree*
by Miriam Moss, Kane/Miller, 2005.

# BRANCH PUZZLES

- **Science A-1** Begins to use senses and a variety of tools and simple measuring devices to gather information, investigate materials and observe processes and relationships.

- **Science B-1** Expands knowledge of and abilities to observe, describe and discuss the natural world, materials, living things and natural processes.

- **Language Development B-1** Develops increasing abilities to understand and use language to communicate information, experiences, ideas, opinions, needs, questions and for other varied purpose.

- **Mathematics C-2** Shows increasing abilities to match, sort, put in series, and regroup objects according to one or two attributes such as shape or size.

- **Creative Arts A-1** Participates with increasing interest and enjoyment in a variety of music activities, including listening, singing, finger plays, games and performances.

- **Physical Health & Development A-1** Develops growing strength, dexterity and control needed to use tools such as scissors, paper punch, stapler and hammer.

*Source: "Head Start Child Outcomes Framework." See Appendix A in this book for the framework.

## What To Look For

| Not Yet | Child does not participate or shows no interest in investigating branches and pieces of a branch. |
|---|---|
| Emerging | Child imitates others when investigating branches and is not fully involved; is not talkative. |
| Almost Mastered | Child puts together the branches, but incorrectly; does not see connections (e.g., thicker part, straight edge); is talkative. |
| Fully Mastered | Child puts together branches with adult's help; notices mistakes and fixes them; sees connections (e.g., thicker part, edge, texture) and describes them (has vocabulary); is very talkative and matches similar textures and sizes. |

## BRANCH PUZZLES

### Family Science Connection:

Go for a walk with your child and observe trees, bushes, and branches. Notice how the parts of a bush or tree get thinner the farther they are from the base of the trunk. Feel the difference in texture between the trunk and a small branch. Look for "Ys" in the branches. Look for differences in colors on the branches.

**Comments or questions** that may add a *sense of wonder* to this activity:

· Your arm is thick and your fingers are thin. Where is the thickest part of this branch or tree? What is the thinnest part?

· What different colors can we find on this branch or tree?

· How many different "Y" shapes can we find in this branch?

· I wonder which part of the tree is the youngest and which is the oldest.

· How big will this tree be next year? When the tree grows, what do you think will happen to this branch?

## TRAMAS DE LAS RAMAS

### Ciencia en familia:

Salga a caminar con su hijo y observen árboles, arbustos y ramas. Vea como las partes de un arbusto o árbol se hacen más delgadas entre más lejos estén de la base del tronco. Sienta la diferencia en textura entre un tronco y una ramita. Busquen las "Y" en las ramas. Vean las diferencias en los colores de las ramas.

**Comentarios o preguntas** que pueden *despertar curiosidad* en esta actividad:

· Tu brazo es grueso y tus dedos son delgados. ¿Dónde está la parte más gruesa de esta rama o árbol? ¿Cuál es la parte más delgada?

· ¿Qué colores podemos encontrar en esta rama o árbol?

· ¿Cuántas diferentes figuras de "Y" podemos encontrar en esta rama?

· Me pregunto qué parte del árbol es más nueva. ¿Más vieja?

· ¿Cuán grande será este árbol el próximo año? Cuando crezca el árbol, ¿qué piensas que le pasará a esta rama?

# LEAVES: FALLING FOR YOU!

**Investigation:** Exploring the shapes, sizes, and colors of fall leaves

**Process Skills:** Observing, comparing, and classifying

**Materials:** Leaves of different sizes and colors, including green, from under two different kinds of trees; leaves that show that some critter has been eating the leaves.

## Procedure:

*Getting started:*
With the children go on a walk to collect leaves. Make sure the collection includes two different kinds of leaves and one green leaf and one multicolored leaf of each kind. Encourage the children to explore the leaves and try to see how the leaves are different and how they are alike. Challenge the children to find something interesting about the leaves. (CAUTION: Check the area ahead of time to make sure it is free of poisonous plants.)

*Questions and comments to guide children:*
  • What other leaves are like this one?
  • This leaf is from one kind of tree. What other leaves are from the same kind of tree?
  • Are all the leaves from the same kind of tree the same size? The same color?
  • Will this green leaf change colors? What colors?
  • Is any part of the leaf missing? I wonder where it went.

*What children and adults will do:*
Children will create two piles of leaves, each pile with similar characteristics. Leaves might be grouped by size, color, shape, or kind of tree. Encourage children to group leaves in different ways.

*Closure:*
Ask the children to show you two leaves that come from the same tree. Ask them to pick out leaves that show that the same kind of leaves can be different sizes and can be different colors. (CAUTION: Have children wash their hands with soap and water after doing this activity.)

## Follow-up Activity:

To show the children how leaves change from green to other colors in the fall, put a piece of tape around the "stems" of a number of green leaves growing on trees. Watch these leaves for color changes and watch what happens to these leaves after they fall from the tree. Also, you may want to dry and press leaves between pages of a newspaper or magazine. Use a heavy weight to press the leaves flat.

## Center Connection:

Make a "leaf zoo" with as many different kinds of leaves as you can find. Challenge children to place leaves that are alike in boxes (cages).

## Art Connection:

Brightly colored leaves can be pressed, using a warm iron, between contact paper or waxed paper and can be hung as colorful transparencies in sunlit windows. Children can paint leaves and then press them on sheets of paper to make leaf prints.

## Literature Connection:

*Growing Colors*
by Bruce McMillan, HarperCollins, 1988.

*A B Cedar: An Alphabet of Trees*
by George Ella Lyon, Franklin Watts, 1989.

*Autumn Leaves*
by Ken Robbins, Scholastic Trade, 1998.

# LEAVES: FALLING FOR YOU!

## Assessment Outcomes & Possible Indicators**

- **Science A-1** Begins to use senses and a variety of tools and simple measuring devices to gather information, investigate materials and observe processes and relationships.

- **Language Development B-1** Develops increasing abilities to understand and use language to communicate information, experiences, ideas, opinions, needs, questions and for other varied purpose.

- **Mathematics C-2** Shows increasing abilities to match, sort, put in series, and regroup objects according to one or two attributes such as shape or size.

- **Mathematics C-3** Begins to make comparisons between several objects based on a single attribute.

*Source: "Head Start Child Outcomes Framework." See Appendix A in this book for the framework.

## What To Look For

| **Not Yet** | Child does not participate or shows no interest in gathering and examining leaves. |
| --- | --- |
| **Emerging** | Child gathers leaves but doesn't look for different attributes, doesn't sort, is not involved with discussion. |
| **Almost Mastered** | Child gathers leaves, looks for a different kind of leaf, and sorts into one or two groups; is talkative and answers some adult's questions. |
| **Fully Mastered** | Child gathers leaves, looks for different kinds, and makes many discoveries and shares with group; sorts into more than one group (i.e., by color, shape, or kind); is very talkative and describes what is different or similar. |

## LEAVES: FALLING FOR YOU!

### Family Science Connection:

Explore your home and neighborhood to look at leaves. You may want to collect as many different kinds of leaves as you can. Don't just look at tree leaves but look at grass and leaves of bushes and weeds. Look closely at any leaves on plants in your home. Notice that some leaves are shiny, other leaves are dull, some are soft, and some have many points. Notice that not all the leaves on the tree turn from green to other colors at the same time.

**Comments or questions** that may add a *sense of wonder* to this activity:

· How are leaves on the same tree alike? How are they different?

· I wonder why leaves change colors in the fall.

· I wonder where the leaves go after they fall from the trees.

## ÁRBOL: ¡TE DESPOJAS DE TUS HOJAS!

### Ciencia en familia:

Explore su hogar y su vecindario para ver hojas. Tal vez quieran colectar diferentes clases de hojas. No sólo vean las hojas de los árboles; también vean césped, hojas de arbustos y hierbas. Miren detenidamente las hojas de las plantas de su hogar. Vea que algunas hojas son brillantes, otras hojas son pálidas; una son tersas y otras tienen muchas puntas. Vea que no todas las hojas del árbol cambian de verde a otros colores al mismo tiempo.

**Comentarios o preguntas** que pueden *despertar curiosidad* en esta actividad:

· ¿En qué se parecen las hojas del mismo árbol? ¿En qué son diferentes?

· Me pregunto por qué cambian de color las hojas en el otoño.

· Me pregunto adónde van a parar las hojas cuando se caen de los árboles.

# HEAD START CHILD OUTCOMES FRAMEWORK

| Domain | Domain Element | Indicators |
|---|---|---|
| 1. Language Development | A. Listening and Understanding | 1. Demonstrates increasing ability to attend to and understand conversations, stories, songs, and poems. |
| | | 2. Shows progress in understanding and following simple and multiple-step directions. |
| | | 3. Understands an increasingly complex and varied vocabulary. |
| | | 4. For non-English-speaking children, progresses in listening to and understanding English. |
| | B. Speaking and Communicating | 1. Develops increasing abilities to understand and use language to communicate information, experiences, ideas, feelings, opinions, needs, questions and for other varied purposes. |
| | | 2. Progresses in abilities to initiate and respond appropriately in conversation and discussions with peers and adults. |
| | | 3. Uses an increasingly complex and varied spoken vocabulary. |
| | | 4. Progresses in clarity of pronunciation and towards speaking in sentences of increasing length and grammatical complexity. |
| | | 5. Associates sounds with written words, such as awareness that different words begin with the same sound. |
| 2. Literacy | A. Phonological Awareness | 1. Shows increasing ability to discriminate and identify sounds in spoken language. |
| | | 2. Shows growing awareness of beginning and ending sounds of words. |
| | | 3. Progresses in recognizing matching sounds and rhymes in familiar words, games, songs, stories and poems. |
| | | 4. Shows growing ability to hear and discriminate separate syllables in words. |
| | | 5. Associates sounds with written words, such as awareness that different words begin with the same sound. |

| Domain | Domain Element | Indicators |
|---|---|---|
| 2. Literacy (cont.) | B. Book Knowledge and Appreciation | 1. Shows growing interest and involvement in listening to and discussing a variety of fiction and non-fiction books and poetry. |
| | | 2. Shows growing interest in reading-related activities, such as asking to have a favorite book read; choosing to look at books; drawing pictures based on stories; asking to take books home; going to the library; and engaging in pretend-reading with other children. |
| | | 3. Demonstrates progress in abilities to retell and dictate stories from books and experiences; to act out stories in dramatic play; and to predict what will happen next in a story. |
| | | 4. Demonstrates progress in abilities to retell and dictate stories from books and experiences; to act out stories in dramatic play; and to predict what will happen next in a story. |
| | | 5. Progresses in learning how to handle and care for books; knowing to view one page at a time in sequence from front to back; and understanding that a book has a title, author and illustrator. |
| | C. Print Awareness and Concepts | 1. Shows increasing awareness of print in classroom, home and community settings. |
| | | 2. Develops growing understanding of the different functions of forms of print such as signs, letters, newspapers, lists, messages and menus. |
| | | 3. Demonstrates increasing awareness of concepts of print, such as that reading in English moves from top to bottom and from left to right, that speech can be written down, and that print conveys a message. |

| Domain | Domain Element | Indicators |
|---|---|---|
| 2. Literacy (cont.) | C. Print Awareness and Concepts (cont.) | 4. Shows progress in recognizing the association between spoken words and written words by following print as it is read aloud. |
| | | 5. Recognizes a word as a unit of print, or awareness that letters are grouped to form words, and that words are separated by spaces. |
| | D. Early Writing | 1. Develops understanding that writing is a way of communicating for a variety of purposes. |
| | | 2. Begins to represent stories and experiences through pictures, dictation, and in play. |
| | | 3. Experiments with a growing variety of writing tools and materials, such as pencils, crayons and computers. |
| | | 4. Progresses from using scribbles, shapes or pictures to represent ideas, to using letter-like symbols, to copying or writing familiar words such as their own name. |
| | E. Alphabet Knowledge | 1. Shows progress in associating the names of letters with their shapes and sounds. |
| | | 2. Increases in ability to notice the beginning of letters in familiar words. |
| | | 3. Identifies at least 10 letters of the alphabet, especially those in their own name. |
| | | 4. Knows that letters of the alphabet are a special category of visual graphics that can be individually named. |
| 3. Mathematics | A. Number and Operations | 1. Demonstrates increasing interest and awareness of numbers and counting as a means for solving problems and determining quantity. |
| | | 2. Begins to associate number concepts, vocabulary, quantities and written numeral in meaningful ways. |

| Domain | Domain Element | Indicators |
|---|---|---|
| 3. Mathematics (cont.) | A. Number and Operations (cont.) | 3. Develops increasing ability to count in sequence to 10 and beyond. |
| | | 4. Begins to make use of one-to-one correspondence in counting objects and matching groups of objects. |
| | | 5. Begins to use language to compare numbers of objects with terms such as more, less, greater than, fewer, equal to. |
| | | 6. Develops increased abilities to combine, separate and name "how many" concrete objects. |
| | B. Geometry and Spatial Sense | 1. Begins to recognize, describe, compare and name common shapes, their parts and attributes. |
| | | 2. Progresses in ability to put together and take apart shapes. |
| | | 3. Begins to be able to determine whether or not two shapes are the same size and shape. |
| | | 4. Shows growth in matching, sorting, putting in series and regrouping objects according to one or two attributes such as color, shape or size. |
| | | 5. Builds an increasing understanding of directionality, order and positions of objects, and words such as up, down, over, under, top, bottom, inside, outside, in front and behind. |
| | C. Patterns and Measurement | 1. Enhances abilities to recognize, duplicate and extend simple patterns using a variety of materials. |
| | | 2. Shows increasing abilities to match, sort, put in series, and regroup objects according to one or two attributes such as shape or size. |
| | | 3. Begins to make comparisons between several objects based on a single attribute. |
| | | 4. Shows progress in using standard and non-standard measures for length and area of objects. |

| Domain | Domain Element | Indicators |
|---|---|---|
| 4. Science | A. Scientific Skills and Methods | 1. Begins to use senses and a variety of tools and simple measuring devices to gather information, investigate materials and observe processes and relationships. |
| | | 2. Develops increased ability to observe and discuss common properties, differences and comparisons among objects and materials. |
| | | 3. Begins to participate in simple investigations to test observations, discuss and draw conclusions and form generalizations. |
| | | 4. Develops growing abilities to collect, describe and record information through a variety of means, including discussions, drawings, maps and charts. |
| | | 5. Begins to describe and discuss predictions, explanations and generalizations based on past experiences. |
| | B. Scientific Knowledge | 1. Expands knowledge of and abilities to observe, describe and discuss the natural world, materials, living things and natural processes. |
| | | 2. Expands knowledge of and respect for their body and the environment. |
| | | 3. Develops growing awareness of ideas and language related to attributes of time and temperature. |
| | | 4. Shows increased awareness and beginning understanding of changes in materials and cause-effect relationships. |
| 5. Creative Arts | A. Music | 1. Participates with increasing interest and enjoyment in a variety of music activities, including listening, singing, finger plays, games and performances. |
| | | 2. Experiments with a variety of musical instruments. |

| Domain | Domain Element | Indicators |
|---|---|---|
| 5. Creative Arts (cont.) | B. Art | 1. Gains ability in using different art media and materials in a variety of ways for creative expression and representation. |
| | | 2. Progresses in abilities to create drawings, paintings, models, and other art creations that are more detailed, creative or realistic. |
| | | 3. Develops growing abilities to plan, work independently, and demonstrate care and persistence in a variety of art projects. |
| | | 4. Begins to understand and share opinions about artistic products and experiments. |
| | C. Movement | 1. Expresses through movement and dancing what is felt and heard in various musical tempos and styles. |
| | | 2. Shows growth in moving in time to different patterns of beat and rhythm in music. |
| | D. Dramatic Play | 1. Participates in a variety of dramatic play activities that become more extended and complex. |
| | | 2. Shows growing creativity and imagination in using material and in assuming different roles in dramatic play situations. |
| 6. Social and Emotional Development | A. Self-Concept | 1. Begins to develop and express awareness of self in terms of specific abilities, characteristics and preferences. |
| | | 2. Develops growing capacity for independence in a range of activities, routines and tasks. |
| | | 3. Demonstrates growing confidence in a range of abilities and expresses pride in accomplishments. |
| | B. Self-Control | 1. Shows progress in expressing feelings, needs and opinions in difficult situations and conflicts without harming themselves, others or property. |

| Domain | Domain Element | Indicators |
|---|---|---|
| 6. Social and Emotional Development (cont.) | B. Self-Control (cont.) | 2. Develops growing understanding of how their actions affect others and begins to accept the consequences of their actions. |
| | | 3. Demonstrates increasing capacity to follow rules and routines and use materials purposefully, safely and respectfully. |
| | C. Cooperation | 1. Increases abilities to sustain interactions with peers by helping, sharing and discussion. |
| | | 2. Shows increasing abilities to use compromise and discussion in working, playing and resolving conflicts with peers. |
| | | 3. Develops increasing abilities to give and take interactions; to take turns in games or using materials, and to interact without being overly submissive or directive. |
| | D. Social Relationships | 1. Demonstrates increasing comfort in talking with accepting guidance and directions from a range of familiar adults. |
| | | 2. Shows progress in developing friendships with peers. |
| | | 3. Progresses in responding sympathetically to peers who are in need, upset, hurt or angry; and in expressing empathy or caring for others. |
| | E. Knowledge of Families and Communities | 1. Develops ability to identify personal characteristics, including gender and family composition. |
| | | 2. Progresses in understanding similarities and respecting differences among people, such as genders, race, special needs, culture, language and family structures. |
| | | 3. Develops growing awareness of jobs and what is required to perform them. |

| Domain | Domain Element | Indicators |
|---|---|---|
| 6. Social and Emotional Development (cont.) | E. Knowledge of Families and Communities (cont.) | 4. Begins to express and understand concepts and language of geography in the contexts of their classroom, home and community. |
| 7. Approaches to Learning | A. Initiative and Curiosity | 1. Chooses to participate in an increasing variety of tasks and activities. |
| | | 2. Develops increased ability to make independent choices. |
| | | 3. Approaches tasks and activities with increased flexibility, imagination and inventiveness. |
| | | 4. Grows in eagerness to learn about and discuss a growing range of topics, ideas and tasks. |
| | B. Engagement and Persistence | 1. Grows in abilities to persist in and complete a variety of tasks, activities, projects and experiences. |
| | | 2. Demonstrates increasing ability to set goals and develop and follow through on plans. |
| | | 3. Shows growing capacity to maintain concentration over time on a task, question, set of directions or interactions, despite distractions and interruptions. |
| | C. Reasoning and Problem-Solving | 1. Develops increasing ability to find more than one solution to a question, task or problem. |
| | | 2. Grows in recognizing and solving problems through active exploration, including trial and error, and interactions and discussions with peers and adults. |
| | | 3. Progresses in abilities to classify, compare and contrast objects, events and experiments. |
| 8. Physical Health and Development | A. Fine Motor Skills | 1. Develops growing strength, dexterity and control needed to use tools such as scissors, paper punch, stapler and hammer. |
| | | 2. Grows in hand-eye coordination in building with blocks, putting together puzzles, reproducing shapes and patterns, stringing beads and using scissors. |

| Domain | Domain Element | Indicators |
|---|---|---|
| 8. Physical Health and Development (cont.) | A. Fine Motor Skills (cont.) | 3. Progresses in abilities to use writing, drawing and art tools including pencils, markers, chalk, paint brushes and various types of technology. |
| | B. Gross Motor Skills | 1. Shows increasing levels of proficiency, control and balance in walking, climbing, running, jumping, hopping, skipping, marching and galloping. |
| | | 2. Demonstrates increasing abilities to coordinate movements in throwing, catching, kicking, bouncing balls, and using the slide and swing. |
| | C. Health Status and Practices | 1. Progresses in physical growth, strength, stamina and flexibility. |
| | | 2. Participates actively in games, outdoor play, and other forms of exercise that enhances physical fitness. |
| | | 3. Shows growing independence in hygiene, nutrition and personal care when eating, dressing, washing hands, brushing teeth and toileting. |
| | | 4. Builds awareness and ability to follow basic health and safety rules such as fire safety, traffic and pedestrian safety, and responding appropriately to potentially harmful objects, substances and activities. |

Source: *Head Start Bulletin*. 2003. Issue No. 76. U.S. Department of Health and Human Services, Head Start Bureau. *www.headstartinfo.org/publications/ hsbulletin76/hsb76_09.htm*

# "A HEAD START ON SCIENCE" PROJECT STAFF AND OTHER COLLABORATORS

Project Director.................................... William C. Ritz

Project Coordinator............................ Ann Wilmshurst

Project Research................................. Maureen McMahon

Greg Potter

Project Evaluator................................. Ruth Von Blum

**California State University, Long Beach Curriculum Development Team:**

Ann Wilmshurst (Leader, Curriculum Development)

Colleen Triesch (Developer, Family Extensions)

Ann Wilmshurst, Deborah Greenwade, and Cynthia Meyer (Developers, Outcomes Assessment Materials)

Maureen McMahon (Additions/ Modifications for the NSTA Press Volume)

**Additional Activities and Center Connections suggested or written by**

Rebecca Agdigos, Dolores Almaraz, Rachel Cortes, Mary Cunningham, Maria Garcia, Bonita Gilbert, Esther Hernandez, Laurethia James, Greg Kelehan, Matt Kelly, Emely Lek, Marjorie Leone, Veronica Orozco, Kay Pandya, Odessa Peraza, Robin Ryan, Larry Schafer, Carmen Simbillo, Beverly Smith, and Martha Walejko.

Logo by...................................................... Graphic Design Concepts, Long Beach, California

Original Illustrations by...................... Aimee Carlson

Workshop Leader / Coordinator........ Ray Casillan

Spanish Translations of

Family Connections............................. Colleen Triesch (1996)

Nydia Hernandez (2003)

Aaron Salinger (2003)

2003 Web Design by.............................. Emily Bonham and Charles Brackman

**Project Funding:**

U.S. Department of Health and Human Services, Head Start Bureau grant 90-CD-119 (1995–1998) and the American Honda Foundation (1999–2003)

**Other Important Collaborators:**

James Matlack, Head Start Director, Long Beach Unified School District, at the time the project was conceived and started

Suzan Hubert and Mary Picone, Los Angeles County Office of Education, Head Start / Pre-School Division

Lisa D. Alford, Director of Child Development, Head Start, P.E.A.C.E., Inc. Syracuse, New York

Larry Schafer, Department of Science Teaching, Syracuse University.

**...and:**

Rebecca Agdidos, Shellinda Barre, Ray Casillan, Maria Contreras, Mary Cunningham, Ruth DeSilva, Kacy Evans, Delia Flores, Esther Hernandez, Donna Iwagaki, Natasha Jackson, Matt Kelly, Steve Kemp, Carolyn Loveridge, Greg Potter, Nona Reimer, Loida Spicer, Colleen Triesch, Maudie Williams.

**"A Head Start on Science" Leadership Teams 2000**

| | |
|---|---|
| Monterey, CA: | Guadalupe Root-Perez, Theresa Truenfels |
| Tampa, FL: | Joyce James, Patricia Horvath, Timothy Hill |
| East Lansing, MI | Marcia Bareis, Norman Lownds, Lisa Brewer |
| Salisbury, MD: | Paula Isett, Starlin Weaver, Debra Thatcher |
| Des Moines, IO | Nancy Duey, Natalie Adams, Josie Floerchinger |
| Toledo, OR: | Elise Bales, Linda Brodeur, Nancy Tido |
| Texarkana, TX: | David Alard, Judy Sander, Deborah Cody, |
| Lubbock, TX: | Claire Dulaney, Carol Vaughn, Mary Hobbs |
| Rutland, VT: | Shawn DuBois, Micki Blanchette, Tom Smith |
| Colville, WA: | Nancy Cannon, Robin Raine, Gretchen Koenig |

**"A Head Start on Science" Leadership Teams 2001**

| | |
|---|---|
| Miami, FL: | Giselle Dove, Lesia Crawford, Maria Rubio |
| Muncie, IN: | Resa Matlock, Steve Newman, Laurie Habich |
| Grambling, LA: | Gloria Ard, Mary Booker, Danny Hubbard |
| Clinton, MN: | Jean Fuhrman, Janell Kleindl, Dawn Stary, |
| Natchez, MS: | Fannie Brown, Tony Johnson, Margaret Minor |
| Yonkers, NY: | Robin Laufer, Betty Terry, Kristy Gopel |
| Toledo, OR: | Ragan Kinney, Lupe Smith |

| Pittsburgh, PA: | Phyllis Esch, Mary Ellen Jones, Ann Ensminger |
| Florence, SC: | Barbara Cooper, Bill Kubinec, Josephine Gilchrest |
| Houston, TX: | Kay Timme, Daniel Felske, Lisa Boone, Pauline Monsegue-Bailey |
| Roanoke, VA: | Barbara Boyd, Scarlette Hicks, Carolyn Butcher |

## "A Head Start on Science" National Advisory Board, 1995–1998

Millie Almy, PhD
Emeritus Professor of Psychology
University of California at Berkeley

Mary S. Lewis, PhD
National Head Start Consultant
Berkeley, CA

Christopher Steinhauser
Area C Superintendent, Long Beach Unified School District

James Matlack, Director (Deceased)
Head Start Program, Long Beach Unified School District

Suzan VanPelt Hubert
Coordinator-in-Charge, Head Start/Pre-School
Los Angeles County Office of Education

Karen Lind, PhD
Professor of Science and Early Childhood Education
University of Louisville

Mary Rivkin, PhD
Professor of Early Childhood Education
University of Maryland–Baltimore County Campus

Mary Budd Rowe, PhD (Deceased)
Professor, College of Education
Stanford University, CA

ınal Science Teachers Association